Dear Tripp,
 Herb passed on to us your condolences & we thank you for that and your prayers too.
 Sherry is at home now which is a blessing to us; she's with her son & grandmothers & fathers & so many of the family, not lonely or sick or afraid.
 The Lord has it all under control, right? Amen. I love you,
 Shirley

The Restoration of Biblical Prayer

Elton and Shirley Gillam

Cover design: Alice Anne Ong

First Printing 2009
Second Printing May 2010
Third Printing November 2011

Copyright © 2009 by Elton Gillam. All rights reserved. No part of this book may be used in any manner whatsoever without written permission of the publisher, except in the case of brief quotations in articles and reviews.

For information write: Chambers College Press, 1300 Ninth Street, Greeley, CO 80631. Phone 970-346-1133.
Email: chamberscollege@msn.com

Scripture references are generally from the King James Version or NASU, New American Standard Bible®, ©copyright the Lockman Foundation 1960, 1962, 1963, 1968, 1971, 1972, 1973, 1975, 1977, 1995.

ISBN: 0-9770217-6-9   978-0-9770217-6-5

Library of Congress Control Number: 2009940351

Chambers College
Press

www.chamberspress.com
www.chamberscollege.com

Table of Contents

Foreword i
Acknowledgments iii
Introduction: The Bag Lady 1
Chapter 1: What Is Life Without Prayer? 9
Chapter 2: Approaching Prayer 19
Chapter 3: The Mind-set That Transforms
Gaze and Glance 31
Chapter 4: The Transformed Mind-set in Action 63
Chapter 5: Nuts and Bolts: Praying Scripture 73
Chapter 6: Conformed to His Image:
Claiming the Promises of God 91
Chapter 7: Biblical Prayer May Change the Way You Pray
The Transforming Power of Praise 103
Chapter 8: All Prayer Leads to Calvary 129
Chapter 9: A Brief Look at Faith 143
Chapter 10: Prayer Partners: AKA Back to Back 155
Chapter 11: Prayer: Who Hears? Who Answers? 187
Chapter 12: Praying Scripturally for the Sick 199
Chapter 13: The Word and Prayer for the Lost 237
Chapter 14: The First Command with a Promise 261
Appendix 271
Endnotes 274
Index 276

Foreword

Early in the ministry God placed in me a strong desire to be effective for Christ. Residing in my mind was a vague notion that prayer would somehow play a role in being effective. But how – I was not sure. After a few years I found out how prayer would be crucial for effective ministry.

While I was starting a mission church in Greeley, Colorado, a member encouraged me to go hear a man he had heard teach on prayer. I was a young pastor and had no desire to go, but to fulfill my pastoral duty to this member I decided to go for an hour or so to show that I respected his opinion. I went mainly to fulfill an obligation. I had no sense of going to learn anything.

When I arrived for a Saturday morning session, I noticed that there were not many people in this big church coming to learn about prayer –mostly women and old people. I had enough surface appreciation for prayer to be saddened at this poor turnout, overlooking the fact that I hadn't wanted to come and learn about prayer either.

What I heard from Elton Gillam that morning immediately gripped my heart. I decided to stay for all the sessions. At the end of the sessions, I asked Elton what his schedule was like and if he would be in the area on Wednesday and could he speak at our church? He came to speak to our small church. We have had him back numerous times. We are slow learners.

My hunch had been more right than I ever calculated about the role of prayer in the Christian walk and in the church. I personally think that a knowledge and practice of prayer might be the weakest area in personal lives and in the church today. If we were to gauge the spiritual health of the church by the prayer meeting attendance and prayer requests we hear, it should cause us to weep. Most prayer requests are for fleshly well-being and detract from spiritual requests for advancement or the kingdom of God. Elton Gillam covers this topic masterfully.

For the investment-minded, you will learn from this book how prayer has a tremendous return for the time and effort expended, when done properly. For those who have been praying and have been frustrated, you will learn the reasons for prayer and the hindrances to prayer. Knowing these things will help you become effective. For all of us, we will learn, perhaps learn again, the importance of using prayer to gaze upon God.

Stephen Ong
Chambers College
and Reformation Baptist Church

Acknowledgments

I have so many people to be thankful for, first and foremost, Shirley. This writing was hard work, but eventually, with much encouraging, it came about as we worked together writing God's story in our lives. I praise the Lord for her ability and dedication to decipher my thoughts and type them all. Thank you, Shirley and my family, for hanging with me!

Thanks to Reverend and Mrs. Stephen Ong. Without their help and encouragement this book would never have come about or been finished. Thank you, Steve and Teri and all your family.

Thank you to our prayer and financial support team, who not only pray for us, and many write their prayers to us, which are so uplifting, but also sustain us financially in this God-given ministry of prayer.

Thank you all very much, and may God bless you for your love of Christ.

Scripture Quote Clarifications

The author has highlight key words in verses in bold to convey their importance to the points being made. The bold text has been added by the author.

Some verses in this book are from the New American Standard Bible. It is the practice for this Bible to place references to the Old Testament in uppercase letters to show they are quotes from the Old Testament. This designation is added by the editors of the New American Standard Bible.

Introduction
The Bag Lady

Have you ever wondered why we don't teach one another to pray more effectively? I had been a Christian for 20 years before I began to study prayer. I had been trained in evangelism, witnessing, tithing, even how to take up an offering, but I had never been in a class on prayer. I heard a lot of messages about prayer. I was told I should pray, especially when the church was in trouble, needed money, etc. When I talked to my pastor about it, he said the church was 120 years old and as far as he knew, there had never been a class on prayer. "What would you teach? You just pray when you are in trouble." What do you pray for when you are in trouble? To get out of trouble!

I am not talking about praying when we are in trouble; even the heathen do that. I'm not talking about taking prayer requests. Everyone takes prayer requests whether they pray for them or not. The requests are generally focused on temporal needs. Praying for temporal things is not wrong, it just has little benefit to the soul, to our relationship with the Lord.

I'm talking about prayer that transforms lives in the midst of circumstances, prayer that is Christ-centered, not crisis-centered. Christ-centered prayer is a ministry to the soul (the mind, will, and emotions) that strengthens our faith and clarifies our view of God. Praying **with** one another for our walk with the Lord is even better than praying just **for** one another. It has unlimited spiritual benefit.

Many years ago I was conducting a Prayer Enrichment Seminar in a very exciting church. This church had four Sunday morning worship services and one Saturday night. Our schedule for the week, apart from Sunday, was morning prayer from 6:00 to 7:00 a..m., evening prayer from 6:00 to 7:00 p.m., and the seminar from 7:00 to 9:00 p.m. Around 30 percent of the regular church attendance registered in the seminar. This is very exceptional. It was exceptional, as well, that this church canceled all activities for the week so that all could participate in the prayer seminar. Why would a church, being so "successful" set aside a whole week for prayer? Because the pastor recognized that biblical prayer was the weakest aspect of everything they were doing.

After the Monday morning prayer time, the church prayer coordinator/seminar facilitator, "Bob," and I were walking down the hall of this beautiful new multimillion dollar facility. Bob had taken me on a guided tour. It was about 9:00 a.m., and Bob was sharing with me about the church program of feeding the homeless. People who came in off the streets had to attend a one-hour Bible study each week before receiving food. Bob said this was his day to do the Bible study with them. He asked, "Would you be interested in sharing something about prayer with this group?"

I responded, "Of course, I'd love to."

About that time we walked into a fellowship hall that was breathtakingly beautiful. The sun was shining through the stained glass windows, and it was like standing in the middle of a rainbow. In this room there were about twelve of the most broken pieces of humanity I've ever seen. They were so out of place. I have seen the homeless under bridges, in the parks, and on the streets. In this beautiful room they looked extra ragged and dirty. I was shocked. I asked myself, "What are you doing here?" I've been blessed in sharing with a number of rescue missions over the years, but never in a setting like this.

To begin with, my thoughts were, "What do I have to share with these people? I have nothing in common with them." After all, I was in this church to guide the leadership to a closer walk with God through biblical prayer! Then God pierced my heart with the thought, "Gillam, apart from Me, there goes you." I silently confessed my arrogance and pride and asked the Lord what on earth I could share that would be of any help to these people. As this was taking place, I was unaware of Bob introducing me. I turned to ask him what he thought I should share. He was gone! Now I was standing in the need of prayer!

So, I decided we needed to pray—duh—so I would have time to consider what to share. I was mentally oblivious to what the Lord was going to do. I asked the group if they had their Bibles. Only one lady said she had a Bible. I didn't see any Bibles in the room to give to the others. She said, "I'm not sure they can read, or if they would even if they could."

I wondered if they might be too embarrassed to pray out loud. I was praying silently, "Lord, HELP!"

I asked the lady with the Bible to turn to Psalm 103, which she did immediately. That was an indication to me that she knew her Bible. I asked her if she would read Psalm 103, verse one, and she did. "Bless the Lord, O my soul, and all that is within me, bless His holy name."

I asked her, "What does that tell us about God?"

She said. "He is holy."

I said, "Yes. Now can you, in a short sentence prayer of praise, say 'Lord, I praise you for being holy'?"

And she did just that.

"Wonderful! That's a wonderful prayer. You have just prayed a prayer of praise based on the Word of God." I said to the person next to me, "Do you agree with what she prayed?"

He thought a moment and said, "Yes, I do."

"Would you be willing to pray and say, 'Lord, I agree with that prayer'?"

He said yes and did it.

I said, "Now, I'll read the second verse–'Bless the Lord, O my soul, and forget none of His benefits.'"

Then I asked the group, "Would you all agree that there are benefits of knowing the Lord—of being a Christian?"

One lady said, "God forgives our sins."

"Yes," I said. "Would you be willing to pray, 'Lord, thank You for forgiving our sins'?"

She did, and I complimented her on her prayer. Then I asked the lady with the Bible if she could continue to do the same with a group of four or five others. I went over it again, to read a verse, look for a characteristic of God and praise Him for that in a simple short sentence prayer of praise. We divided them up into two groups. I was the reader for one group, and the lady with the Bible was the reader for the other group.

I told them, "Listen to the verse that is read and praise God from something in the verse that tells us about Him. Another verse will be read and the next person pray about that one. If nothing to praise God about comes to mind right away, you can just say, 'I love You, Lord—next.' That's a wonderful prayer of praise."

After going over it for the second time, I asked the lady who read if she thought she could do that and she said, "Yes, I think I can"

So we began, starting over with verse one. I read the verse and praised the Lord for His holiness. Then I said to the person on my right, "This is your verse," and I read the second verse. He thanked the Lord for forgiving sin. So we progressed around the group.

I got to the fourth person, a very little old lady –at least I thought she was old until I looked closer. Her skin texture revealed that she was much younger than I thought. I don't have the words to adequately describe to you how she looked. The best

The Restoration of Biblical Prayer

I can say is that she looked like a bag lady that pushes a shopping cart, very ragged, dirty, and she smelled so bad! When I said to her, "Now this is your verse," the whole room became silent. I looked up and saw that everyone in the other group was watching me.

After a few moments of hesitation, the lady in the other group said, "She doesn't talk."

I said, "Do you know her name?"

"No, I've never heard her speak a word."

"Do you know if she can't or if she just won't?" She said that she didn't know.

So I asked the group if any of them had heard her speak.

"No."

"Does anyone know her name?"

"No, she just shows up here."

I asked, "Does she come and leave with anyone?"

"No, she's always alone."

The Lord seemed to impress me to just reach out and put my hand on her shoulder. I really didn't want to touch her, but I did—gently. I know the Lord was helping me. I asked her, "Has anyone ever told you that they love you?"

No response. I repeated it again, louder and slower. "Has. . .anyone . . .ever . . . told . . .you . . . that . . . they . . . love . . . you?

Everyone knows when you are in a foreign country, you speak louder and slower. That's where I was and what I was trying to do. I was trying to find out if she could hear. Still no response. Then I said, "Do you know God loves you? Though no one loves you, God loves you. I think it would have made a big difference in my life if just once my father had told me that he loved me. I know now that he did, and he showed it in many ways, but he just couldn't bring himself to put it in words. So I believe God brought me here today to tell you (I got down below her eye level, looked up into her eyes and said) God loves you." Then I said in a louder voice, "Do you know that? Do you believe that?"

In the slightest movement, she nodded, "Yes."

Then I knew she could hear! I said, "Wonderful!" Then I read a verse for the next person. She prayed a little prayer. Then the next person and the next. Then it was the little bag lady's turn again. Everyone was silent again. Every eye in the room was on the little bag lady. I said, "It's your turn. Do you know that God loves you? Do you know that?" I looked at her and there was a little tear coming down her cheek, and I said, "That tear is a liquid prayer! And that's because God is more concerned with the attitude of your heart than He is with your words." I still didn't know if she could speak.

I read a verse for the next person and the next, and they prayed and became slightly more comfortable. Then it was her turn again. I put my hand on her shoulder and said, "You know God loves you, right?" She made a little nod of yes. Then I said, "Do you love God?" Another nod. So I said, "God knows that you love Him, but He will be so pleased if you tell Him in your own words that you love Him. Could you just say, 'I love you, Lord'?" I had to repeat it several times.

In the faintest voice she said, "I love you."

Wow! She can speak! As I wiped a tear, I noticed tears in every eye. God was at work! As we resumed praying and went around the circle, it was her turn again.

This time, she added a couple of words, much louder and more distinct: "God, I love you!" Next time around she stood up and said with an excited voice, "God, I love you. I really do love you!" And her arms were flying about and the tears were flowing down her cheeks. She was radiant. She was transformed before our very eyes. The joy of the Lord was so evident. Then she paused in silence a moment and said something I shall never forget as long as I live. She said, "I can talk to God. I can talk to GOD! I can *talk* to God!" The tears streamed down her cheeks. The rest of the group gathered around her and hugged her and said that they loved her too!

I wish I could tell you that now she is teaching Sunday school or has became a missionary, but I can't. I really don't know what happened to her. But the message sent to my heart was, "Elton, why are you not as excited as this one is to talk to Me? I've only begun to work in this child's heart. I've been working in yours for years. I've shown you my love in so many ways. I've forgiven your sins. I've sent the Holy Spirit to live in your heart. Why then are you so hesitant to talk to Me?"

God used this lady to remind me how important it is to disciple His children to pray, and to use His Word in prayer. If we can't or won't talk to God, we are impudent, powerless, crippled, indigent, and destitute.

Chapter 1
What Is Life Without Prayer?

In 1992 I attended a three-day church growth seminar. In my opinion, it was one of the most sophisticated and well-researched in the country. There were eighteen hours of instruction on church growth but not one word on prayer! I was sure that I must have missed something, so I asked the leader, "How can you talk so much about church growth and never mention prayer?"

His response still rings in my ears as I write this. He said, "That is assumed." I could not believe what I heard. But I know that assumption is still in many people's minds today. Mission organizations, evangelistic crusades, churches, etc., take it for granted that Christians pray. I dare say they do, but with little to no eternal results.

My purpose in writing is to share with you something that has so impacted my life I feel compelled to pass it on. It is God's purpose for true prayer. Coming to a fuller understanding of God's design and requirements for prayer has changed my life and blessed me so much. I trust the Lord will use this information to cause you to make Luke 11:1 your most heartfelt fervent prayer: Lord, teach me to pray.

How's your prayer life? Does it have intimacy with God? Does it have power? Are you receiving clear and unmistakable answers to your prayers? Are you living an abundant, exciting, and fulfilling life with meaning and purpose? If you have answered no to any of these questions, I have good news for you. You are on the verge of the most remarkable experiences of your life—experiences that will never end and will only deepen with the passage of time –communion with the Sovereign Lord.

I found it helpful to understand that communion, or communication, with a Holy God is basically what biblical prayer is all about. C. H. Spurgeon has said, "The highway of holiness is the highway of communion (communication)."

Virginia Satir, secular writer and author of *People Making*, has stated, "I see communication as a huge umbrella that covers and affects all that goes on between human beings. Once a human being has arrived on this earth, communication is the largest single factor determining what kinds of relationships he makes with others and what happens to him in the world about him."

If you want to be a successful business man, you must learn to communicate. If you want to be a successful father, husband, or wife, you must learn to communicate. How far would a football team get without having huddles?

The Christian "umbrella," to use Satir's terminology, is the Word of God and prayer. Do you want to be used of God to be a good preacher, teacher, missionary, businessman, or parent? You must be a Christ-centered communicator. As C. H. Spurgeon said, "A fish could more easily live in a tree than a Christian can live without (biblical) prayer."

Because I had such a distorted view of prayer, God had to show me that talking to Him must be a two way conversation, not just a speech from me (a monologue), which it mostly was. A monologue is not good communication; it only goes one way. Good communication requires that the person to whom you are speaking be able to hear and interpret and respond back. Biblical prayer is two-way communication; we talk to God in prayer and He talks to us through His Word. No one can fulfill God's will or calling apart from the Word of God and prayer.

All relationships are dependent on communication. If you are having difficulty in your marriage, whether you are a Christian or not, any pastor/counselor will say you must establish or reestablish communication. Without communication no relationship can be sustained, including our relationship with the Lord.

All warfare is dependent on communication. You may recall that in World War II the allies had significant victories because the Japanese could not break our communication code, which was the Navajo Indian language. One of the difficulties in the Korean and Vietnamese wars was the lack of good communication. What was our first strike in Desert Storm? Take out Iraqi communication. What is the whole space program all about? Communication. What are computers all about? Communicating. What is the visible evidence to us today of the importance of communication? Satellites – cell phones – computers. All relationships are dependent on communication.

Some would say that Ronald Reagan was perhaps the greatest president we've ever had. What was the key to his success? Communication. He was and is often referred to as the "great communicator."

The following is "The Importance of Dialogue," an excerpt from *Miracle of Dialogue*, by Reuel Howe (pp. 3 and 4)[1].

> Only through dialogue are we saved from this enmity toward one another. Dialogue is to love, what blood is to the body. When the flow of blood stops, the body dies. When dialogue stops, love dies and resentment and hate are born. But dialogue can restore a dead relationship. Indeed, this is the miracle of dialogue; it can bring relationship into being, and it can bring back once again a relationship that has died.
>
> There is only one qualification to these claims for dialogue: it must be mutual and proceed from both sides, and the parties to it must persist relentlessly. The word of dialogue may be spoken by one side but evaded or

ignored by the other, in which case the promise may not be fulfilled. There is risk in speaking the dialogical word—that is, in entering into dialogue—but when two persons undertake it and accept their fear of doing so, the miracle-working power of dialogue may be released.

If the claims we are making here for dialogue are a cause for surprise to the reader, the reason may be that dialogue has been equated too exclusively with the conversational parts of a play. We think of it differently—as the serious address and response between two or more, in which the being and truth of each is confronted by the being and truth of the other. Dialogue, therefore, is not easy and comfortable to achieve, a fact which may explain why it occurs so rarely. And its rare occurrence accounts for the frequent absence of its benefits in our communication with one another."

To say that communication is important to human life is to be trite, but that bit of triteness witnesses to an invariable truth: communication means life or death to persons and relationships in and under heaven. All communication begins and ends with God, the Alpha and Omega, the Beginning and the End.

Where do we start?
1. You must be born again.
   For there is one God, and one mediator also between God and men, the man Christ Jesus. (1 Timothy 2:5)
2. You must be in a right relationship with the Lord.
   If I regard wickedness in my heart, the Lord will not hear. (Psalm 66:1)
3. You must be filled and controlled by the Holy Spirit.

*With **all** prayers and petitions pray at **all** times in the spirit.* (Ephesians 6:18)

These three principles are essential and build on one another. You can't be sure of being forgiven if you are not sure of cleansing, and you can't be sure of cleansing if you are not sure of your salvation. This is what I call being on praying ground. Assurance of these three factors gets us ready to pray.

Christ-centered prayer is a holy occupation; it is influenced positively or negatively much more by our relationship to God than by our circumstances. Prayer is not a heavenly welfare program that God has for us. If God is Sovereign, and He is, and He already knows our needs, why has God commissioned us to pray? God's purpose of prayer is that we may know Him and make Him known to others. I will state here unequivocally that significant answers to prayer will not sustain our prayer life if our only motivation is to get the need met. So what will? The only way to sustain intimacy in prayer is to:

1. Focus on the attributes of God.
2. Focus on the works of God.
3. Focus on the purposes of God.

Prayers focused on the temporal will not, for the most part, change lives, at least not permanently. Prayers focused on the eternal are sustained by the Holy Spirit and have eternal results.

One of the many truths I have learned was expressed by Samuel Chadwick:

"Though a man shall have all knowledge about prayer, though he knows all the mysteries of prayer, unless he prays, he'll never learn to pray,"

We must pray. God told His people through King Solomon, *If my people, which are called by my name, shall humble themselves and seek my face, and turn from their wicked ways, then will I hear from heaven...* (I Chronicles 7:14) God has also revealed to us that His desire is for His house to be called a "house of prayer." (Isaiah 56:7) God's people laboring in prayer is very important to Him. Praying together builds the temple, His life in us.

In Him the whole structure is joined (bound, welded) together harmoniously; and it continues to rise (grow, increase) into a holy temple in the Lord—a sanctuary dedicated, consecrated and sacred to the presence of the Lord. In Him—and in fellowship with one another—you yourselves also are being built up [into this structure] with the rest, to form a fixed abode (dwelling place) of God in (by, through) the Spirit. (Ephesians 2:21-22, Amplified Bible)

This cannot be a reality in our lives apart from the Word of God and prayer.

Almost from the time I put my faith in Christ, I sensed God had something for me to do. But I strongly resisted that thought for more than twenty years. Every time I felt the "calling," I would give more money because that seemed to be the real need. Once the feeling was so strong that I talked to a pastor about it. As I look back on it, I probably went to a pastor I thought would discourage me in the whole thing. The pastor asked me how many children we had (four) and how much schooling I had. I told him I had graduated from high school only because of sports. I believed I could never go back to school. The pastor said that he understood and that the real movement was with the laymen at that time. I was greatly relieved and proceeded to forget about it.

In 1970 I was challenged to attend a Lay Institute for Evangelism (LIFE) at Arrowhead Springs, California. Shirley and I were thinking about divorce, our oldest daughter was in the drug scene, and her younger sister seemed to be going her own way. We were Christians, but had no answers to life's problems.

It was Memorial Day weekend, May 29, 1970. At the Lay Institute for Evangelism conference we learned more about the Christian life than we had in the previous twenty years. We learned how to allow the Holy Spirit to reveal the sin in our lives and how to confess it. For the first time in our lives we knew for sure God had heard and answered our prayer of repentance. Now we had the same confidence in cleansing as we did for salvation. We learned how to keep Christ on the throne of our lives. Shirley and I fell in love all over again, and now we had some answers for our kids. Praise God! He is so merciful and He is so good to us.

Shirley and I made application for staff of Campus Crusade for Christ (CCC) about six months later and were accepted. It was the most exciting time of our lives. We were involved in Explo '72 in Dallas, Texas, the largest conference held up to that time—100,000. Most of those were students. Next was the "I Found It" campaign in 1976, a world-wide evangelistic campaign meaning "I found new life in Christ." Those exciting activities made us feel we were a part of changing the world.

Then we noticed a troubling pattern taking place. For example, we would hold a LIFE conference in a church and see people come to Christ and Christians grow in their walk with the Lord, but as far as church growth was concerned, we did not see the fruit remain and multiply. When we would go back to the church three to six months after the LIFE conference, there was very little difference from the way things were before the training. It seemed to me we were putting out a ton of effort to get an ounce of results.

With my business background, this was not acceptable. For instance, if the church had a Sunday morning attendance of 300, we would get about thirty or, about 10 percent, to go through the training. On Saturday, when we would go out witnessing, fifteen would show up. We accepted that as normal because we were looking for a core group. This group would be the church visitation team. The first week of visitation, all fifteen might show, but the next week only thirteen, next week eleven, and so forth until it was just the pastor and me. So the "program" was dropped for the summer with the intention of starting up again in the fall. However, the fall came and went without a visitation program. Then the church would have to find another program and call it something else to get the people interested.

Whatever the program –the Winsome Program, the New Life, the Way of Life, Evangelism Explosion –it didn't matter. They all ended up the same. Most only lasted a few months. A few lasted a year. I don't mean to be critical, because even though they were not ongoing as we would like, they were certainly better than doing nothing! My point is this: if I experienced that kind of return in business, I'd go broke in a hurry.

About that time I went to a prayer conference. It was the first of its kind as far as I know. What I learned began to give me stability in my walk and ministry. I discovered I could help a pastor start a pastor's prayer support team and train those on the team in biblical prayer. It would do more to strengthen the church than all the other programs we tried to start. I'm not saying those programs weren't good or that they weren't important; they were very important. However, what I discovered was that you can't sustain any of them without a scriptural prayer base.

It became clear to me that true prayer, biblical prayer, was a missing element in evangelism. It was a missing element in all aspects of Christian ministry and outreach. My wife and I found that our praying together from the Bible did more for our marriage and our ministry than all the marriage conferences we had attended. The information from these conferences was very helpful, but without scriptural prayer it was short-lived. A cliché from the 1950s said, "A family that prays together stays together." That is so true if that prayer is Christ-centered. It is true of a physical family, but it is also true of the spiritual family of God.

We started allowing God to use us to help other Christians learn to pray from the Bible. As we did, the Lord began to bless us with insights that empowered our prayer life, and we have never been the same. *Behold, all things became new.* (2 Corinthians 5:17)

Now our ministry is the prayer ministry entrusted to us by God. Our prayer for you is that as you read and apply these biblical truths, they will be used of the Lord to bless you and glorify the Lord Jesus Christ through you.

True prayer, in the biblical meaning of the term, is an exciting adventure. What you're about to read will perhaps be a new way of looking at the principles and practices of prayer, as taught within the pages of Scripture. This is more than just another book about prayer: it is in part a humble testimony of how God broke into the life of an ordinary Christian—a Christian full of sins and foibles and fears, like any other—and showed him the wonders of a deep, dynamic prayer life.

Chapter 2
Approaching Prayer

Most Christians don't want to hear anything more about the need for prayer or the power of prayer. They've heard too much about it already—and more information just adds to their guilt. They are quick to say prayer is the greatest power, but it is the last thing people try. Actually, down deep, they are hungry to know and understand how to pray more effectively, because for the most part they are not praying with any sense of power or assurance. Their experience does not square with what they have read or heard about God and prayer in the Bible.

The way most Christians approach prayer reminds me of the way elephants are trained. An elephant is a powerful animal. He can pull 70-foot power-line poles out of the ground with his trunk all day long, even when they are planted six feet deep. But once his circus trainer puts a steel bracelet around his leg to tether him to the stake, he won't pull a four-foot stake two feet out of the ground.

When the elephant is young, his trainer puts a bracelet on one leg and chains it to a steel anchor that won't give way. For two weeks or more the elephant will do everything he can to get free. The steel bracelet cuts into the flesh around his leg, causing it to bleed and sometimes cutting it to the bone. The object, of course, is not to cripple the elephant for life, but to hurt him deeply enough that he will give up trying to free himself. Eventually, all elephants stop testing the steel bracelet. Some, while chained, have lost their lives in circus fires simply because they wouldn't lift their leg to walk out. They are in bondage because of their earlier defeat and conditioning they've undergone.

Most of us Christians are like the elephants. We've been conditioned not to strive with God in prayer because our previous experiences have been unproductive and not all that pleasant. Or perhaps we prayed and still remained in pain. Or perhaps we've had so little training in scriptural prayer that our efforts resulted in defeat because we misapplied God's promises in the situations we were facing, never understanding the prerequisites to effective prayer.

Shirley's father died of cancer in a Denver, Colorado, hospital on May 28, 1950, just three weeks after we were married. We lived in a little basement apartment in Scottsbluff, Nebraska. About eight months after he died, there was a knock at our door. It was a Berean missionary, Howard Herbst. He and his wife came in answer to Shirley's father's dying request: "Share with my daughter Shirley what you've shared with me!"

Carl Friehauf, Shirley's father, had prayed to receive Christ on his deathbed and was immediately concerned for his daughter. Shirley wanted to hear everything the missionary had to tell her about her dad. The missionary told her that her dad recited Scriptures and sang hymns in German. He had learned the German Catechism in his youth, but seldom attended church as Shirley was growing up. He and Shirley's mother saw to it that Shirley was in church and went to the catechism class as they had. Oh, what a joy this was for Shirley to hear about her father's salvation. Now she cried for joy!

Shirley was so open and prayed with all her heart to invite Christ into her life to forgive her sins and help her obey Him. She received the assurance that she would see her father again in heaven. She had spent many afternoons crying because she had never told her dad that she loved him, and now it seemed too late. Her family was not emotionally expressive with hugs and the like. But now it was okay with her about her Dad; she had genuine peace about their love for each other. Now she cried for joy. Missionary Herbst said her father asked him to tell her to share the Gospel with her two younger brothers as well.

I prayed the salvation prayer too, but with my fingers crossed, so to speak. It was not from my heart. Shirley was eight months pregnant and I didn't want to cause her any unnecessary grief, so I went through the motions. However, in that process, I heard that I could know, not guess or hope, where I would spend eternity. Having gone through the act of praying to receive Christ, it bothered me that I had no assurance or change in my life. Shirley's prayer had made such a difference in her life.

Finally, a few months later, on a lonely stretch of dirt road between Scottsbluff and Chadron, Nebraska, I stopped the car, got out, knelt down on the edge of the road and asked Jesus to forgive my sins and come into my heart. I don't like to think about where I'd be today had I not done that. Howard Herbst had read Revelation 3:20 to us, which says, *Behold, I stand at the door and knock; if anyone hears my voice and opens the door, I will come into him, and will dine with him, and he with Me.* I made that verse mine. From that moment on I had a serene peace about where I would spend eternity, BUT the Christian life dealt me a fit! We went to church and were active there. We tried to live for God on Sunday, but lived the world's way the rest of the week.

I'll share just one example that may help you understand or appreciate where I come from in my Christian experience.

From 1962 to 1970 I worked for Garriott Crop Dusting in Bakersfield, California. The company paid for my flying lessons

The Restoration of Biblical Prayer

while I sold crop dusting to the farmers and did public relations work. I earned my multi-engine agriculture pilot's licenses. I loved my dream job. The owner's father told my wife that if she wanted a divorce, she could sue for alienation of affections. "Elton just petted those planes!"

I had an unlimited expense account, a company boat on the Colorado River at Lake Mojave, several company planes and a car. Shirley and I would fly couples to Calgary, Lake Louise, Banff, etc. Sometimes guys would call me and ask if I would like to go to lunch. Often I would say,"OK. Where do you want to go? How about Vegas?" So we would fly to Vegas just for lunch. Other times we would go hunting or fishing in Wyoming and Montana. I loved flying and the company paid for it all.

I had opportunities to fly for multi-millionaires – customers of the company. One was J. G. Boswell, founder of Kern County Land Company, the largest land company in the world at that time. It was said that Mr. Boswell could go from Mexico to Canada by covered wagon and camp every night on his own land. That should give an idea of the size and scope of my so-called"job." Now you would think, wouldn't you, that an uneducated boy from Nebraska would feel like he had really made it?

I had managed to graduate from high school, the first in my family of seven kids to graduate, mostly because of sports. I graduated 154th out of 156; I wasn't too interested in the academics. At 40 years of age, I had never read a single book all the way through. In English you just read the first and last chapter, turned in a book report, and got D-; you made it! However, I was street smart and could make a lot of money. Why would I need school?

But let me be honest, while I was working for Garriott, I was a Christian but not living for the Lord; I was running from His call for my life. Sometimes when coming back from a very expensive hunting or fishing trip with customers, I would get so upset with my passengers griping and complaining about an insignificant incident, like the waitress pouring them a cold cup of coffee, I wanted to just climb up to 15 or 20,000 feet and turn off the oxygen. I knew that would put them out like a light, and I would have a nice quiet flight home!

Some of my passengers were very intellectual men. One was instrumental in the first moon flight, but because of his mental capacity, his company could not give him enough money to fully express his mind. They didn't understand him; neither did his wife and kids, so he wasn't good company.

I also had opportunity to fly for wealthy men—even multi-millionaires. They could do anything they wanted to do, anytime they wanted to do it. They were unlimited in time and money; some were immoral, but most were very unhappy. They had come to know from experience that money couldn't buy happiness. If perhaps you doubt that, just watch the evening news!

Remember I graduated 154 out of 156. Only two kids in my class were dumber than me, and they were friends of mine. So, if it doesn't make any difference how smart or dumb, how rich or poor you are, if that doesn't have to do with happiness and fulfillment in life, where is it?

We were going to church and active in it, but I had as much or more trouble in church as I did at work. Working in the crop dusting business, I felt I dealt with stark reality. There were only two questions we asked a duster pilot who wanted to work for us: one was, "Are you legally licensed?" We didn't care about how a pilot got his licenses, but he had to be legal because we were always being sued about something. The second was, "Can you fly?" We would tell him, "There is a loaded Stearman, a crop duster airplane, loaded with parathion (an insecticide). Go put it on that cotton field." If he came back, he could fly; if not, we went to his funeral or sent flowers. I am being a little facetious, but in reality it would happen just like that. You get the idea; we were not in the crop dusting business just for fun and games.

I have shared all of that to say my experience working in the church was just the opposite. The more involved I'd get, the less I dealt with reality; like the time I sat for three hours with three other reasonably intelligent business men discussing how the communion cup goes back in the wooden holder that is attached to the back of the pew. When the glass cups went back in, they would make a clicking sound out across the congregation. Some felt that it detracted from the service.

One fellow wanted to buy rubber bumpers, but the bumpers we could get wouldn't fit the hole. Another wanted to throw away the glass cups and get plastic communion cups that wouldn't make that awful noise; besides, you didn't have to wash them, just throw them away. We went back to the holder and talked about taking the wooden bracket off of the pew, but that would mar the pew, and after all, these were memorials to saints that had passed on. We just couldn't do that. Can you believe three hours? What was very obvious to all of us was that we would not put up with that for five minutes in our own businesses, or we would go broke; but there we were in God's business, just Mickey Mousing around, playing church. The final decision was postponed until our next meeting, which never took place!

After being a Christian for 20 years at the time, I did not realize, I *really* did not realize that the enemy of my soul had given me such a distorted view of prayer that he had robbed me of the power base to live the Christian life with the same degree of authenticity and realism as I lived the rest of my life. The Word and prayer are as essential to living the Christian life as the Pratt & Whitney engine is to the crop duster! Without them, you die!

Wednesday night prayer meeting was the dullest meeting you could go to in our church. Sometimes the pastor would call on Tuesday and inform me he was going to be out of town and asked me to take Wednesday night prayer meeting. I would do anything to get out of it. I would give more money, be on another committee or whatever, because for me it was a real downer.

The usual format was to have a little sermonette and then ask for prayer requests. If the first one was for sickness, then the next one was too, and so it went until you had a sick list. I got sick praying for the sick. Please don't misunderstand me, we must pray for the sick. God commands we do so, but if that is all we pray about, we have a "sick" prayer life. Sometimes I would tell someone who was sick that I would pray for him and I would forget, and he would get better! The one I remembered to pray for got worse! That will do a lot for your prayer life. At times I would go to Wednesday night prayer meeting feeling pretty good and leave depressed because I didn't know there were so many problems. Can you relate to my experience?

During twenty years of going to church (we were religious) we received training in how to teach Sunday School, how to lead people to Christ, and even how to take up an offering, but never a class on how or what to pray. I heard a lot of messages about prayer, devotionals on prayer, testimonies of answered prayer, but I was never discipled in prayer. My past experiences never gave me a hunger for God.

After being a Christian for twenty years and in full-time Christian work for a few years, a friend in ministry asked me, "Gil, do you pray?"

"Of course I pray," I said, "I'm a Christian."

"When do you pray?" he said.

"Well, sometimes in the morning and sometimes in the evening."

"No, I mean what motivates you to pray?"

I thought about it a moment and said, "Well, I guess when I get into trouble."

"What do you pray for when you get in trouble?"

"To get out of trouble," I replied.

Then my friend said, "Gil, do you believe the heathen pray?"

"They sure do," I said.

"When do the unbelievers pray?"

"When they get in trouble." I could feel his point coming like the blow of a sledgehammer.

He said, "So, Gil, how then are you praying any differently than the heathen?"

I had to admit I wasn't. If I wasn't sick or broke, I didn't have a prayer request.

In 1974 a number of Christian leaders decided to get together and share with one another what they had learned about prayer. These men included Bill Bright, President/Founder of Campus Crusade for Christ; J. Edwin Orr, an authority on revival; Robert Coleman, professor at Asbury Seminary and author of many books including *One Divine Moment*, a record of the 1970's revival starting at Asbury; Chuck Smith, pastor of Calvary Chapel, Costa Mesa, California, a man of prayer used of God in the Jesus Movement during the 1970's; Armin Gesswine, founder of Pastors' Prayer Fellowship; Howard Hendricks, professor at Dallas Theological Seminary; Ron Dunn, pastor and conference speaker; and Dr. Curtis Mitchell, professor at Bible Institute of Los Angeles (Biola) and teacher of prayer.

I was a staff member of Campus Crusade for Christ, working with some pastors and businessmen who were struggling in their churches or families or business. I'd tried everything I knew to

The Restoration of Biblical Prayer

help them, but it wasn't working, so I thought they might get help at the prayer conference. I wasn't going –I knew how to pray! After twenty years as a salesman in the agriculture line, working for a crop-dusting company and learning to fly, I'd prayed my way onto the Campus Crusade for Christ staff, prayed in my support, and I wasn't sick or broke. But these men I'd invited said they wouldn't go unless I did, so I decided to go for their sakes. Well, as you can imagine, I was the one that got zapped.

Those Christian leaders, men of prayer, were not praying for Aunt Merna's bad toe or Uncle Pete's bad back. These men were sharing how prayer was used of God to fulfill His plan for their lives. I can't remember that we prayed for one sick person. We prayed to know God!

I left that weekend conference convinced that I was an illiterate Christian in the area of biblical prayer. God "flung a cravin' on me," as my friend Jim Hatfield would say. God put a hunger in my heart to learn everything I could about prayer.

It took a year or so for some of the truths I'd heard that weekend to begin to sink in. I didn't realize how deeply I was indoctrinated with myths about prayer such as, it's the women's job or the elderlies' job. Little did I know that you couldn't delegate the responsibility of prayer. I didn't understand that God had ordained every child of His to be a praying Christian. Sometimes I think we need to put up signs around the church: *No Prayer Dumping Allowed*. We cannot have our praying done for us. God has ordained each one of us to stand before Him in person. *You also, as living stones, are being built up as a spiritual house for a holy priesthood, to offer up spiritual sacrifices acceptable to God through Jesus Christ. But you are a Chosen race, a royal priesthood, a holy nation, a people for God's own possession, that you may proclaim the excellencies of Him who has called you out of darkness into His marvelous light.* (1 Peter 2:5,9)

Then one Sunday morning, the Sunday School teacher didn't make it to church, so I volunteered to share some things I'd learned about prayer and some contents of the Ninth Transferable Concept published by Campus Crusade for Christ. It is a short introduction to prayer with subjects of "Who can pray?, why pray?," etc. There were so many questions raised that I couldn't answer, so I started to read and study everything I could on prayer. I became very troubled. Why, with all the knowledge about prayer, do we not pray? Everybody would agree it is very important, but I found a sad few who actually prayed. Why? I believe it was C. H. Spurgeon who said, "There are men who teach about prayer, but where are the men who set men to praying?" That is the real need.

As you see, it wasn't until I started teaching a class on prayer that I realized that I had a hunger for knowledge of prayer, but not necessarily a passion for God. I didn't put the two together until problems and questions developed in the classes, like: "What about speaking in tongues, what is a prayer language, what about signs and wonders, healing, fasting, praying for the lost?" I found help in a lot of books, but also I discovered that I had to pray! Truths about prayer are of little value apart from praying. I found that only the Word of God and prayer could satisfy the thirst.

That's when I began to pray Luke 11:1: *Lord, teach me to pray.* That is a prayer that God always hears and answers. I discovered it is a somewhat dangerous prayer from man's perspective because we seldom like the way God chooses to teach us to pray. Luke 11:1 is to this day, after thirty years, one of my most heart-felt prayers.

My primary motivation to teach classes on prayer is that I may learn to pray and to know Him. *For my determined purpose is that I may know Him—that I may progressively become more deeply and intimately acquainted with Him, perceiving and recognizing and understanding the wonders of His person more strongly and more clearly.* (Philippians 3:10, *Amplified Bible*)

Prayer is about knowing God and making Him known. Prayer is God's only means of harmonizing His sovereignty with man's responsibilities. It is my conviction, founded on Scripture, that Calvary-based prayer and the Bible are God's major means of conforming us to His image. *For by these [His own glory and excellence] He has granted to us His precious and magnificent promises, in order that by them you might become partakers of the divine nature, having escaped the corruption that is in the world by lust. (*2 Peter 1:4) In the light of biblical truth on prayer, I hope my message encourages and strengthens Christians' prayer life, thereby transforming them into the likeness of God's Son.

Chapter 3
The Mind-set That Transforms:
Gaze and Glance

Philippians 3:10 in the *Amplified Bible* says, *"For my determined purpose is that I may know Him--that I may progressively become more deeply and intimately acquainted with Him, perceiving and recognizing and understanding the wonders of His person more strongly and more clearly."*

When I purpose, by an act of my will, to set my mind on the Lord to know Him better and to become more like Him, my mind is transformed, causing me to think about my circumstances from a spiritual perspective. In the same passage in the *New American Standard Bible*, verses 10 and 11 say, *"That I may know Him, and the power of His resurrection and the fellowship of His sufferings, being conformed to His death; in order that I may attain to the resurrection from the dead."* That is the mind-set that transforms us into the image of our Savior, Christ Jesus. That mind-set gives us assurance of knowing Christ's victory as the way of life, allowing us to respond to all life situations as Christ did, does, and will. It is the opposite of reacting humanly to my circumstances.

As I have kept my gaze on God and have only glanced at all the circumstances of life, I have gotten to know Him better and have deepened my relationship with Him. My Christian walk has become more intimate with God. Being intimate from God's perspective was foreign to me until I started practicing this simple concept. Practicing the "gaze and glance" principle continues to be the most life-changing truth I've learned during my many years as a Christian.

A frequent question is, "Do you believe in miracles?" I say, "Yes, I are one!" The foundational "gaze and glance" teaching of God's Word in relation to prayer has produced the most consistent positive growth in my life and my family's life, far more than any other miracle I have known. God has saved me from hell and from myself. He saved my marriage, my children, and my loved ones, and brought many spiritual healings.

God, the Holy Spirit, is the only source of true intimacy, the kind of intimacy Paul was talking about in Philippians 3:10. Pascal, the great philosopher, said that there is a God-shaped vacuum in the heart of every man that cannot be satisfied by any created thing, but only by the Creator, God Himself. God has created us with a need for intimacy, a fact I've realized only recently. Dialogue with God through His Word and prayer is God's primary way for attaining spiritual intimacy—being in tune with Him. Your mind and heart say, "God would like this" —or —"God would not like this." Intimacy with God is when your heart, soul, and mind are at peace with God. It is being one with the One who created you, the One who knows you inside out (Psalm 139).

On a spiritual level, I have no human ability to be intimate with my wife or family and friends apart from my intimacy with God. Intimacy with your mate means you know what they're thinking before they say it because you are both responding in concert with God's spirit. For example, I was invited to Sudan to teach on prayer. Sudan is not a very safe place for a white American Christian, but the most dangerous place to be is out of God's will. I know that and I know my wife knows that. Even before we prayed about it together, I was confident that I would be going with her blessings. It's a oneness that only God can give, through the Word and prayer.

Discovering this concept began under the teaching of Sergio Garcia, director of Campus Crusade for Christ (CCC) in Mexico. He emphasized seeking and focusing on God's eternal perspective. This sensitized me to Ron Dunn's teaching on Christ-centered prayer, which led to applying CCC's teaching on the filling of the Holy Spirit to the Christian's prayer life.

In the late 1970's, someone sent us a *2959 Plan* by Peter Lord. On page 12, under the title, "Some Secrets of Prayer," the second secret is the "gaze and glance" principle. The simple diagram presented there was for me the beginning of defining the Biblical and theological basis of effective prayer, that is, praying from an eternal perspective.

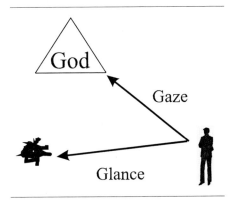

I discovered that unless one's prayers are Christ-centered, one cannot sustain a vibrant prayer life. Allowing God to enlighten me, through prayer, to the "gaze and glance" principle in relation to prayer is one of the major reasons I am in the prayer ministry today.

What does the "gaze and glance" principle mean in relation to prayer? It means:

1. Realizing that my greatest need in life is to know God–not my physical/temporal needs (Philippians 3:10-11). Knowing Him begins by believing in the saving work of Christ done at Calvary.

2. Seeking God's face before seeking His hand (Matthew 6:33), allowing God to give us His eternal perspective on our temporal needs (Colossians 3:1-2).

3. Understanding that in God's sovereignty, everything touching our lives is designed and/or allowed by Him in order to conform us to His image (Romans 8:26-30).

4. Trusting God enough to willingly allow Him to work in us in any given circumstance so that His attributes are made visible through us (Philippians 3:17-21), rather than our own human reactions.

The "gaze and glance" concept transforms our view of God and our view of our circumstances. The adage that says that prayer changes things is a partial truth. More often prayer changes us.

Let's look at each one of these crucial transformations.

1. Realizing that my greatest need in life is to know God. Knowing Him begins by believing in the saving work of Christ done at Calvary.

Many Christians think prayer is just telling God about their needs. That certainly is an aspect of prayer, but they have forgotten, or have never been taught, that prayer is primarily a means of knowing God. A pray-er, with a heart to know God, will ask God to teach him how to pray, show him His truth and what to pray for. *Lord, teach me to pray.* (Luke 11:1) Biblical prayer is primarily, though not exclusively, asking God to teach us how to pray, for we don't know how to pray as we should. (Romans 8:26,27) A Christian with an eternal mind-set does not assume that he knows what to pray or how to pray.

To illustrate my point, look at almost any prayer list or chain of prayer requests. How many requests do you find asking God for His view of the need? How many do you find asking to know God better? How many do you find asking God to give them strength to walk uprightly in their situation? Or even asking, "Lord, change me!" I have found exceptions, but for the most part, prayer is focused on the need from man's point of view —what he thinks should be done. Oswald Chambers said in *My Utmost for His Highest,"The idea of prayer is not in order to get answers from God; prayer is perfect and complete oneness with God. If we pray because we want answers, we will get huffed with God.*[2] Why would that be so? Because frequently, our earthbound solutions are very different from God's best for us.

The Biblical idea of prayer is to get to know God Himself, and every other thing we need will be taken care of in the process. Matthew 6:33 says, *"But seek first His kingdom and His righteousness; and all these things shall be added to you."* Jesus teaches us to seek His kingdom, to become a Christian, before we seek anything else. If we are not a child of the King, He has no obligation to impart His provision.

The next step is to seek His righteousness; ask Him to reveal the sin in us so we can confess it, in order to have access to the Father. (Ephesians 2:18) The fact that God does not hear the prayer of an unrepentant sinner, except a prayer of repentance, is a fundamental doctrine of prayer. We have no access to the righteousness of the Holy God apart from going through Christ's righteousness.

Without a doubt, this truth is often misunderstood, abused, and/or ignored. A lot of well-meaning Christians fall into the enemy's ploy of praying to have "all these things added" with known sin in their lives, without righteousness. This practice has resulted in establishing a myth that no matter how you live your life, when you get into trouble, just call on "the man upstairs"; he will hear and answer, because he is loving and understanding. This thought is straight from the pit!

It's true that anyone, through God's grace, can call on the name of the Lord to repent, to be saved (Romans 10:12,13), but only a child of God in a right relationship to Him can pray about temporal things with confidence that God will hear and answer. John 9:31 states, *We know that God does not hear sinners, but if anyone is God-fearing, and does His will, He hears him.*

To keep this in balance, we must also keep in mind that the Lord blesses whomever He pleases. (Psalm 115:3 and Matthew 5:45) But we can't take a blessing and call it answered prayer. The blessing could be an answer to the prayer of a sanctified Christian or a provision of God's common grace. Accepting a blessing from God as an answer to prayer is dangerous when we know we are out of fellowship with Him. It allows Satan to have a decisive victory in distorting our view of God by making us think that righteousness is not a prerequisite for getting an answer to prayer. If a Christian or a non-Christian could receive an answer to prayer without getting right with the Lord, Calvary was not necessary. The enemy, Satan, will try to use such a misunderstanding to entice us to bypass Calvary.

Biblical prayer is Calvary-based prayer. I have a bumper sticker I like that says, "If you don't know Jesus, you don't have a prayer." That's right. *For there is one God and one Mediator between God and men, the Man Christ Jesus.* (1 Timothy 2:5) The only access for sinful man into the Holy of Holies is through Jesus Christ. This is where our prayer life is born and this is where it is sustained. C. H. Spurgeon said, "You misread Calvary if you fail to see its role in prayer." What does he mean? To me he is saying that without Christ's work at Calvary, you cannot pray a prayer that is acceptable to God. I think he is saying you have no assurance of God hearing or answering apart from a personal relationship to the Father through Jesus Christ. Apart from Christ's shed blood, we have no covering for our sin, and God cannot look on sin. He cannot hear us. *If I regard iniquity in my heart the Lord will not hear.* (Psalm 66:18)

Biblical prayer is based on Christ's righteousness and, because of that truth, leads to the cross. What do I mean by that? Let's say God gives you a burden for your mother or father's salvation. You will need to ask the Lord to search your heart to confirm your righteousness in Jesus based on what He did at Calvary. *The fervent prayer of a righteous man avails much.* (James 5:16 b) Then as the Lord leads, you will need to go to Him based on His work of redemption in your life to seek light, strength, encouragement, etc. Like the song says,"There is power in the blood."

How do you pray for someone who is sick or dying? I can only pray effectively for them on the basis of Christ's death on the cross. Apart from Christ's blood, there is no basis for healing. *Confess your trespasses* (that's based on Calvary) *to one another, and pray for one another that you may be healed. The effective fervent prayer of a righteous man avails much.* (James 5:16)

Biblical prayer is communication with a Holy God, based on Christ's righteousness imputed to the redeemed by His death on Calvary. Biblical praying revolves around the hub of Christ's death on the cross. The pray-er's commission is to draw on the whole counsel of God; the cross is the center of that counsel, and the pray-er who loses sight of the hill called Calvary will soon find himself praying in the flesh —an abomination to the Lord.

Oswald Chambers wrote, "We look upon prayer as a means of getting things for ourselves. The Bible idea of prayer is that we may get to know God Himself."[3] What is Chambers saying? It seems to me that he is saying man is temporally minded and self-centered, which is true of all of us apart from Jesus. What I hear Chambers saying is "don't look at prayer from man's point of view. Prayer is a godly practice and we must look at prayer from the Word of God." The Word says in Colossians 3:1, *If then you have been raised up with Christ, keep seeking the things above, where Christ is, seated at the right hand of God.* If you are a child of God, stop seeking only the provision/hand of God, and seek Him, because of the command of Matthew 6:33: *Seek first the kingdom of God and His righteousness and all these things will be added unto you.*

Christ knows our physical needs, so our real need is to know Him. *Set your mind on the things above, not on the things that are on the earth.* (Colossians 3:2) That is supernatural. It is the nature of a man to seek God's hand to meet earthbound, temporal needs. But if I am a child of God, I can choose to set my mind on eternal things. The Bible idea of prayer is to talk to God about spiritual things so that we will know how to pray about the temporal needs.

It is important to be reminded there is nothing wrong with seeking the hand of God. He is merciful. Often we just cry out to God, "HELP!" and He hears and answers. During one of our prayer seminars, a lady shared that the lights went out on her car as she drove home the night before. She was on the freeway; she didn't have time to consider which attributes of God she needed just then —she just cried, "HELP!" and He did!

However, when we are wrestling with God about an issue, God's command is that we seek His face first (2 Chronicles 7:14), so that we get His truth about the situation and ask for those things that are in harmony with His will, for we are to pray about everything. When we pray for temporal things without thought of what God has for us, we give prayer a poor or weak reputation because of our ineffective praying, thus God's reputation comes into question or doubt.

2. Seeking God's face before seeking His hand. Allowing God to give us His eternal perspective on our temporal needs.

The Bible teaches seeking God's face before seeking His hand, seeking the Mountain Mover before endeavoring to move a mountain, knowing the Provider before seeking the provision.

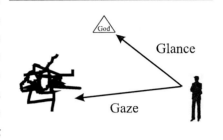

In Numbers 13, twelve men were sent to spy out the Promised Land. How many had their eyes on the Lord? Two, right? Were the two spies ignorant of the problem in the land? No, they knew there were giants in the land, but their gaze was on the Lord, and their God was able. Those giants just made better targets! But what was the report of the ten of the twelve spies? They said they couldn't go in and possess the land because their focus was fully on those giants; their gaze and glance were reversed. When our gaze and glance are reversed, problems loom bigger and bigger and darker and darker in our mind. At the same time, our view of and faith in God diminish, until our God looks like a grasshopper compared to our need.

We find in 2 Kings 6:8-17 another wonderful story illustrating the gaze and glance principle. The king sent a great army to surround the city of Elisha and his attendant. The attendant rose early in the morning and saw the great army circling the city and cried to Elisha, who said, "Do not fear, for those who are with us are more than those who are with them." Then Elisha prayed and said, "O LORD, I pray, open his eyes that he may see." The Lord opened the servant's eyes and he saw; the mountain was full of horses and chariots of fire all around them. The attendant could only see the temporal, the army of the enemy, but Elisha prayed for him and his eyes were opened to see the eternal.

What was Apostle Peter's problem when he began to sink after walking on the water? He took his eyes off the Lord and looked at the waves. When he began to focus on his problem and on his fear, he began to sink. The same thing is true of us today. We must learn to keep our eyes on the Problem Solver, the Lord, and not on the problem.

In 1 Corinthians 12, the Corinthians were so caught up in their gifts and the exercise of their gifts that they had forgotten the Giver. Their eyes were on the hand of God, rather than on his face. I know of no portion of Scripture that has been so abused or misunderstood as 1 Corinthians 12 (concerning spiritual gifts, especially the gift of tongues). In the flesh, often under the guise of prayer, misunderstandings about the gifts have damaged many churches and caused trouble in families and relationships. We must remember that no gift makes us spiritual; the only thing that makes you and me spiritual is the absence of sin through the power of the Holy Spirit.

If I have the gift of giving, I can give with the wrong motive. If I have the gift of preaching, I can preach with sin in my life. Any gift can be exercised in the flesh. Praise God for the gifts, but if the gift has higher priority than the Giver, we are in trouble; our gaze and glance are reversed. Following 1 Corinthians 12, the Apostle Paul wrote 1 Corinthians 13, which is the love chapter, to get their eyes off their gifts and back on the Giver.

Our view of God is distorted when our gaze and glance are reversed. Why? Because we evaluate the effectiveness of our prayer by what He is doing for us rather than by what He is doing in us! Whatever view we have of prayer is our view of God. It is not possible to have a high view of God and a low view of prayer. Don't tell me you love me if you won't talk to me! Don't say that you love God if the only time you talk to Him is when you get into trouble.

When Shirley and I went into the ministry with Campus Crusade for Christ, we had to raise our support, as you know most missionaries do. When our account would get in the red, we would do everything we could to get it out of the hole. If our newsletter wasn't in the mail, we would hurry and get one out, just in case that would remind someone to send in his or her support. If someone said to me, "Charlie has really been strengthened through your ministry, and I think if you were to share with him that you have a financial need, he would want to have a part," as long as my account was in the black, I didn't need to talk to him. But when it was in the red, I would do that. After we had done all that we could, and our account was still in the red, I would say to Shirley, "This is getting serious. I think we're going to have to pray about this." Shirley would respond, "Has it come to that?" The last resort—so we would pray.

If a little money came in, we thought God still loved us— *a little bit*. But if a whole lot of money came in, we were a whole bunch in love with the Lord! Our gaze and glance were upside down; we still loved the Lord, we had a glance at Him, but our gaze was fixed on our need. What we didn't realize was that we were allowing our circumstance to dictate to us the extent of God's love for us. Our need, rather than the objective truth of God's Word, dictated our view of God.

When Christians seek the hand of God before the face of God, they can have sin in their life and not know it. If they pray with sin in their life, God does not listen to their prayer. *"So when you spread out your hands in prayer, I will hide My eyes from you, yes, even though you multiply prayers, I will not listen. Your hands are covered with blood."* (Isaiah 1:15)

If God doesn't hear their prayer, guess who could? When anyone prays while not in a right relationship with the Lord, they give Satan an opportunity to falsify or counterfeit an answer to prayer. But when people seek the face of God first, if anything in their life displeases the Lord, He has obligated Himself to reveal that to them, so that they can confess. *"The effective prayer of a righteous man can accomplish much"* (James 5:16); the prayer of an unrighteous man can only confuse.

When we seek only the hand of God and not the face of God first, our view of God is based only on what He does for us. The nations' or unbelievers' view of God is often determined by what God does for his followers. Psalm 115:1 and 2 say, *"Not to us, O Lord, not to us, but to Thy name give glory because of Thy lovingkindness, because of Thy truth (faithfulness). Why should the nations say, 'Where now is their God?'"* Our selfish demands are often made without consideration of God's will. We sound like we are our own gods. When believers are asking for things out of the will of God, the heathen perceive this as a sign that there is no God. On the other hand, when a Christian seeks only the hand of God and perceives he's being blessed, he, the pray-er, is glorified more than the Lord is. Attention is drawn to the ability of the pray-er rather than to the power of the Lord. That's why the Psalmist prays, *Not to us, O Lord, not to us, but to Thy name give glory*.

The pray-er who seeks the face of God before he seeks His hand gives God glory and attention is drawn to who God is and not to the pray-er. Peter Lord says in his *2959 Plan*, "If we allow our gaze to be on our request, it will dominate our prayers; we will tell God what we see and what needs to be done. However, if our gaze is on God, we will ask Him to interpret the situation from His viewpoint (tell us what He sees), and to tell us what needs to be done."

The Psalmist goes on in Psalm 115:3, *"But our God is in the heavens; He does whatever He pleases."* Prayer must not be a means of manipulating God to get our needs met. To *only* seek the hand of God is in reality an attempt to manipulate God. We tell Him what to do, how to do it and when to do it! I didn't realize I was doing just that during the first twenty years of being a Christian. I thought God loved me if He answered the way I wanted, assuring me that I had prayed correctly. In reality, I had an idolatrous view of prayer; I had made my need the number one thing in my life.

Psalm 115:4-8 says, *"Their idols are silver and gold, the work of man's hands. They have mouths, but they cannot speak; they have eyes, but they cannot see; they have ears but they cannot hear, they have noses, but they cannot smell; they have hands, but they cannot feel; they have feet, but they cannot walk; they cannot make a sound with their throat. Those who make them will become like them, everyone who trusts in them."* We become like whatever is number one in our life. That is a law of the universe. It doesn't matter if we are Christians or not. A friend of mine in high school, whose father was an alcoholic, always said that he would never be like his father. Whenever the opportunity arose, he would say,"I'll never be like my father; nothing can make me be like him; no matter what happens, I won't be like him!" What do you think happened to him? You're right, he became just like his father. Why? Because we become like that on which we focus.

If money becomes more important to us than our relationship to the Lord, we become like money. "How do you become like money?" you ask. We turn hard, cold, indifferent, inconsistent, fluctuating with the circumstances. We will gladly meet the need one day and not give one thing the next day. Money buys a lot one day and the next day we never have enough. *"For as he thinks within himself, so he is."* (Proverbs 23:7) If we focus on the problem instead of the Problem Solver, we become more a part of the problem than a part of the solution.

When our minds are not set on things above they will naturally concentrate on the things on the earth and they become temporal. Time-bound, earth-bound concerns easily become flesh-bound as well. *"For those who are according to the flesh set their minds on the things of the flesh, but those who are according to the Spirit, the things of the Spirit. For the mind set on the flesh is death, but the mind set on the Spirit is life and peace, because the mind set on the flesh is hostile toward God; for it does not subject itself to the law of God, for it is not even able to do so; and those who are in the flesh cannot please God."* (Romans 8:5-8)

Prayer exclusively focused on the temporal cannot please God. Man is made up of body, soul, and spirit. When the body (the flesh) is more important than the spirit (the eternal), our gaze and glance are reversed. When our gaze and glance are reversed, emotions will surface and take control. Man's soul is made up of mind, will, and emotions. With emotions in control, the will is subject to the emotions, the mind becomes subject to the will and we are controlled by our circumstances. I will do this or that if I feel good about it. If I don't feel like going to church, I won't go. If I don't feel like tithing, I won't tithe. I am controlled by my feelings because I have allowed myself a temporal mind-set. When emotions are in control, you make up your mind about what you'll do based on how you feel.

This was really brought home to me through an experience with a man in our church whom I had been working with. He had just received a letter from the church saying that the leadership had decided to take money out of the general funds to pave the parking lot. The congregation was not consulted. After receiving this letter, he came by and asked me if I could go with him for a couple hours; he just wanted to take me for a ride. I agreed to go. He drove to a men's clothing store that was having a sale. He said, "I want to buy a nice suit for you." I was a little uneasy and asked why he wanted to do that. He said he would feel much better with me wearing his tithe than having it laying in the parking lot! I can honestly say I tried to talk him out of it, but he was so emotional about it, I relented. Every time I wore that suit I was a little uncomfortable. The tithes should go in the storehouse. When emotions are in charge, your will is subject to the emotions and your mind is subject to your will and you will satisfy your emotions. We have a human tendency to justify anything we want, but often we do it irrationally.

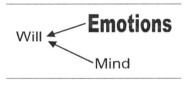

The more emotional a prayer request or concern is, the more caution we should exercise to be sure to pray with our mind. "... *I shall pray with the spirit and I shall pray with the mind also.*" (I Corinthians 14:15) The will is subject to either the mind or the emotions. If we don't seek to get God's mind first, our mind is tossed by every wind of doctrine. Ephesians 4:14 says, *"As a result, we are . . . children, tossed here and there by waves, and carried about by every wind of doctrine, by the trickery of men, by craftiness in deceitful scheming."*

No one can sustain a vital prayer life with their mind set on temporal things; there will be no stability in their prayer life. Why? Because we have no ability to see temporal needs from God's perspective if the spirit of prayer has been mortified. Remember that the mind set on the flesh is death (Romans 8:6).

We will have no confidence in our prayers in this condition because God has not obligated Himself to answer in the temporal as He has in the eternal.

However, if by an act of my will I set my mind on eternal issues, things above, my mind is in control instead of my emotions. My will is subject to my mind and my emotions are subject to my will. It is with the mind that we understand God's truth. Our minds are to be renewed with God's truth so that our very lives will be transformed (Romans 12:2). God desires that the spiritual predominate and that our minds control our wills.

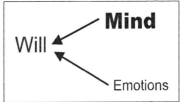

The Apostle Paul says in Colossians 3:3, *For you have died and your life is hidden with Christ in God.* If we have been raised up with Christ, we are dead to self. Does a dead man care about what he wears or what he has to eat? Why would a dead man pray about his health? Paul is teaching that temporal issues will have no power over us if we understand that the old man is dead.

Juan Ortiz, a South American evangelist, tells the story of Poncho, who asked his pastor, "What does it mean, dead in Christ?"

"Poncho, remember we buried Manuel last week. You go out to his grave and tell him all the bad things you know about him, you tell him how you remember when he lied to you and how he stole from his friends. Don't hold back anything, then come back and tell me what happened." Poncho did as the Pastor suggested.

When he came back, the pastor asked Poncho what had happened. Poncho said, "Nothing!"

"Well then, go back to Manuel's grave and tell him all the good things you know about him. Tell him how you remember when he helped you get your car going. Just really praise him for everything you can think of, then come back and tell me what happened."

Poncho went again to the grave and praised Manuel as he was instructed. Then he went to the pastor, who asked what had happened. "Nothing!"

Pastor said, "That's dead."

When neither praising nor cursing brings a reaction, that's dead!

There is nothing wrong in praying about our own health; in fact, we are commanded to pray about everything. James 5:16 says, *Pray for one another, so that you may be healed. The fervent prayer of a righteous man can accomplish much.* Also Philippians 4:6-7 says, *Be anxious for nothing, but in everything by prayer and supplication with thanksgiving let your requests be made known to God.* But when we pray about our health, it should be from an eternal perspective; that is, how does my health help or hinder me doing the Father's will? This is a prayer focused on the eternal, which equips us to pray in the Spirit.

Praying in the Spirit will focus on transforming us into His image. *He condemned sin in the flesh, in order that the requirement of the Law might be fulfilled in us, who do not walk according to the flesh, but according to the **Spirit**.* (Romans 8:4) Our flesh prays in the temporal. Our spirit prays in the eternal. *But their **minds** were hardened; for until this very day at the reading of the old covenant the same veil remains uplifted, because it is removed in Christ. But to this day whenever Moses is read, a veil lies over their heart; but whenever a man turns to the Lord* (seeks His face), *the veil is taken away. Now the Lord is the Spirit; where **the Spirit of the Lord is**, there is liberty. But we all, with unveiled face beholding as in a mirror the glory of the Lord, are being transformed into the same image from glory to* *glory, just as from the Lord, **the Spirit**.* (2 Corinthians 3:14-18) Praying in the Spirit will focus on transforming us into His image. Praying in the flesh will conform us to the world.

> *The God of this world has blinded the **minds** of the unbelieving, that they might not see the light of the gospel of the glory of Christ, who is the image of God.* (2 Corinthians 4:4)

Praying to change the circumstance without knowing the mind of Christ in the circumstance will lead our mind astray. It is temporal prayer.

> *But I am afraid, lest as the serpent deceived Eve by his craftiness, your **minds** should be led astray from the simplicity and purity of devotion to Christ.* (2 Corinthians 11:3)

> *Be anxious for nothing, but in everything by prayer and supplication with thanksgiving let your requests be made known to God. And the peace of God, which surpasses all comprehension, shall guard your **hearts** and your **minds** in Christ Jesus. Finally, brethren, whatever is true, whatever is honorable, whatever is pure, whatever is lovely, whatever is of good repute, if there is any excellence and if anything worthy of praise, let your **mind** dwell on these things.* (Philippians 4:6-8)

This is the content of eternal prayers in the Spirit of God. Such prayer empowers us to take every thought captive to the obedience of Christ. (2 Corinthians 2:5)

3. Understanding that in God's sovereignty, everything touching our lives is designed and/or allowed by him to conform us to His image.

An eternal mind-set in prayer transforms us into the image of God. Being conformed to Christ is the ultimate good that God has in mind for us.

And we know that God causes all things to work together for good to those who love God, to those who are called according to His purpose. (Romans 8:28)

And what is His purpose? Paul tells us in the next verse.

"For whom He did foreknow, He also did predestine to be conformed to the image of His Son."

When we are confronted with an emergency, like a loved one being injured in an automobile accident, we can think for a moment and ask ourselves or the Lord, what attribute of God is most needed in this situation? By that act of the will, we have set our mind on the things above and are *taking every thought captive to the obedience of Christ.* (2 Corinthians 10:4, 5) We are not presuming that we know how to pray, like telling God what to do for our loved one. We should be careful not to pray someone out of their Gethsemane when God is leading them to Calvary. Discomfort is sometimes necessary to accomplish God's will, just as it was necessary for Jesus.

The gaze and glance principle teaches that our attitude about being unemployed, for example, is more important to the Lord than our being without a job. An unemployed Christian who is seeking God's face to be sure his relationship is right and asking the Lord to open his understanding of God's purpose in the situation is being conformed to the image of Christ. He is internalizing peace, patience, self-control, etc. –the fruit of the Spirit. Because he puts his relationship to the Lord above his circumstances, he will definitely grow spiritually.

And we know that God causes all things to work together for good to those who love God, to those who are called according to His purpose. For whom He foreknew, He also predestined to become conformed to the image of His Son, that He might be the first-born among many brethren" (Romans 8:28, 29).

4. Trusting God enough to willingly allow Him to work in us in any given circumstance, so that His attributes are made visible through us, rather than our own human reactions.

If we don't want to distort others' views of God, we need to make God's attributes visible. When the Israelites were allowed to go back to Israel after the exile in Babylon, their grief was intensified when they realized how bad things were in their homeland. God was certainly grieved too. Back in Babylon, the king noticed Nehemiah's countenance and asked, "Why is your face sad, though you are not sick?" The king noticing the plight of the Jews was an answer to Nehemiah's prayer. See Nehemiah 1 and 2 for this record of God working through prayer. The remarkable way in which God caused the King to provide for the rebuilding and resettlement of Jerusalem brought great glory to God, even from a heathen king.

Here's an experience out of our lives when we applied the principle of making God's attributes visible through prayer. Please remember that we should not form a doctrine of prayer based on experiences. Our personal testimony only illustrates my point.

In 1971, Shirley and I were assigned at headquarters of Campus Crusade for Christ in Arrowhead Springs near San Bernardino, California. We were learning so much that we could hardly wait to share it with our church. Our church had introduced us to CCC and helped us to be staff members. We felt we owed them so much and needed to share anything with them that would strengthen and advance the cause of Christ. Up to that point, very little of what we shared had made a difference. Then God began burdening us to pray. The church had problems, but we were learning not to focus on the problem so much, but to seek the spiritual issues.

As we drove from San Bernardino into the desert, my thoughts and prayers were about how ineffective we had been. What could I do to gain a positive position to intercede effectively for the church? The thought came, "What about relinquishing their financial support to us?" They gave us $50 a month and were the largest supporter we had at the time. We had gone from $1,000 a week at my job to $500 a month on staff. What's more, not even that much was coming in. When I got that thought, I immediately dismissed it. I thought, "Lord, it's not possible for us to continue without this support!"

Then came that still small voice, not audible: "Gil, who are you trusting?"

My words can't explain the struggle going on in my mind and heart. It was one thing for me to go without, but did I have the right to put the needs of my wife and four children on the line? Finally, two hours later I said, "Okay, Lord, I will give up the support the church gives me."

When we got to town, I met the pastor and shared my decision. I said, "The Lord has impressed upon me to offer to give up my support. Then perhaps some men in the church, who have questioned my motives, would be open to what I share that could strengthen the church."

Pastor said, "No. I don't think that would make any difference to our financial problems. You are the only missionary this church has ever helped send to the mission field and the church needs to have a part." He dismissed that idea. I took a deep breath of relief! We departed and I felt so spiritual for having offered.

But one hour later, the pastor called me and said, "I've been thinking about your offer. Were you serious?"

I took another breath and said, "Yes, I was serious."

The pastor said, "I think there is one person who is most concerned about the finances that I think your offer will speak to, loud and clear. Would you go with me to tell him about your decision?"

I smile to myself as I think about it today, but at the time I really felt like I had died to self. This is a very significant principle of prayer. Often we have to die to self to gain a favorable position to pray effectively. When the pastor and I shared my decision with this man, he accepted it and asked me to share in the midweek service. It really wasn't that much money, but it established an attitude that took a lot of pressure off the pastor. As we returned to the church, we were rejoicing and decided to pray, following the pattern of adoration, confession, thanksgiving, and supplication. We went to a back room where we wouldn't be disturbed and began praising the Lord for His faithfulness to us, asking forgiveness for our unbelief, and thanking God for one another. We were consciously in the presence of the Lord. *Where the Spirit of the Lord is there is liberty.* (2 Corinthians 3:17) The Holy Spirit had enabled me to make visible the selfless spirit of Christ to those men in our church.

The pastor began to share his heart, saying things he had not shared with anyone. He had an inward spiritual struggle much like I had just gone through several hours earlier. He said he had not had a good relationship with his father since he became a pastor. Now for the first time his dad was coming to visit him. Pastor had a deep desire to take his father to Disneyland and show him a good time. However, he didn't have the money, his car had bald tires, etc. But he had an idea. His rental house needed painting. He thought if he painted it himself, maybe the landlord would give him a month's free rent. That would give him enough money to meet the need, if the landlord would agree. But he was concerned what the congregation would think when they saw him painting his house. He envisioned they would be critical, that he should be working on his sermon or making hospital calls. I suggested that we pray from Psalm 37:4 and 5: *Delight yourself in the LORD; and He will give you the desires of your heart. Commit your way to the LORD, trust also in Him, and He will do it.* We had learned that putting scripture with our prayers gives us confidence, knowing we are praying in His will.

As we discussed the verse, we determined that our responsibility was to rejoice in God. And God's responsibility was to put the right desires in our hearts. It was our understanding that if we rejoiced, in spite of the circumstance, we could take it by faith that our desire was of the Lord. So we prayed in agreement, with a spirit of expectancy, "Father, if it is your will for Pastor to paint that house, thank you for working in the heart of the landlord to approve this plan. Thank you, too, for working in the heart of the congregation to be grateful, so that every stroke of the brush would be glory to you, Lord. If the desire we have in our hearts is not of You, we commit our prayers and these plans into Your hands, based on Proverbs16:3: *Commit your works to the Lord, and your plans will be established.* We pray this in unity in Jesus name. Amen."

We rejoiced, and I went home. Shortly thereafter, we heard the fire sirens. Then the phone rang. A man from church said the pastor's house was on fire! We hurried to his house. The fire trucks and firemen and the neighborhood had all gathered around. Within a few minutes, his house and all their possessions were burned to the ground. After watching in amazement, I asked the pastor if the Lord wanted him to paint that house? His response was, "We did ask Him to make it clear, didn't we? I think He answered our prayers!"

The fire chief standing nearby was telling some of the firemen that there was a gas leak that filled all the walls with gas. Pastor had come home to change into his jogging suit and then had gone out to jog. A few minutes later, his daughter had come home, washed her hands with warm water, and left; the house was empty. She had used enough hot water for the water heater to light. When it did, the gas in the walls ignited, causing an explosion throughout the house. There was no chance to save anything. The fire chief said it couldn't have been leaking very long. It seemed obvious to Pastor and me that the leak started about the time we finished praying. The pastor had a confident peace in his heart that the Lord had been attentive to our prayers.

Businessmen, community leaders, and the man on the street would ask him, "How can you be so calm? How can you be so joyous after losing your home?" He shared how the Lord gave him the inner peace and joy of knowing that he was a child of the King and he knew God meant the situation for good, even though we saw no good reason for it at the time. He had numerous opportunities to share the Gospel at the Rotary Club, the Lions Club, Kiwanis Club, etc. Headlines in the local paper said the pastor's response to his house burning down was, *"God is our refuge and strength. A very present help in trouble."* The pastor had such a positive witness in the community that, as a result, he was given a new residence, clothes, furniture, a new car. The church doubled his salary, and he took his father to Disneyland for a marvelous vacation. The desires of the pastor's heart were abundantly fulfilled. Many leaders and individuals who had been unapproachable before surrendered their lives to Christ. The incident gave the pastor a position in the community that had not been available to him. Many Christians were strengthened as a result. His supernatural response to adversity made many attributes of God visible to those in the community.

Another example of making God visible through a proper gaze and glance is the story of a lady in Chicago who had a coal furnace. She ran out of coal and ordered a truckload. The truck arrived, the driver put the steel chute down into the coal bin, and just as he began to dump the coal, the wind shifted. The lady of the house had four lines of partially dried white clothes. If you know anything about coal dust, you know that was a disaster. The driver just wanted to get out of there. You can't keep your job doing dumb things like that. But, before he could move, the lady came out on the porch, saw her clothes that were now covered with black coal dust, and said, "My! I'm going to have to wash those all over again."

The driver said, "Lady, what church do you go to?" God wasn't mentioned, but here's a probable non-Christian relating the lady's actions to God. Why? She was making visible various attributes of God. This may have happened to her so that she could manifest God's calmness, patience, understanding, forgiveness, and longsuffering, to mention a few. That's God's purpose for biblical prayer–to know Him and to make Him known.

The Restoration of Biblical Prayer

Does everything really belong to the Lord?

Shirley and I did not have reliable transportation very early in our ministry. As we got going, my brother Don and his wife Nancy supplied us with a very nice, almost new car for the ministry. I was able to go places and do things without ever worrying about getting there or about making car payments or repairs. We were so blessed with that car. We loved it! Shirley especially loved the stereo.

One afternoon we were on our way to the airport to pick up a missionary couple with Campus Crusade for Christ, coming home from overseas ministry. We arrived at the airport about 5 p.m. It was just beginning to get dark. About 50 miles from the airport on the freeway headed for San Jose where we lived and headquartered, I noticed other drivers blinking their light and honking their horns. At first I thought they wanted to pass, but I was doing over the speed limit, ashamed to say. As they persisted, I saw sparks and fire coming from the rear of my car!

I immediately pulled off the freeway onto the shoulder and discovered my car - rather, Don's car - was on fire! We hurriedly got the missionaries' luggage unloaded and tried to put out the fire. Several drivers with fire extinguishers tried to help us, and with their help, we were able to put out the fire; but as soon as the fire extinguishers ran out of chemical, the flames returned – hotter and more fierce than before. We threw dirt on it to no avail. I thought at the time, if we only had a bucket of water. I prayed in my heart,"Lord, could you cause it to rain right now? Just a little would help."

By this time the car was totally engulfed in flames. I was sure the gas tank was ready to blow. The interior was completely gutted and blackened. Shirley's elderly uncle, Henry Lenhart, was visiting us at the time and accompanied us on this trip. As the flames burned hotter and higher, Uncle Henry yelled with a strong forceful voice, from quite a distance,"Men, get away from that car!" At that moment I realized no one was hurt; Praise the Lord! After all, it was Don's car; NO — it was the LORD'S. We had given it to the Lord the day we received it.

My thought was,"Lord, why do you want to burn up Your car?" We had no answer at the time, but we did know and believe that the Lord was watching over us. Eventually, the fire department arrived and finished putting out the flames. The whole thing had been quite traumatic.

That evening when I called my brother and told him that the Lord had burned up his car, he was a little taken back, but not too much. He was used to me somewhat pushing the envelope. Anyway, he said he would need the police report and he would check with his insurance the next day. If I remember right, the insurance had a $1,000 deductible that we didn't have.

The following Sunday, we shared with our church family what had happened. None of them had ever burned up a car and neither had I. What we discovered afterwards was that the left rear wheel bearing went out, and the excessive friction caused the tire to catch fire. That melted the spare tire compartment and the tire caught fire. It was the burning rubber that we couldn't put out.

We prayed at the time for help to put the fire out. God didn't answer in the way we wanted. We finally accepted the fact that God had something else in mind. The peace of God we had once we gave the situation to the Lord was amazing. In a couple of weeks, Don sent his son Mark from Nebraska to California with a replacement car – newer and better!

Shirley and I have a friend who has supported us financially and prayerfully for 20 years or more. He has told us on numerous occasions how our testimony about that car and the fire has ministered to him over the years. The confidence God gave us to trust Him and acknowledge that He is the owner of our possessions built up our friend's confidence as well. We have many other testimonies of how God encouraged us to walk closer with Him.

The point of all of this is that if we don't hold on too tightly to material things, we can often pray much more effectively. The moral of the story is keep your eyes on the Lord – the gaze and glance principle!

In Colossians 3:4, Paul says, *When Christ, who is our life, is revealed, then you also will be revealed with him in glory.* When knowing Christ is our very life, when our relationship to Christ is the most important thing in life, we are then being conformed to His likeness. What does it mean to be revealed with Christ in glory? It means to be disclosed, to be open to view. In other words, we will not only be with Him, we will be like Him. (Romans 8:29-30) Not only will we be with Him in glory, but also He is with us right now. The life you and I are now living is a very real part of our eternal life. That's good news, but it can't happen without prayer. You can't become a Christian apart from prayer because calling upon the Lord is an act of prayer as we see in Romans 10:9. Prayer is necessary for the Christian life, because prayer is one of the vital means of communion with God to understand His will and to ask for grace to perform His will.

John Wesley has gone so far as to say, "God does nothing but in answer to prayer." It is my understanding that God, working in the world today to fulfill His will, has chosen to work primarily –not exclusively, but primarily –through man. And man cannot fulfill the Father's calling apart from prayer.

> *Pray without ceasing; in everything give thanks for this is the will of God for you in Christ Jesus.*
> (1 Thessalonians 5:17, 18)

> *Through Him then, let us continually offer up a sacrifice of praise to God, that is, the fruit of lips that give thanks to His name.* (Hebrews 13:15)
>
> *Now He was telling them a parable to show that at all times they ought to pray and not lose heart.* (Luke 18:1)
>
> *Therefore I want men in every place to pray, lifting up holy hands, without wrath and dissension.* (1 Timothy 2:8)
>
> *Be anxious for nothing, but in everything by prayer and supplication with thanksgiving let your requests be made known to God.* (Philippians 4:6)

I am sure you would agree with me that one of the major reasons Jesus came to earth was to glorify the Father. How did He do that? He did that primarily by making the attributes of God visible. How do you and I know and believe that God is love? We know and believe that God is love because Jesus was a loving man. How do you and I know and believe God is forgiving? We know and believe that God is forgiving because Jesus was forgiving. Jesus was the visible, physical manifestation of God and of His attributes so that you and I may know Him.

Then what is man's purpose on earth? The same thing—to manifest the attributes of God in our life: that is, to make those attributes visible and real to those in our sphere of influence—to glorify God and to be glorified with Him. It means to be identified in a positive way as a Christian. That's the Biblical idea of the outcome of prayer, to know God and make Him known.

Perhaps an illustration would help us get a better handle on this. Years ago a lay couple invited us to do the Prayer Enrichment Seminar in their church in a small, isolated community in the Deep South. The small country church had little exposure to this kind of teaching on prayer, so I was careful to teach with clarity and simplicity. One of the couples in the seminar sat in the front row the entire week. This couple had just recently given their lives to Christ. They had many problems –physical problems, financial problems, marital problems, and relational problems –with her kids, his kids, their kids, and their ex-mates, who all lived in this little rural community. They were there because someone had said, "Look, you've tried everything in the world (which they had) –why not try Jesus?" And they thought that was true, so they were trying Jesus!

The husband was an ex-merchant marine with absolutely no biblical knowledge or exposure to Christianity. If I had had a double-doctorate in counseling, I wouldn't have known where to start to help this couple. When I explained the gaze and glance principle and asked how many of the spies who went into the Promised Land had their eyes on Jesus, he asked what the Promised Land was and if the spies were Russians! But they were trying Jesus and came every night. At the conclusion of the week, I had no idea how much they were able to understand about communicating with God. I didn't have great faith that they would be able to apply what I had been teaching.

I had the opportunity to return a year or so later and my friend had to introduce them to me again, because I didn't recognize them. They had changed so much. They not only were still together as a couple, but they were a couple that looked like they had spent most of their life with Jesus Christ. They were radiant, happy, fulfilled, and joyous. I was so amazed that I asked the wife to what she attributed this great change. She got a little smile on her face and took me to her kitchen. She pointed to the refrigerator door. There was about an eighteen-inch-high gaze-and-glance diagram. I said, "OH!"

She said, "That's not all," and took me into the hallway of their long double-wide mobile home. There at the end, on the linen closet door was an even bigger gaze-and glance-diagram!

I said, "Oh, I'm beginning to understand."

She said, "That's not all," and walked into the bedroom. On the inside of the footboard of their bed was, you guessed it, another big gaze-and-glance diagram. She said, "We don't know a lot about the Bible, and we don't fully understand how or why it works. All we know is, the minute our heads come off the pillow in the morning, we have to get our eyes on Jesus, not on our problems."

Chapter 4
The Transformed Mind-set in Action

Prayer really works when you purpose to seek the Counselor before you seek to eliminate the problem! When our relationship to the Lord is right, then all our other relationships fall into place. Christ is glorified and we are glorified with Him. To use the terms from Campus Crusade for Christ, when Christ is on the throne of our life, the fruit of the Spirit is evident: love, joy, peace, patience, kindness, gentleness, self-control, etc.

How do I know if my gaze is on the Lord? If I am experiencing the fruit of the Spirit in my life, I can be sure God is active in my life (Matthew 7:20). If I am becoming a little more loving in an unloving situation, I know my gaze is on the Lord; I have an eternal mind-set and I am praying kingdom prayers.

What are kingdom prayers? Kingdom prayers are based on the concept found in the Lord's Prayer, His model for the disciples: *Thy kingdom come, Thy will be done...* The focus of such prayers is the advancement of God's program for mankind. They are prayers prayed in the Spirit. *With all prayer and petition pray at all times in the Spirit!* (Ephesians 6:18) The spiritual man has set his mind on things above, and his prayer life is based on a relationship with Christ. He prays with an eternal mind-set resulting in being conformed to the image of Christ. Notice that Ephesians 6:18 emphasizes to pray at "all times."

The Spiritual Man

The spiritual man is Christ-centered, is empowered by the Holy Spirit, introduces others to Christ, has an effective prayer life, understands God's Word, trusts God, and obeys God. His prayers produce love, joy, peace, patience, kindness, faithfulness and goodness. The Christ-centered man understands that Christ is at the right hand of the Father, interceding for him, with the mind and will of the Father. He accepts the reality of Christ's prayer for himself and others.

For example, in John 17:17 Christ prays, *Sanctify them in the truth; Thy word is truth*. The spiritual man realizes that the Holy Spirit has obligated Himself to lead us into all truth. That does not mean that we'll become all-knowing, but it does mean that God has obligated himself to lead us into all the truth we'll need at any given moment to walk uprightly in any given circumstance. (John 16:13)

Now what does that mean to this man's prayer life? It means that he does not rely on his own intellect or experience to pray in a given situation. He realizes that he first must seek God's enlightenment as to how to pray from God's perspective. His prayers for others who don't know the Lord might go something like this: "Heavenly Father, I know Bill has a distorted view of You. Please enlighten me to his misconception about You, or of Christianity, so that I might pray that attribute of Yourself into my life and make it visible to him—so that it will dispel his misconception! I pray this in the name of Jesus, Amen." This is Christ-centered praying because it is based on the known, revealed will of God. This is kingdom prayer. This type of prayer is heard and answered 10,000 out of 10,000 times when uttered by a believer who is in a right relationship with the Lord, who has set his mind on things above, on the kingdom.

A spiritual man's prayer life is empowered by the Holy Spirit. This means that his prayer life is directed by Christ, and results in being in harmony with God's plan. This person acknowledges in his prayer that apart from the Holy Spirit, he can do nothing that counts for eternity. He understands that the Holy Spirit must help him recognize sin in his life, just as the Apostle Paul says in 1 Corinthians 4:4: *I am conscious of nothing against myself, yet I am not by this acquitted; but the one who examines me is the Lord*. This believer is totally dependent; he has come to have full confidence in the Lord.

To expand on this, when I was born physically, I weighed two and a half pounds. In 1929 it was no small miracle that I survived. I was totally dependent. If my mother and my nurse had not watched over me constantly, I would not be here today. As I grew, I grew to independence. However, when I was born again spiritually, I was born independent. I only received Christ as "fire insurance." I just didn't want to go to hell. I did not trust or rely upon God for anything else. But as I grew spiritually, I became more and more dependent on Him. Physically we are dependent and grow to independence. Spiritually we are born independent and grow to dependence. The spiritual man has accepted the reality of his inability to exist or flourish on his own. He must have the power of the Holy Spirit in his life.

An illustration that has helped me to understand the spiritual man's dependence upon Spirit-empowered prayer is a story about a young man who went to see the evangelist D. L. Moody. Moody's secretary said that she was sorry, but that Mr. Moody was in prayer. If he would care to wait, she was sure Moody would want to see him. So the young man chose to wait. The only chair was near Mr. Moody's office door. After a few minutes the young man heard a voice coming from the office and assumed that it was Mr. Moody. He heard, "Oh, God!" The young man perked up, thinking he was going to hear Mr. Moody pray. He was interested in what a godly man's prayer life consisted of, but he heard nothing else. So he thought Moody was finished and would be out in a minute, but he wasn't. After a time of silence, he heard again, "Oh, God!" There was silence again for a while. Then finally he heard, "Oh, God, *empower* me." That was his prayer for 45 minutes—"Oh, God, empower me."

Let me ask you, how long has it been since you've been in a prayer meeting when a sincere Christian was simply crying out to God for power—for power to love the unlovable, power to live the Christian life, power to share his faith? "God, empower me" is another prayer that is heard 10,000 out of 10,000 times, for it's a prayer of a Spirit-filled Christian. It is kingdom prayer. The flesh never prompts that kind of prayer. It is Christ-centered, powerfully effective, and counts for eternity!

A spiritual man's prayer life is effective because it is based on his relationship with Jesus Christ through the Word of God, empowered by the Holy Spirit. It glorifies Christ. His prayer life brings glory to the Father, not to the pray-er.

A spiritual man's prayer life is permeated by a deep need to understand God's Word. He makes the Bible his prayer book, which brings to light the purpose and plan of God. We will find this man praying often to be empowered to understand the Word of God. This man, for example, might remind God in prayer of His response to King Solomon when he prayed for understanding in 1 Kings 3:9: *So give Thy servant an understanding heart to judge Thy people, to discern between good and evil...* This prayer pleased the Lord.

Note verses 10-14. In parentheses I have noted the things we typically ask for, which are in contrast to what Solomon asked for. *Because you have asked this thing and have not asked for yourself long life* (heal our sicknesses), *nor have asked riches for yourself* (improve our finances), *nor have you asked for the life of your enemies* (change others to please us), *but have asked for yourself discernment to understand justice, behold, I have done according to your words. Behold, I have given you a wise and discerning heart, so that there has been no one like you before you, nor shall one like you arise after you. And I have also given you what you have not asked, both riches and honor, so that there will not be any among the kings like you all your days. And if you walk in My statutes and commandments, as your father David walked, then I will prolong your days.*

Because of the spiritual nature of what Solomon did ask for, God took care of his material needs in a super-abundant way. Solomon sought God's kingdom first, and God added everything else to him!

The spiritual man who trusts God prays, "Lord, help me to trust You for a job. I know You love me unconditionally and I praise You for being love. I praise You, knowing that Your plan for my life is so much greater than my own. Lord, I trust You to enlighten me to trust and obey in this opportunity to grow spiritually. Thank You, Father. Amen."

A spiritual man's prayer life is undergirded with his commitment to trust and obey. His first response to adversity is not necessarily to change it. The apostle Paul never asked anyone to pray him out of jail. His request was always for his inner person to be strengthened that He would glorify his Lord in his imprisonment. He would not allow himself to entertain the thought that he was chained to those guards. No! Those guards were chained to him—that they might come to know his Lord.

The Carnal Man

Colossians 3:5 says, *Therefore consider the members of your earthly body as dead to immorality, impurity, passion, evil desire and greed, which amounts to idolatry.* When temporal things are more important than the eternal, we begin to make visible the works of the flesh instead of the fruit of the Spirit. When our gaze and glance are reversed, our prayers become idolatrous. Why would our prayers be idolatrous? Because our prayers have become greedy, self-centered, and worldly.

What is an idol? It is using anything to meet needs that God should meet. The carnal man's prayer life is an abomination to God because it is temporally motivated. *He who turns away his ear from listening to the law, even his prayer is an abomination.* (Proverbs 28:9) We manufacture a god who responds to our desires. *For it is on account of these things that the wrath of God will come.* (Colossians 3:6) On account of what things? The works of the flesh!

When a Christian begins to make visible in his life the attributes of the flesh rather than the attributes of the Spirit, God is not glorified. He is dishonored.

Some or all of the following traits may characterize the Christian who does not fully trust God: ignorance of his spiritual heritage, unbelief, disobedience, loss of love for God and for others, poor prayer life, no desire for Bible study. His prayer life may produce a legalistic attitude, impure thoughts, jealousy, guilt, worry, discouragement, a critical spirit, frustration, and aimlessness.

This describes a praying Christian who has set his mind on the temporal things. Let's look at these traits more closely in relationship to prayer.

Ignorance of his spiritual heritage commonly characterizes a carnal man's prayer life. We know that the Bible tells us to go boldly into the throne room of God. The carnal man would not do that. He would tend to go to the back door, so to speak, and beg alms. His prayers would be making deals and bargains with God, such as, "Lord, if you save my daughter, I'll quit smoking." Or "Lord, if you get me out of this mess, I'll serve you the rest of my life." Or "Lord, if you heal my eyes, I'll live for you." Or "Lord, if you give me a raise at work, I'll start tithing." Because of his ignorance, his prayers require God to perform for him before he'll obey.

A man who does not fully trust God, prays to prove to himself who God is through the answer or lack of an answer. A Christian living in disobedience often prays to justify his disobedience. He may pray for God to bless his Sunday school class when he is not obeying God's command to tithe. He may even have an attitude that God isn't going to answer anyway, but thinks he looks good to others when he is praying. His life is void of love and joy. Because he loves himself so much, he has a loss of love for God and for others. Since he wants to look "more spiritual," his prayer is, "God, change them." The problem is always with others. He's critical and thinks he can do it better. This is a very poor prayer life! He doesn't pray from his Bible. He has neither time nor desire for Bible study. His prayers are based on his own desires and interpretation of God's will and way. His prayer life is legalistic, critical, and frustrating, and its aim is always temporal, because he has a temporal mind-set.

Paul says in Colossians 3:7, *And in them you also once walked, when you were living in them.* We all can identify very easily with the fleshly man's prayer life because we have all walked that way. In Colossians 3:8-11, Paul also tells us that we are to put the old ways aside and put on the new self: *But now you also, put them all aside; anger, wrath, malice, slander and abusive speech from your mouth. Do not lie to one another, since you laid aside the old self with its evil practices, and have put on the new self who is being renewed to a true **knowledge** according to the image of the One who created him—a renewal in which there is no distinction between Greek and Jew, circumcised and uncircumcised, barbarian, Scythian, slave and freeman, but Christ is all, and in all.*

In summary, Paul is saying that if we claim to be Christians we must set our minds on eternal issues. As we do, we will be renewed in our mind, soul, and spirit, in the knowledge of our Creator. This will result in renewal, whether we are Baptist, Presbyterian, or Pentecostal; whether we have great talent or little; whether we teach a first grade Sunday school class or seminary graduates. When Christ is exalted and our relationship to Him is number one in our life, Christ is all and in all.

The fruit of the Spirit in our lives makes our relationship to Christ visible to the world. If our relationship to God is number one in our life, the fruit of the Spirit is being produced. But, for example, if our ministry is more important than our relationship to the Lord, our gaze and glance are reversed and the fruit we bear is of the flesh. If what we are doing for God is more important to us than what God is doing in us, our gaze and glance are reversed.

Effective Praying

How do I know if I am praying effectively when I pray for $50? Before I understood the gaze and glance principle, I would have said to wait until I get the $50. I now know that using the visible evidence to affirm my effectiveness in prayer can be a trap. On the other hand, if I am praying for someone's salvation and it seems to me that the more I pray the worse they get, but in spite of that, I become more caring, more creative in the way I love and respond to them, then I know I am praying effectively. The Bible teaches that we are to measure the effectiveness of our prayers by the fruit of the Spirit internalized in the pray-er.

Prayer is God's major means of manifesting or internalizing His attributes in our lives. *For by these He has granted to us His precious and magnificent promises, in order that by them you might become partakers of the divine nature, having escaped the corruption that is in the world by lust.* (2 Peter 1:4)

How can Elton Gillam, with all his imperfections, possibly escape the corruption that is all around him? Is there any place you and I can go where we won't be surrounded by sin, corruption, and lust? What is our hope? Is it to become more knowledgeable, to work harder, to give more? I believe the Bible teaches that my only hope is to become more like Christ. How do I become more like Him? Second Peter 1:2 and 3 gives us some help: *Grace and peace be multiplied to you in the knowledge of God and of Jesus our Lord; seeing that His divine power has granted to us everything pertaining to life and godliness, through the true knowledge of Him who called us by His own glory and excellence.* I first must know Him.

This is the primary purpose of prayer—to know God. If we are growing in our knowledge of God, as evidenced by living more like Him, we are praying effectively.

Chapter 5
Nuts and Bolts: Praying Scripture

What does praying Scripture mean? Basically it means making your Bible your prayer book. For example: Psalm 100:4 says *Enter His gates with thanksgiving and His courts with praise* (a command.) Based on that verse we may praise Him for being our King and inviting us into His presence. By using praise to start our prayer, we are allowing God's majesty to fill us, thus giving the Holy Spirit an opportunity to guide our prayers. We will be less apt to use prayer merely to tell God how we feel about our life. Praise acknowledges God's attributes. Praise acknowledges the greatness of God. It is different from thankfulness, which acknowledges specific things He has *done* for us. We praise God for who He is and thank Him for what He has done. For example, we praise Him that He is a God of love; we thank Him for loving us.

Nothing can hinder a true prayer of praise. It goes directly to God's heart. It is the highest form of prayer. However, when we thank God for what He has done, it brings our prayer to more earthly things, a horizontal view rather than vertical. When we praise Him for being a God of love, we are praying eternal prayers. When we thank Him for what He has done, we acknowledge our temporal perspective of what we see and understand.

The Bible commands us to do both, to praise and to give thanks. However, if we begin to make a distinction between the two it will have an enduring effect on all our prayers.

Using the Scriptures to Build a Foundation for Communion with God

"Holy men of old spake as they were moved by the Holy Ghost. Their utterances, whether in adoration, thanksgiving, confession, or supplication, were controlled by the Spirit of God.

Hence they expressed the mind of the Spirit; they are the most appropriate vehicles for the expression of those feelings and desires, which the Spirit awakens in the minds of God's people. No prayers, therefore, are more edifying, other things being equal, than those which abound in the appropriate use of Scriptural language." (From *Unto Every Good Work*, published by Reformed Presbyterian Church in America)

I noticed an unusual thing when I attended the Arrowhead Springs prayer conference: the men there were spending more time talking about which Scripture would apply to certain needs than talking about the needs! It was revolutionary for me. In all the prayer meetings I had attended, we spent most of our time talking about the problems or needs. At this conference I heard, "Our prayers must be based on Scripture." I didn't know just what that meant. When we prayed in small groups, everyone had a Bible, and it was open! They were praying what they read. I had never experienced praying the Word like that before.

In all the church prayer meetings I had previously attended, we always had a short Bible study, but I can't remember that the Bible study had anything to do with what was prayed. Generally, after the Bible study we closed our Bibles and were asked, "Are there any prayer requests?" The first was usually for someone's sickness. Then the second one was too, and the third, etc. For twenty minutes or so we would talk about the problems as the pastor took notes on the requests; then we were out of time. So the pastor or another person would pray for the needs. The majority of the group was not expected to pray.

What I experienced in praying the Word at that conference was so uplifting and encouraging to me that I purposed to learn all I could about biblical prayer. I am sure that today I still don't fully understand or appreciate how essential the Bible is in praying. However, what I have learned I would like to share with you.

The frustration that I felt in many of those early church prayer meetings, and which I am sure many of you have felt too, was due to praying "in the flesh," rather than "in the spirit." Praying in the flesh means praying according to the fruit of the flesh. This type of praying almost always springs from and/or results in some of the following:

    Legalistic attitude   Discouragement
    Impure thoughts   Critical spirit
    Jealousy   Frustration
    Guilt   Aimlessness
    Worry

When our prayers are based only on the needs or desires of our fleshly bodies, they are temporal. Praying for temporal things is good and necessary; God expects us to pray about our "daily bread." But time-bound needs should not be dominant in our prayers.

Another frustrating aspect of the common experience of prayer falls under the heading of "vain repetitions." Church prayer meetings, prayer chains, and prayer circles sometimes develop a "prayer list" that varies little from week to week or month to month. Pray-ers easily fall into a habit of praying, "God, heal Mrs. A, Mr. B, Miss C, and God bless all the missionaries."

The great English Puritan John Owen wrote, "Nothing is more detrimental to the reality of *true* prayer than the mere thoughtless repetition of words."

When we learn to pray based on God's Word, we can bring a spiritual perspective even to temporal needs, our prayers are based on the eternal nature of God as revealed in His Word, and

God's Spirit witnesses with our spirit bringing insight and creativity to our praying.

To illustrate this technique, take your Bible and turn to Psalm 100. The basic idea is to seek God's face, His righteousness (Psalm 27:8) and to consciously come into His presence with praise and thanksgiving (Psalm 100:4) before seeking His hand with requesting or petitioning. This is not to gain favor or butter up God just to get Him to answer us favorably, but to accept His invitation to commune with Him.

Whether you are alone or in a group (you may want to try it with your family or Sunday School class), read aloud the first verse of Psalm 100: *Shout joyfully to the Lord, all the earth.* Pause a moment and look for an attribute, a characteristic, or a name of God and praise Him for it. Endeavor to keep your prayer short because longer prayers make it hard for those who are just learning (see Ecclesiastics 5:1, 2). Your short sentence prayer may be, "Lord, I praise You for being the God of joy and the Creator of all." Then read verse two. If you are in a group, take turns reading and praying. *Serve the Lord with gladness; come before Him with joyful songs.* Pause a moment to reflect on this. You may pray, "Father, I praise You for being the Creator of music and the Source of gladness, joy, and gratefulness." Continue through Psalm 100 by reading each verse, pausing to let the Holy spirit direct your thoughts, and then pray.

There are many other psalms of praise, such as Psalms 34, 84, 103, 145, 147, and others. We can pray through any of the books of the Bible in this manner, praying praise, confession, thanksgiving, petitioning for ourselves, and supplications for others. Include singing in your prayer time as well. Hymns, choruses, and songs of worship lift our spirits and nourish our souls: songs such as "Alleluia," "Seek ye first the Kingdom of God," "Turn your eyes upon Jesus," and "Holy, Holy, Holy."

Charles Wesley said, "He who sings prays twice." What does this mean? It means we make the words we sing our prayer, as well as lift up in our minds whatever burden the Lord lays on our heart as we sing.

Praying the Word has many advantages. One of the major ones is that we know we are praying in the will of God and not in the flesh. Read all of Isaiah 55. Verses 6, 8, and 11 say, *Seek the Lord while He may be found: call upon Him while He is near.* "*For My thoughts are not your thoughts, neither are your ways My ways," declares the Lord. "So shall My word be which goes forth from My mouth; it shall not return to me empty, without accomplishing what I desire, and without succeeding in the matter for which I sent it."* God's word is a revelation of His ways to us. Praying God's Word gives us confidence that our prayers are not empty and that they will succeed.

Another advantage is that Scripture helps keep our minds from wandering and helps us concentrate on Christ. We are edified, encouraged, and uplifted with hope. Jesus used the Scriptures to thwart Satan's offers in Matthew 4. The Word keeps us from praying with wrong motives, according to James 4:3. It gives us a track to run on and keeps our minds focused upon God and His will as in 1 John 5:14. This brings creativity to our prayer and gives us new insights about requests. It greatly reduces the repetitiveness of overused or trite phrases that tend to lose their meaning.

We quoted Oswald Chambers earlier: "We look upon prayer as a means of getting things for ourselves; the Bible idea of prayer is that we may get to know God Himself." As we seek God's face through His Word, we are enlightened to the truths that transform and conform us into the image of His Son. *And we know that God causes all things to work together for good to those who love God, those who are called according to His purpose. For whom He foreknew,* ***He also predestined to become conformed to the image of His Son,*** *that He might be the first-born among many brethren.* (Romans 8:28-29, my emphasis added)

Persistence Versus Vain Repetition

In Luke 11:1-4, after the disciples heard Jesus pray, they asked him to teach them to pray like John taught his disciples. Jesus answered them with what we call "The Lord's Prayer." Then in verses 5-8 Jesus shares the parable of the man who had no bread for his friend. He went to his neighbor and asked him for bread. This story illustrates persistence. Verses 9 and 10 teach us to "keep on asking and it shall be given you. Keep on seeking and you shall find. Keep on knocking and it shall be opened."

Jesus reinforces this idea in Luke 18:2 and following in the parable of the unjust judge. In verse 5 the judge says, *Yet because this widow bothers me, I will give her legal protection, lest by continually coming she wear me out.* Jesus said, *Hear what the unrighteous judge said; Now shall not God bring about justice for His elect, who cry to Him day and night, and will He delay long over them? I tell you that He will bring about justice for them speedily. However, when the Son of Man comes, will He find faith on the earth?*

To balance that, however, Jesus also teaches that we should not expect to be heard because of our many words. *And when you are praying, do not use meaningless repetition, as the Gentiles do, for they suppose they will be heard for their many words. Therefore do not be like them; for your Father knows what you need, before you ask Him.* (Matthew 6:7-8)

So the question is, how do I know when my persistence becomes vain repetition? One good way is when my persistence in prayer does not lead to action. Almost all true prayer leads to an action. When I am disobedient to do that action or if I am ignoring it, my prayers become vain repetition. *Even so faith, if it has no works, is dead, being by itself* (verse 17 of James 2:14-26).

Using God's Word can be a safeguard, but in our flesh, if we repeat the Word over and over, it becomes an abomination to the Lord. This is often done with "The Lord's Prayer." I have found that when my persistence loses, or is tending to lose, its creativity or spirit of expectancy, I am on the verge of vain repetition. That's when I need to stop the way I am praying –not stop praying altogether –but rather go back to Luke 11:1, *Lord, teach me to pray.* That helps me refocus on the Word and my spirit is lifted. The light of His Word increases my creativity in the way I pray. *For with thee is the fountain of life; in Thy light we see light* (Psalm 36:9) As a result I have peace, joy, love,... the fruit of the Spirit in my praying.

Peter Lord, founder of Agape Ministries and author of the *2959 Plan*, a private prayer journal, says, "If we allow our gaze to be on our request, it will dominate our prayers; we will tell God what we see and what needs to be done. However, if our gaze is on God, we will ask Him to interpret the situation from His viewpoint, and to tell us what He wants done." Using Scripture as the basis of our prayers helps us keep our eyes on the Author of those Scriptures.

This is what one writer said about praying based on Scripture:

"The Word and prayer to me are constantly interwoven. I don't read the Bible longer than a minute without praying, and I don't pray longer than a minute without some Scripture on my mind. If I start churning out prayers that aren't informed pretty explicitly by the Bible, I'm probably going to wind up praying carnal prayers; and if I try to read the Bible extensively without constantly sending my heart up to God, it will become an academic exercise that doesn't move my heart. I'm not just reading a document about a historical man, I'm reading an inspired Word from a living Christ, and my prayers are to a real, living person.

"This is a conversation. God is telling me what to do and I'm saying "Yes, yes!" I'm crying out to Him for help and I'm pleading for insight and I'm laying all my burdens before Him, and He's able to bear them. 2 Chronicles 16:9 says, "For the eyes of the Lord run to and fro throughout the earth, to give strong support to those whose heart is blameless toward him." (ESV) I love to think of prayer as giving God an occasion to show off how broad His shoulders are.

"I had a grandmother who opposed prayer because she felt it bothered God. I remember my father feared my visiting this woman because he was such a man of prayer and he knew that her views were so wrong. She thought that she was doing God an honor by saying, "I won't bother You with my little problems." But that attitude is highly dishonoring to God, as if somehow His circuits can be overloaded and our prayers are too much for Him to handle. God's circuits are infinite. You cannot but honor God when you go to Him for help. Psalm 50:15 says, "Call upon me in the day of trouble; I will deliver you, and you shall glorify me." (ESV) Prayer is the great means by which I get all the help I need and God gets all the glory He should have." (Source unknown)

In addition to praying based on God's Word, we need to make our requests based on the revealed character of God. That is what it means to pray "in the name" of Christ. Names reveal and represent the nature of the one named. We will now look at some aspects of God's character that can enlighten our praying.

The Attributes of God

When we have trouble recalling people's names, we often remember them by their unique characteristics such as the color and length of their hair, tall or short, thin or heavy, race or nationality, or the kind of personality that they may have (calm, hyper, critical, encourager). The characteristics of people describe the real them, and the more we are around a person, the more we know that person. The same is true with our Lord. The more we are around Him, studying His characteristics, the more we will know Him.

Since we are going to study the Lord's attributes, we must first study His essence, for His attributes come out of His essence. One cannot effectively grasp the attributes of God unless he understands His essence.

A good definition of essence is "that which underlies all outward manifestation, the reality of a being. The real thing." A good definition of attributes is "the distinguishing qualities or characteristics of the Divine nature."

He is **immaterial**. *A spirit has not flesh and bones . . .* (Luke 24:39)

When body parts are ascribed to Him, it is to make God real to the human mind and to express His various interests, powers, and activities. He is not limited by a physical body; therefore, all have access to His attention and care. We don't have to "wait for an appointment" to talk to Him.

He is **invisible**. *Who is the image of the invisible God . . .* (Colossians 1:15)

When the Scriptures give an account that somebody saw God, it was not His essence that they saw, but a reflection of His glory. (Exodus 33:21-23; Hebrews 1:3)

He is **alive**. *Hereby shall you know that the living God is among you* . . . (Joshua 3:10) Since He is alive, we can know that we are praying to a living God who hears, answers, and cares for His own—whereas, the idols of the heathen are dead. (Psalm 115:3-9)

He is **a person**. Since man has a personality, it is taken for granted that his Creator must also have a personality. If God did not have a personality, then man would be of a higher nature than God, for he would have something that God does not have. And if that be the case, then God would not be sovereign because He would not be able to control man or know man. Because God has a personality, we know that we are praying to someone who feels what we feel and therefore understands our circumstances. (Hebrews 4:14-16.)

He is **self-existent**. *I am that I am.* (Exodus 3:14)
God is not dependent upon anyone or anything in order to exist. Therefore, we know that our God cannot be influenced in any direction or be held in the hands of anyone else. What He has said will come about.

Mahatma Gandhi was once approached by an atheist with the request to organize and promote an anti-God society. Gandhi replied, "It amazes me to find an intelligent person who fights against something which he does not at all believe exists." [4]

He is **immense**. *...the heaven and heavens cannot contain thee.* (2 Kings 8:27)
God is not limited or circumscribed by space.

He is **eternal**. *...even from everlasting to everlasting thou art God.* (Psalm 90:2) *Who only has immortality* . . . (1 Timothy 6:16)

He is without beginning or end. He is free from any constraints of time.

An attribute is an inner quality that makes a person who he or she is. God wants very much for us to know what He is really like, so He has told us much about Himself in the Bible. Take time to think about God's attributes. Ask Him to help you know Him better and better. Then watch Him build His wonderful character into your life. *The fear of the LORD is the beginning of wisdom and knowledge of the Holy One is understanding.* (Proverbs 9:10)

Let him who glories glory in that, that he understands and knows Me, that I am the LORD, exercising lovingkindness, judgment, and righteousness in the earth. For in these I delight, says the LORD. (Jeremiah 9:24)

Attributes of God

Triune	Although we cannot understand it, God is a trinity—One God, yet three persons, all in perfect agreement. Deut. 6:4; Matt. 3:16, 17:2 Cor. 13:14
Eternal	God has no beginning. He has always been and He will always be, forever and ever. Gen. 21:33; Deut. 33:27
Infinite	God is a Spirit. He is not limited by place; even the heavens and the earth cannot contain Him. He is not limited in time; He sees all things, past, present, and future. 1 Kings 8:27; 2 Pet. 3:8
Holy	God is completely pure and perfect—so much so that we can't even imagine it. He never sins and He cannot tolerate sin. All that God does is right and good. 1 Sam. 2:2; Ps. 99:5; Isa. 43:15
Love	God always seeks our highest good. That is why He sent His Son to pay for our sin. He wants you to know His love and to show it to others. Jer. 31:3; Matt. 22:37-40; 1 John 4:16
Truth	God sees and knows all things as they really are. He never lies. His word is totally trustworthy; you need never doubt any promises He makes. Ps. 117:2; Titus 1:2
Just	God is always just. He always makes the right decision. He must punish sin, so He sent His own Son to pay for all sin on the cross. Now because the price is paid, God is "just" not to give us the punishment we deserve if we will turn to Him. Because of God's love, His justice works perfectly with His mercy. Deut. 32:4; Isa. 45:21; Rom. 3:22-26; 1 John 1:7
All-knowing	God knows everything—past, present and future. He is omniscient. He knows all about you, even what you are thinking. He knows your deepest needs and desires, and He knows how to meet them.

All-wise (Omniscient)	God, the great Creator, made and understands all things. He has perfect plans and always carries them out in the best possible way. That is why we may trust Him completely. Ps. 104:24; Isa. 40:28; Rom. 11:33
All-powerful (Omnipotent)	God can do anything He wants to do. His power is greater than we can imagine. He always uses it for our good. Job 42:2; Rev. 19:6
All-present (Omnipresent)	God is always present everywhere at the same time. He is with you all the time. He sees everything you do and hears everything you say. Ps. 139:7-12; Prov. 5:21; 15:3; Acts 17:28
Good	God is full of kindness, sympathy, and tenderheartedness. He takes pleasure in providing for His people. Ps. 34:8; 100:5 103:22-4; 145:9
Faithful	God always does what He says He will do. You can trust His Word completely. Lam. 3:22, 23; 1 Cor. 10:13; 1 Thess. 5:24
Merciful	God cares about us more deeply than we can understand. He sent His Son to die so that He can justly choose not to give us the punishment our sin deserves. Num. 14:18; Ps. 130:3; Eph. 2:4
Unchanging (Immutable)	Because God is perfect, He never changes in any way. He never changes His moods or lessens His love. Mal. 3:6; James 1:17
Majestic	God is matchless in goodness, beauty, power, and excellence. He is great in dignity. He is awesomely wonderful. We bow our heads and worship Him. Ps. 29:2, 4; 95:6; 96:9; 104:1; Isa. 24:14
Sovereign	God is Ruler over all. No one can tell God what to do. All earthly rulers and angelic powers must submit to Him. He cares for all creation and does His will in the affairs of men. Although He allows you free will, He wants you to submit to His right to plan your life. Ps. 22:28; 47:2; Isa. 44:6; 66:1,2; Dan 4:34, 35

Primary Names of God

Hebrew Name	English rendering NKJV	Scripture Reference	Meaning
Elohim	God Used over 2,500 times	Genesis 1:1	Mighty God or supreme God with reference too His faithfulness
Yahweh, YHWH	"LORD" (all capitals) Found over 7000 times	Psalm 110:1 Found over 7,000 times	Self-existent or Eternal One Speaks of His holiness, justice, hatred of sin. The One who exists because of Who He is.
Adonai	"Lord" used for God 300 times referring to God ("lord" used for men) 200 + times for man	Psalm 8;9 1 Peter 3:6	Master or owner of all things. Master, sir, or lord

Compound Words for God

Name	Meaning	Scripture	Practical meaning
El Shaddai	"Almighty God"	Genesis 17:1, 2	El ("strength") Shaddai ("life-giver") All-bountiful supplier of all things.
El Elyon	"God Most High"	Genesis 14:18	God above all as King of universe.
El Gibbon	"Mighty God"	Isaiah 9:6, 7	God Who can do anything.
YHWH Yireh	"The-Lord-Will-Provide"	Genesis 22:7,8,14	God Who will provide all your needs.
YHWH	Sabaoth "LORD of Hosts"	Psalm 24:10	God of heaven's armies.
YHWH Shalom	"The LORD-is-Peace"	Judges 6:24	God can give you peace
YHWH Rophe	"The-LORD-Who-Heals"	Exodus 15:22-26	God Who restores, strengthen, Heals.
YHWH Nissi	"The LORD-My-Banner"	Exodus 17:15	God your authority to follow.
YHWH Tsidkenu	"The Lord Our Righteousness"	Jeremiah 23:6	God Who thinks & acts in all that is just, right and good.
YHWH Roii	"The Lord Our Shepherd"	Psalm 23	God Who tenderly cares for, guides,& protects like a shepherd.
YHWH Shammah	"The LORD Is There"	Ezekiel 48:35	God Who is present at all times.
THWH M'Kaddesh	"The LORD Who Sanctifies"	Leviticus 20:8	God Who brings you to the place of separation from sin and dedication to stay there.

Peter Lord, in the *2959 Plan*, uses the acronym ACTS to help us remember key elements in Biblical prayer. The *A* stands for adoration; that is what we are doing when we are praising the Lord exclusively for who He is, based on His character as revealed in His Word and by His names. The *C* stands for confession; we must not harbor known sin in our lives if we want God to hear our prayers. The *T* stands for thanksgiving; that is what we are doing when we are expressing our gratitude for specific things the Lord has done for us and for those around us. The *S* stands for supplication; that is a broad word that covers the various types of needs and requests that we lay before God's throne.

Adoration

Adoration is appreciating and worshiping God for His nature and His program. It is not focusing on what God has done as much as what He is.

Confession

In our seminars we like to use a little booklet called, *Prayer Without Purity Is Function Without Effect*. Working through this little booklet helps believers make sure they have no known, unconfessed sin in their lives that can hinder their prayers. We have also found the procedure we call the "discipline of silence" helpful in the process of confession.

The following pattern is helpful with confession.
- Praise God from Psalm 111:1-6
- Sing: *Cleanse Me* by J. Edwin Orr:

    "Search me, O God, and know my heart today;
    Try me, O Savior, know my thoughts I pray.
    See if there be some wicked way in me;
    Cleanse me from every sin and set me free."
- Ask God to search your heart from Psalm 139:23,24. List anything that comes to mind.[5]

If time allows, and you need God to search your heart further, read and pray through Psalm 51, listing everything that comes to mind.

- ☐ As you confess each sin by name, claim I John 1:9.
- ☐ Write out the entire verse across the list and destroy it.
- ☐ Thank God for His forgiveness and cleansing, then praise Him from Psalm 111:7-10.
- ☐ Meditate on Colossians 2:6-15, The Living Bible.

   "You were dead in sins, and your sinful desires were not yet cut away. Then he gave you a share in the very life of Christ, for he forgave all your sins, and blotted out the charges proved against you, the list of his commandments which you had not obeyed. He took this list of sins and destroyed it by nailing it to Christ's cross. In this way God took away Satan's power to accuse you of sin, and God openly displayed to the whole world Christ's triumph at the cross where your sins were all taken away."

- ☐ Sing:

   "Thank you, Lord, for saving my soul,
   Thank you, Lord, for making me whole;
   Thank you, Lord, for giving to me
   Thy great salvation so rich and free." (Repeat)

Thanksgiving

Not only do we thank God for His nature but we can also thank Him for specific things He has done for us and others. When we do not feel thankful we can still adore God for Who He is.

Supplication

These are prayers of asking of God for yourself and for others. In following chapters we will be looking in depth at principles to guide our supplications in a variety of settings and for a variety of needs.

Chapter 6
Conformed to His Image:
Claiming the Promises of God

Charles Haddon Spurgeon's commentary on Psalm 92:5-6 in *The Treasury of David* contrasts the great works of God and the mind of the foolish man. A praying Christian can expect to know these great works, but the foolish cannot understand them. The deep mysteries, truths, and benefits of biblical praying are foolishness to the senseless person. As you read this, think in terms of the rewards of biblical praying. The Lord's plans are as marvelous as His acts. To know God and His works is a very high calling. Here are Spurgeon's comments.

O Lord, how great are thy works! and thy thoughts are very deep. A brutish man knoweth not; neither doth a fool understand this.

O Lord, how great are thy works! He is lost in wonder. He utters an exclamation of amazement. How vast! How stupendous are the doings of Jehovah! Great in number, extent, glory, and design are all the creations of the Infinite One.

And thy thoughts are very deep. The Lord's plans are as marvelous as His acts; his designs are as profound as His doings are vast. Creation is immeasurable, and the wisdom displayed in it unsearchable. Some men think but cannot work, and others are mere drudges working without thought; In the Eternal the conception and execution go together. Providence is inexhaustible, and the divine decrees which originate it are inscrutable. Redemption is grand beyond conception, and the thoughts of love which planned it are infinite. Man is superficial, God is inscrutable; man is shallow, God is deep. Dive as we may we shall never fathom the mysterious plan, or exhaust the boundless wisdom of the all-comprehending mind of the Lord. We stand by the fathomless sea of divine wisdom, and exclaim with holy awe, "O the depth!"

A brutish man knoweth not; neither doth a fool understand this. In this and the following verses the effect of the Psalm is heightened by contrast; the shadows are thrown in to bring out the lights more prominently. What a stoop from the preceding verse; from the saint to the brute, from the worshipper to the boor, from the psalmist to the fool! Yet, alas, the character described here is no uncommon one. The boorish or boarish man, for such is almost the very Hebrew word, sees nothing in nature; and if it be pointed out to him, his foolish mind will not comprehend it. He may be a philosopher, and yet be such a brutish being that he will not own the existence of a Maker for the ten thousand matchless creations around him, which wear, even upon their surface, the evidences of profound design. The unbelieving heart, let it boast as it will, does not know; and with all its parade of intellect, it does not understand. A man must either be a saint or a brute, he has no other choice; his type must be the adoring seraph, or the ungrateful swine. So far from paying respect to great thinkers who will not own the glory or being of God, we ought to regard them as comparable to the beasts which perish, only vastly lower than mere brutes, because their degrading condition is of their own choosing. O God, how sorrowful a thing it is that men whom thou hast so largely gifted, and made in thine own image, should so brutify themselves that they will neither see nor understand what thou hast made so clear. Well might an eccentric writer say, "God made man a little lower than the angels at first, and he has been trying to get lower ever since."

For many years I wondered, "Why am I here? Who am I? Where am I going? What will I amount to?" These are the great philosophical questions pondered by men of all the ages. Have you, too, asked yourself these questions? Now I know the answers, and you can too, if you know the One who created you. You can know Him if you desire to do so. Let's review Philippians 3:10a from the Amplified Bible: *[For my determined purpose is] that I may know Him–that I may progressively become more deeply and intimately acquainted with Him, perceiving and recognizing and understanding [the wonders of His Person] more strongly and more clearly.*

We are on earth to glorify the Lord! *Glorify* is a very important word. It means the outshining of the deity of God Himself: His person, His power, His purpose. Matthew 5:16 tells us, *Let your light shine before men in such a way that they may see your good works, and glorify your Father who is in heaven.* This is not possible for us without biblical prayer because we cannot show who God is if we do not know Him, and we cannot fully know Him if we do not communicate with Him by means of the Word and prayer.

Jesus, our perfect example, came to earth to glorify the Father. *And this is eternal life, that they may know Thee, the only true God, and Jesus Christ whom Thou hast sent. I glorified Thee on the earth, having accomplished the work which Thou hast given Me to do.* (John 17:3-4) How did Jesus glorify the Father? He primarily did that by making the attributes of God visible.

How do you and I know and believe that God is love? We know and believe that God is love because Jesus was loving. How do you and I know that God is forgiving? We know and believe that God is forgiving because Jesus was forgiving. How do you and I know and believe that God is powerful? We know and believe that God is powerful because Jesus was powerful. Jesus was the visible, physical manifestation of God, **so that** you and I might know Him and believe in Him. That's why Christ became a man – to show us the way to the Father.

> *O righteous Father, although the world has not known Thee, yet I have known Thee; and these have known that Thou didst send Me; and I have made Thy name known to them, and will make it known; that the love wherewith Thou didst love Me may be in them, and I in them.* (John 17:25-26 NKJV)

So, what is your purpose in this world? What is mine? Man's purpose on earth is the same as the Son's—to know God and to make Him known—to glorify the Father by being conformed to the image of Christ so that others will want to know the Lord Jesus Christ as their Savior.

Who am I? I am a child of God. This is where purpose begins. If you don't know for sure that you are a child of God, you will never know for sure who you are or why you are here. Jesus said, *I come that they may have life and have it abundantly.* (John 10:10) The Bible teaches that an abundant life is becoming conformed to His image, to become like Him by internalizing the attributes of God. Can you believe that? We can become like Him!

How does a Christian internalize an attribute of God? How does the process of conforming us to the image of God take place? Scripture tells us that God Himself conforms us through the Word and prayer.

For example, I am walking uprightly with the Lord to the best of my ability and have a need of $500 by the 15th. Today is the 2nd. First, I assume, because I believe in the sovereignty of God, that He is at work! He has allowed or created this situation in my life because He desires that I be conformed to His likeness. Therefore, my first response is not to panic, but to get my focus on the Provider.

For everything created by God is good, and nothing is to be rejected, if it is received with gratitude (and self control)*; for it is sanctified by means of the word of God and prayer.* (I Timothy 4:4-5)

His admonition in Philippines 4:6-8 strengthens me. It says, *Be anxious for nothing, but in everything by prayer and supplication with thanksgiving let your requests be made known to God. And the peace of God, which surpasses all comprehension, shall guard your hearts and your minds in Christ Jesus. Finally brethren, whatever is true, whatever is honorable, whatever is right, whatever is pure, whatever is lovely, whatever is of good repute, if there is any excellence and if anything worthy of praise,* **let your minds dwell on these things.**

My need for $500 can be God's way of having me come to Him in prayer. He loves me and wants to give me what I need. To acknowledge my need is part of His plan for my life.

My second response is to glance at my need long enough to claim a promise and then commit it to Him. The promise may be Matthew 6:33, which tells me to . . . *seek first His kingdom, and His righteousness; and all these things shall be added to you.* What things? Food, shelter, clothing—whatever temporal things I need! Now I praise Him for the faith to trust Him for the $500 and ask Him to teach me how to pray from His perspective. I might ask myself, "What attribute of God do I need in my life to honor my Lord in the next thirteen days?" It might occur to me that I really need wisdom. If so, I would focus my prayers on James 1:5: *but if any of you lacks wisdom, let him ask of God, who gives to all men generously and without reproach, and it will be given to him.* To take a promise of God and make it your own by personal faith is the highest form of wisdom.

Perhaps I need understanding. In that case, I may pray for understanding by faith; that is, to take Him at His Word. *For this reason also, since the day we heard of it, we have not ceased to pray for you and to ask that you may be filled with the knowledge of His will in all spiritual wisdom and understanding, so that you may walk in a manner worthy of the Lord, to please Him in all respects, bearing fruit in every good work and increasing in the knowledge of God.* (Colossians 1:9-10)

And we know that the Son of God has come, and has given us understanding, in order that we might know Him who is true, and we are in Him who is true, in His Son Jesus Christ. This is the true God and eternal life. (I John 5:20)

For if these qualities (self-control, perseverance, godliness, brotherly kindness, love) are yours and are increasing, they render you neither useless nor unfruitful in the true **knowledge** *of our Lord Jesus Christ. For he who lacks these qualities is blind or short-sighted, having forgotten his purification from his former sins.* (2 Peter 1:8-9)

Ephesians 1:7-9 is another great strengthening promise. These are just a very few of the 7,000 promises in the Word of God. Every promise is wrapped around a command to enable us to grab hold of it. Every command is accompanied by the promise of God's grace to help us fulfill it. When I have peace in the midst of my problem, God is glorified. When I have joy in a difficult situation, no matter the answer to my prayer, God is glorified. God gets glory every time His attributes become visible in my life for others to see.

Oswald Chambers wrote in *My Utmost for His Highest* (June 26),

> *We . . . beseech you that ye receive not the grace of God in vain.* (2 Cor. 6:1)
>
> The grace you had yesterday will not do for to-day. Grace is the overflowing favour of God; you can always reckon it is there to draw upon. "In much patience, in afflictions, in necessities, in distresses"—that is where the test for patience comes. Are you failing the grace of God there? Are you saying—Oh, well, I won't count this time? It is not a question of praying and asking God to help you; it is taking the grace of God *now*. We make prayer the preparation for work, it is never that in the Bible. Prayer is the exercise of drawing on the grace of God. Don't say—I will endure this until I can get away and pray. Pray *now*; draw on the grace of God in the moment of need. Prayer is the most practical thing; it is not the reflex action of devotion. Prayer is the last thing in which we learn to draw on God's grace.
>
> "In stripes, in imprisonment, in tumults, in labours"—in all these things manifest a drawing upon the grace of God that will make you a marvel to yourself and to others. Draw now, not presently. The one word in the spiritual vocabulary is *Now*. Let circumstances bring you where they will, keep drawing on the grace of God in every conceivable condition you may be in. One of the greatest proofs that you are drawing on the grace of God is that you can be humiliated without manifesting the slightest trace of anything but His grace.
>
> "Having nothing . . . Never reserve anything. Pour out the best you have, and always be poor. Never be

diplomatic and careful about the treasure God gives. This is poverty triumphant." [6]

Internalizing God's Attributes

An attribute is a quality that is intrinsic to its subject. It is some characteristic by which someone may be distinguished or identified. Some of God's characteristics are unique to Him (incommunicable attributes such as infinity, self-existence, omnipotence, etc.), as we saw in chapter four. Certain other characteristics He desires to share with man. The "communicable" attributes include such qualities as love, forgiveness, mercy, and justice. For our purpose, then, attributes are the characteristics of God in Scripture or visibly exercised by Him in His works of creation, providence, and redemption. Through prayer, based on His Word, we may confidently ask God to manifest His character in our lives. *And this is the confidence which we have before Him that, if we ask anything according to His will, He hears us. And if we know that He hears us in whatever we ask, we know that we have the requests which we have asked from Him.* (I John 5:14-15)

Let's say a man comes to church who was raised in a Christian family, but who has never surrendered his life to Christ. He has done some very bad things, and the guilt is killing him. He can't forgive himself, and no one else will forgive him, but he has been told even if no one will forgive him, Jesus Christ will. The pastor preaches an evangelistic message with an invitation to anyone who wants to receive Christ to come forward. So out of the need for forgiveness, he goes forward and prays to receive Christ. Would you agree that there is a possibility that he became a Christian the moment he got out of the pew? Yes, because God is more concerned with our hearts than with our words.

So what did the prayer do when he prayed to receive Christ? The prayer, based on the Word of God, manifested in his life the reality of God's forgiveness. So, as a new believer, what was the first attribute of God he experienced? Forgiveness!

Let's say there is another person who is very unloving. No one loves him and he doesn't love anyone, but he has been told that God loves him. When he prays to receive Christ, what is the first attribute he experiences? God's love, right?

The Word of God and prayer are God's major means of conforming us to His image. The Lord Jesus manifests His attributes in our lives as we pray through His Word and trust Him to provide that which is declared in His promise.

For by these (His own glory and excellence) He has granted to us His precious and magnificent promises, in order that by them (His promises) you might become partakers of the divine nature, having escaped the corruption that is in the world by lust. (2 Peter 1:4)

We escape the effects of the world on our lives by being conformed to Christ. We may not escape adverse circumstances, but we can, in God's grace, escape the effects such as bitterness, ungratefulness, loss of joy and love, etc.

The Bible sometimes metaphorically compares the great oak tree, the cedar in Lebanon, or the palm tree to the attributes of God. Points of comparison include their strength, fruitfulness, purity, usefulness as a place of refuge, etc. Can you picture in your mind a great oak tree in a green field and you are a seedling a little distance away from the tree? You are predestined to become a great oak tree. How? Reread 2 Peter 1:4 above, and then look up verses 5 through 11 as well.

Fulfilling the 7,000 promises

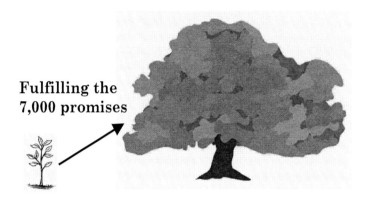

Someone has said that there are 7,000 promises in the Bible. We are given those promises so that we may become like that great oak tree: that is, conformed to the image of Christ.

I came to faith in Christ through Revelation 3:20, which says, *Behold, I stand at the door and knock; if anyone hears My voice and opens the door, I will come in to him, and will dine with him, and he with me.* I invited Christ into my life through prayer, asking Him to come in. At that moment I became what we refer to as a babe in Christ, a seedling of a great oak tree. Now I am on my way to becoming like that great oak tree. I am on the "Holy Highway" as described in Isaiah 35:8-10: *And a highway will be there, a roadway, and it will be called the Highway of Holiness. The unclean will not travel on it, but it will be for him who walks that way, and fools will not wander on it. No lion will be there, nor will any vicious beast go up on it; these will not be found there. But the redeemed will walk there, and the ransomed of the LORD will return, and come with joyful shouting to Zion, with everlasting joy upon their heads. They will find gladness and joy, and sorrow and sighing will flee away.*

As I claimed by prayer the promise of Revelation 3:20, it became mine, and I had 6,999 promises to go to be what Christ would have me to be—like Him!

Before I became a Christian I knew John 3:16: *For God so loved the world that He gave His only begotten son, that whoever believes in Him should not perish, but have eternal life!* It had never changed my life. Sometime after I became a Christian and realized God loves me unconditionally, I internalized John 3:16 through prayer. I began to respond to other people on the basis that God loves me. If others don't love me, I know God loves me. If God be for us, who can be against us? (See Romans 8:31.) After claiming the promise of John 3:16 in prayer, with God's help, my lifestyle was changing. I had 6,998 promises to go. I was further on my way to becoming all that God would have me to be.

7,000 promises	**Great oak tree**
- 1 fulfillment	**Rev 3:20**
6,999 promises to go	**Babe on road to becoming like the great tree**

I had been a Christian for 20 years and knew my sins were forgiven past, present, and future, but until I learned how to claim a promise of God through His Word and prayer, I lived in defeat. I had confessed my sin nature, but not my specific sins. Then I claimed 1 John 1:9, which says, *If we confess our sins, He is faithful and righteous to forgive us our sins and to cleanse us from **all** unrighteousness.* This is a reality in my life today because of God's faithfulness, mercy, and grace to show me the sin in my life. As I confess it, and know God hears and forgives my sin, I have 6,997 promises to go!

I praise the Lord for leading me in the light, for in His light we see the light (Psalm 36:9). It is God's will for us to experience His light as a way of life through the Word and prayer. He desires that others will see His light in us and come to the Light for themselves. (Matthew 5:14-16) But few Christians understand the necessity of being like Christ for effective evangelism of the lost. *Then He said to His disciples, "The harvest is plentiful, but the workers are few. Therefore beseech the Lord of the harvest to send out workers into His harvest."* (Matthew 9:27-28)

Much of our work in God's harvest is making His attributes visible in life's situations. Being in the world but not of it and allowing God's attributes to work through us is not only a blessing, but it also destroys the work of the Devil.

The workers prepare the soil in which the seed is to be planted. (Mark 4:1-20) Different soils require different preparation. The seed is planted, it is watered and nurtured, the Lord causes the growth, and then comes the harvest! The harvest is new converts who display the fruit of the Spirit. Some show love, some joy, some peace, some all of the fruit of the Spirit. All of the converts will also begin to make the attributes of God visible in this world, through the Word of God and prayer, glorifying the Father. The Word and prayer are God's means of bringing souls to Himself as well as the means of maturing the fruit, so that the fruit will remain and multiply.

Chapter 7
Biblical Prayer May Change the Way You Pray: The Transforming Power of Praise

Until I learned to pray from the Scriptures, putting my faith in them and not in what I wanted, I never had the same assurance of cleansing that I had for salvation. I knew my salvation was based on the Word. I was sure I was saved because God says so: *For God so loved the world, that He gave His only begotten Son, that whoever believes in Him should not perish, but have eternal life.* (John 3:16) But learning to pray the scriptures transformed my life because I gained the same confidence in the promises of God's Word for other areas of my Christian walk.

In 1976, I participated in a prayer conference in Kansas City, Kansas. Corrie Ten Boom, author of *The Hiding Place*, was one of the speakers. She always began her time with prayer, and when she prayed, it got very quiet. I noticed how people would sit up straight or reach for their pen and paper. Her prayer would create an anticipation of hearing from God. I felt close to the Lord as she prayed. I was so blessed that I listened closer. I discovered most of her prayers were based on the Bible. She used memorized Scripture like a second language with God. It was wonderful and powerful. I had never heard prayer like that. Her prayers were not about complaints, but were praising the Lord for Who He is. I can't remember that she prayed for "Aunt Merna's bad back" or "Uncle Joe's upcoming surgery" –not that that would be bad, but it just wasn't her focus. It was so different from the kind of prayer I had grown used to in Wednesday night prayer meetings. The more I listened to Corrie pray, the more I wanted to learn to pray better. I left with a sincere desire to know the Word better. I'd like to share what I have learned so far.

What is Biblical prayer?
Let's review:

1. Biblical prayer is communication with the holy, righteous, and omnipotent Father.

Prayer is an exchange of thoughts, the act of consciously coming into the very presence of God, the way He has taught us to do in the Scriptures. Psalm 100:4 instructs us to enter His gates with thanksgiving and His courts with praise. Psalm 118:19 reveals that His gates are the entrance into His righteousness. We are to enter into His righteousness thanking and praising the One who imparts His own righteousness to us.

2. Biblical prayer is based on the Word of God.

As we pray Scripture-based prayers, we focus on God rather than on our need and ourselves. As we focus on God, we come into harmony with the essential biblical principles of effective prayer. We develop a dialogue with Him, an exchange of thoughts that results in renewing our minds in Him.

3. Biblical prayer is seeking to know God.

As we seek God's face through His Word, we are enlightened to the truths that transform and conform us into the image of His Son. *And we know that God causes all things to work together for good to those who love God, to those who are called according to His purpose. For whom He foreknew,* **He also predestined to become conformed to the image of His Son,** *that He might be the first-born among many brethren.* (Romans 8:28, 29)

The Transforming Power of Praise: Praise transforms my view of God and of my circumstances

Praise is the most effective way of seeking God's face. Praise is glorifying God both for who and what He is. Praising God affects the way we think of Him. Praising God is the most appropriate way to enter into His presence. The source of praise is God Himself, so our praise should center on the excellencies, perfections, and glories of His nature, His character, and His role in human affairs.

Paul E. Billheimer, author of *Destined for the Throne*, states on page 126, "The secret of answered prayer is faith without doubt (Mark 11:23), and the secret of faith without doubt is praise—continuous, triumphant, massive praise; praise that is a way of life."[7]

In the book *On the High Road of Surrender*, in the chapter "Praise Transforms," Francis J. Roberts discusses the verse *In everything give thanks; for this is the **will** of God in Christ Jesus concerning you.* I Thessalonians 5:18

> Rejoice in the Lord always, for as you rejoice and give thanks, you release heaven's treasures and shower upon your head blessings of a delighted Father. Nothing so thoroughly delights the Father's heart as the praises of His children.
>
> Praise exercises the heart toward gratitude, and gratitude nurtures contentment, and you may know for a certainty that no fruit ever appears on the tree of discontent.
>
> So praise, My children, and never cease in your praising, for in the midst of it I will manifest Myself, and you will understand that when I demand of you your praises it is for your highest good. Out of praises come courage, faith, strength, optimism, clarity and peace.
>
> Out of praises come health and happiness and the soul satisfaction men seek in the world and do not find.
>
> Praise will transform the humblest dwelling to a hallowed haven. It will light the countenance and make

the plainest face beautiful. It is impossible for the man who has learned unceasing praise to be a failure. God's blessing attends his path, and God's Spirit rules his heart. He is eternally at peace with both God and man.[8]

IN EVERYTHING!! Have you found that absolutely impossible? I'm sure you have, so what do you do? We have no power to give thanks in everything unless the Lord gives us power to obey. I have found that when I am in a circumstance where I can't or won't give thanks, it is because I have become ungrateful for all the Lord has already done for me. So when I praise Him for what I can, He gives me the power to praise Him for what I can't understand.

I know in my heart that God never commands us to do something He is not willing to empower us to do. His grace is sufficient! 2 Corinthians 12:9 states, *And He said to me, "My grace is sufficient for you, for My strength is made perfect in weakness." Therefore most gladly I will rather boast in my infirmities, that the power of Christ may rest upon me.*

2 Timothy 2:1 says, *You therefore, my son, be strong in the grace that is in Christ Jesus.*

When I am unwilling or unable to praise the Lord in a given situation, it is often because I have been negligent or disobedient to give thanks in all things. It seems to me when there is a biggie coming up, God will prepare us ahead of time. When I can't give thanks, I know for sure He is preparing me.

Look again at the first paragraph of "Praise Transforms." Note: "Nothing so thoroughly delights the Father's heart as the praises of His children." Think about that! What would a loving Father withhold when He is pleased with you and me? The answer is nothing that is good for us. Why? Because the Bible teaches us that praise is the purest form of faith, and God has promised to respond to requests made in faith. (Matthew 21:22)

Look at the second paragraph: "For praise exercises the heart toward gratitude, and gratitude nurtures contentment, and you may know for a certainty that no fruit ever appears on the tree of discontent." What fruit is in view here? The fruit of the Spirit: love, joy, peace, patience, kindness, goodness, faithfulness, gentleness, self-control.

I did not realize for so many years how much of my prayer life was really born out of discontent. Proverbs 22:6 states that we are to train up our children in the way of the Lord and when they are old they will not depart. We were trying to bring our children up that way, but they rebelled. And our prayers for them were out of discontent–big time. For years, I was robbing myself of the potential fruit of God's spirit that I could have had by learning to praise Him in faith.

Paragraph three says, "So praise, My children, and never cease in your praising, for in the midst of it I will MANIFEST Myself." I have been a Christian for 57 years and the most consistent miracle I experience in answered prayer is God in the midst of all of life's circumstances with me. WOW!

Paragraph four says man's soul has no satisfaction in this world apart from praise. Man is looking in all of the wrong places for peace and contentment, and Satan is happy to let him do so. Satan is the destroyer of our faith, and inasmuch as praise is an expression of our faith, Satan detests it.

Paragraph five says praise transforms my mind, my will, my emotions, my inner self. It strengthens my weakest faith. "It is impossible for the man who has learned unceasing praise to be a failure."

When my son-in-law graduated from Bible college, the visiting speaker made the statement that "within six months, half of you graduating today will be pumping gas." Ouch! At first I thought it was an awful thing to say. As I thought about the price my daughter and son-in-law paid to get to the point of graduating, with two children and five years of study, why did the man make such a statement?

Then he began to explain. "The ministry is tough, it's hard, and unless you purpose to give thanks in and for all things, you will never make it in the ministry." I'm sorry to say that years later that speaker's prophecy came true. That son-in-law fell and had to leave the ministry. If you do not want to fail in your Christian walk, read this statement again: "It is impossible for the man who has learned unceasing praise to be a failure. God's blessing attends his path and God's Spirit rules his heart. He is eternally at peace with both God and man."

Can you imagine being eternally at peace, not just now and then, but continually forever and ever? That's the power of praise. Sometimes I am at peace with God but not man. At other times I am at peace with man and not God. Think about what that means to you. It means you and I cannot afford to take our eyes off of the Lord!

If then you were raised with Christ, seek those things which are above, where Christ is, sitting at the right hand of God. Set your mind on things above, not on things on the earth. (Colossians 3:1-2)

Praise . . . The purest form of faith

When things go bad and you cannot see any good reason or purpose for praise, be sure to praise the Lord anyway, because God's Word commands it. *In everything give thanks, for this is the will of God in Christ Jesus for you.* (I Thessalonians 5:18)

When I first was confronted with this idea, I agreed we were to praise *in* all things but not *for* all things. How do you praise

God for drugs, rape, or an untimely death? I learned we do not praise God for sin. We praise Him for the good He brings out of it, *by faith*, that He may bless us. Then I read in Ephesians 5:20 that we are to praise Him *for* all things. A friend of mine who knew I was having a hard time with this showed me a companion passage that shed light on my difficulty–I Thessalonians 5:16, which says, *Rejoice always*. That did it for me. I cannot *rejoice always* on my own; it takes God's grace and my faith. The Lord seemed to say in that still small voice, "Now you understand why I demand of you your praises, it is for your highest good." We praise Him not because we feel like it or understand it, but because we know He loves us and has the very best for us that we can have; we accept that truth by faith.

The language of heaven is praise. God actively gets involved with His people when they praise Him. Psalm 8:2 says, *From the lips of children and infants You have ordained praise because of Your enemies, to silence the enemy and the avenger.* Psalm 22:3 says, *But You are holy, enthroned in the praises of Israel.*

Our God functions in an atmosphere of praise. God created the seraphim and the cherubim to surround the throne of God with *"Holy, Holy, Holy is the Lord of hosts; the whole earth is full of His glory!* (Isaiah 6:3). We praise the Lord because the joy of the Lord is our strength; so do not sorrow. (Nehemiah 8:10)

Praise is a command. 1 Thessalonians 5:16-19 states, *Rejoice always, pray without ceasing,* **in** *everything give thanks; for this is the will of God in Christ Jesus for you. Do not quench the Spirit* (by not praising Him).

Ephesians 5:18-20 says, *Be filled with the Spirit, speaking to one another in psalms and hymns and spiritual songs, singing and making melody in your heart to the Lord, giving thanks always* **for** (my emphasis) *all things to God the Father in the name of our Lord Jesus Christ.*

The Restoration of Biblical Prayer

Let me share an experience of giving thanks when my reputation and what I stand for was questioned. Several years ago I was doing a week long Prayer Enrichment Seminar in a church of about 450 to 500 attending members. This church was not noted for showing emotion, but right in the middle of my message on Sunday morning, a little elderly lady stood up and in a very bold voice said, "THIS IS HERESY! This is heresy! I'm never coming back to this church again," and she sat down. To say that I was shocked is an understatement. I was petrified. I had been teaching prayer seminars for about twenty years at that time and never had anything like this happen.

I looked at the pastor behind me. He said, "It's okay, Elton. That's Rosy and she gets a little verbal at times. You go right ahead with your message."

I thought, "Easy for you to say." I had a hard time trying to go on. All I could think about was what the lady had said. What if what I was teaching was not biblical? Was my heart not right? In my flesh I thought, "Lord, if I am right with You and she is not, could you just *zap* her for me?"

The Lord didn't do that, of course, and somehow I went on, but just as I was closing Rosy stood up again. "This is heresy, this is heresy, and this is real heresy. I'm never coming back to this church," and she started walking to the exit. To tell you the truth, I was relieved that she wouldn't be back. I met with the pastor after the service to share my regrets. He assured me that he found no problem with what I had shared and it was okay.

That evening we were assembled in small groups praying for the evening session. I was in a group some distance from the door, and all of a sudden the whole room got quiet, very quiet. I looked up and saw Rosy. She was standing at the door and every eye was on her. In that same commanding voice she said, "I'm just here to check you out, young fellow." I thought, "Oh, no!

Lord, why me?" But somehow I did teach and get through the lesson, even though I didn't cover nearly what I had planned. I was very uncomfortable. Just as I was closing, it was Rosy again, "I have never heard such heresy. For sure, I am never coming back!"

I began to ask the Lord to search my heart, praying Psalm 139:23,24: *Search me, O God, and know my heart; try me, and know my anxious thoughts; and see if there be any hurtful way in me, and lead me in the everlasting way.* Nothing came to mind, so I began to thank God for Rosy and asked Him to bless her. Let me tell you, I did not feel like it – I did not understand any of this. I was sure I could do a much better job of teaching if this situation were better. But by God's grace, I was able to go on; and Rosy, well, she came every night, but after Tuesday night she came and went almost unnoticed.

On Saturday morning at the first break, Rosy came to me with tears, asking me to forgive her.

"Rosy, there is nothing to forgive. God has used you this week in a mighty way."

"Not me!" she cried.

"Yes, you, Rosy. When I came here I didn't know this church or its teaching. You see, Rosy, because you were able to verbalize your thoughts, you caused me to slow down and to be as clear as I could about the doctrine of prayer. I didn't know that a good number of the people in this seminar felt the same way you did but would never have said anything. God used you to confront me so the others would see and understand. God has brought a mini-revival to this congregation through you, and I praise the Lord for you, Rosy."

As we hugged and cried, God touched our hearts. I am a stronger believer in giving thanks. He is faithful!

Now I realize that often the light does not come until I am obedient to give thanks whether I understand it or not. I must give thanks and praise by faith. To refuse to give thanks in all things is a clear indication of a lack of faith. Ungratefulness, truly all complaining, is against God, for He is the cause of all things.

You may have heard of the example of a man crossing the Grand Canyon on a tight wire with a wheelbarrow. After crossing several times, he asked a bystander, "Do you think I can cross this with a wheelbarrow?"

The bystander said, "Yes."

When the man asked him to get in the wheelbarrow, the bystander said, "No way!"

It's easy to agree as long as nothing is required of us. We frequently are willing to agree with God in our heads, unless He requires some measure of obedience on our part.

There is power in praise. I would like to share one example. In our home church a number of years ago, I was walking the hall when a friend of mine who was teaching a new Christians' Sunday School class stopped me to ask if I could teach the last class on prayer. I agreed, and the next Sunday I went to the class. After my friend introduced me, I explained that on the basis of Psalm 100:4 we are to enter His gates with praise and thanksgiving. One of the best ways to do that is to pray through a psalm by reading a verse, looking for an attribute or characteristic of God in that verse, and praising Him for that attribute.

To begin we read Psalm 103:1: *Bless the Lord, O my soul, and all that is within me, bless His holy name.* I prayed, "Lord, I praise you for being holy."

Verse 2: *Bless the Lord, O my soul, and forget none of His benefits.* The next person prayed, "Lord, I praise you, the Benefactor of my soul."

Verse 3: *Who pardons all your iniquities; Who heals all your diseases.* The next person prayed, "Lord, I praise you, the forgiver of my sins and healer of my sickness."

Verse 4: *Who redeems your life from the pit; who crowns you with lovingkindness and compassions.* "I praise You, Lord, for being the Redeemer and the crowner of my soul with love and compassion."

The next person to pray was the husband of a woman we knew quite well. I'll call him Bill. It seemed strange that Bill was in a new Christians' class. His wife had been in several groups with us and in a home Bible study we were in, and she was certain her husband was not saved. I thought perhaps he had become a Christian. Instead of reading the next verse, he said, "You know I am not a Christian!"

I responded, "What are you doing in this class?"

"My wife wanted me to come."

Everyone in the class showed concern for him and hoped that I would not upset him. I said, "You are working in Awana and helping your kids memorize Scripture and you are not a Christian?"

"Yes, I like to help out."

I said, "You come to this church every time the door is open. What are you doing here?"

"I like to be around my friends."

I asked, "Do you realize that you are a stumbling block?"

"Who, me?"

I stated, "Yes, you. Apparently most people in the church know that you are not a Christian. Your lifestyle is more like a Christian's than most Christians. What you are saying is that you don't have to be a Christian to be a good husband and father, and you're right, but you are missing God's best for you. What's the holdup?"

He was a little taken back and our time was about gone. I said, "Friend, do you love God?"

"Yes, but I don't think Jesus was His son."

"Okay," I said, "since you say you love God, would you be willing to praise God with me from Scripture before you go to work for five minutes for the next thirty days?"

"What do you mean?"

"Just like we started to do today. What time do you go to work?"

"7 A.M."

"OK, at 6:45 tomorrow morning call me and we will praise God together from the Bible. Are you willing to do that?"

He said, "Yes, I am willing, but I don't see the point."

"Well, if you are willing, I know it will be good for me. Let's pray and ask the Lord to help us."

I prayed, claiming Proverbs 16:9, "Lord, You say we can make our plans but that the final outcome is in your hands. I pray by faith that our time in the Word will be a glory to you. We come in Jesus' name. Amen."

The next morning Bill called. We praised the Lord from Psalm 100. The next day we prayed from Psalm 103. The next day we picked up where we left off in Psalm 103. I would close our time by asking God to bless our day. By the fourth or fifth day, Bill said, "You know my wife is interested in what we are doing."

"Great," I said, "Do you have another phone?"

"Yes, we do."

"We do too, so I'll have Shirley, get the other phone."

The four of us praised the Lord together for the next few days. Then Bill said his wife was going out of town and he was going to take some time off, so he'd like to change our time of prayer. It was fine with me. We prayed for several more days. He called back later on the fifth day to say he had just asked Christ to forgive his sins and to come into his life! WOW! I had never shared the Gospel with him. You see, he knew the Gospel; he just didn't know God. After praising the Lord for who He is, Bill got to know Him. He wanted Jesus in his life. His conversion was one of the soundest conversions I can recall. By faith, his life to this day is one of praise.

I believe that the reason for that man's confidence in his salvation is because it was founded on knowing God through praising Him. Paul Billheimer, in his book *Destined for the Throne*, gives valuable insights into "The Power of Praise."

> A program of prayer without faith is powerless. The missing element that is necessary to energize prevailing prayer that binds and casts out Satan is triumphant faith. And the missing element that is necessary to energize triumphant faith is praise—perpetual, purposeful, aggressive praise. Praise is the highest form of prayer because it combines petition with faith. Praise is the spark plug of faith. It is the only thing needed to get faith airborne, enabling it to soar above the deadly miasma of doubt. Praise is the detergent which purifies faith and purges doubt from the heart. The secret of answered prayer is faith without doubt (Mark 11:23). And the secrecy of faith without doubt is praise, triumphant praise, continuous praise, praise that is a way of life. This is the solution to the problem of a living faith and successful prayer.

> The secret of success in overcoming Satan and qualifying for the throne is a massive program of effective prayer. The secret of effective prayer is a massive program of praise.
>
> The problem of living faith, faith without doubt, is a very real one. Many who have deep devotional habits and who live disciplined lives of prayer and intercession are never quite sure that they have prevailed because their faith seems tentative, dim, uncertain, and often mixed with doubt. Large segments of the Body of Christ are baffled by this plague. Much of the effectiveness of many well-organized prayer programs is crippled by failure to reach a triumphant faith. Since few know how to obtain and exercise this achieving faith, many prayer efforts bog down in frustration and defeat. HOW CAN THIS DIFFICULTY BE OVERCOME? PRAISE IS THE ANSWER!
>
> We have had much teaching on prayer, but until recently little on praise. Yet there is much more emphasis in the Bible on praise than on prayer.[9]

I will always be grateful for an experience that God blessed us with in a different culture in the Deep South. He worked through a couple we met while in Campus Crusade for Christ. They invited us to do a week long Prayer Enrichment Seminar in their little church. The community was tightly knit and suspicious of outsiders. They truly did love the Lord but had had little training in the Word. They all carried Bibles, but other than the basics of salvation, they knew little about what it said, especially about prayer.

We tried very hard to be sensitive to where they were in the Lord. The congregation and especially the pastor, an older man, were as uncomfortable as we were. We found out later that the pastor felt threatened by us. Also, he and his wife were having a hard time with their teenage granddaughter who lived with them. The couple that invited us had a position in the church such that the pastor could not refuse their desire for us to come.

Because of our confidence in the power of praise, we began each night by praising God from Scripture for a longer time than usual. It was one aspect of prayer in which we were all united. By Wednesday night the pastor and his wife began to warm up and invited us over to their house for coffee after the service. He realized we weren't there to get his job.

The lesson had been about giving thanks in all things from 1 Thessalonians 5:18. They lived in the church parsonage that was on church property about a block away. As we walked there, the pastor began to share all the problems they were having with their granddaughter. He was going into a great detail about the situation and how they were praying, but things were getting worse. She was a dog lover and wanted a puppy. The pastor tried to explain to her how hard it would be for them to have a dog because their home belonged to the congregation and they were liable to drop in at any time. Pastor said he eventually relented and bought her a golden retriever puppy, and it was growing. He detailed all the problems they were having with the dog and that it just wasn't working. He seemed to be challenging me about prayer that didn't work.

He was apologizing for taking me in the back door through the laundry room, but he had locked the dog in there before going to church and needed to check on him. The granddaughter was supposed to do that, but hadn't. About that time we opened the back door. You would not believe what we saw. That puppy had torn up the clothes, and what he didn't tear up, he messed on. The washer and dryer were scratched so badly. The dog had hung himself in the Venetian blinds, upside-down. He was yapping and barking and whining. The pastor really lost it. When he got the dog free, he opened the door and kicked that dog right out the door. He had hit his mark that sent the dog yelping even louder.

Bless the pastor's heart, he was like one demon possessed for a moment. I don't believe a Christian can be demon possessed, *because greater is He who is in you than he who is in the world* (1 John 4:4b), but I use that terminology to communicate what the situation was like. We were truly in a spiritual battle, that was for sure. The pastor was so very embarrassed about the whole thing. As he was trying to explain to me what had led up to this moment, it was as though he were saying, "If you had been through what I have, you would have done the same thing!"

Now, remember, we had been studying that night about why and how we are to give thanks in all things –it's a command. But this was just too much to happen with a visiting preacher! As the pastor was trying to justify his actions and paused for a moment, I said, "Pastor, I think perhaps *God gave* you that dog!"

He almost screamed at me, "No, I bought that dog!"

His wife screamed back even louder, "You what? You bought that dog? You paid money for that thing?"

As you can imagine, we had a very cold cup of coffee, but all the time we had spent in praising the Lord together that week gave us a foundation to go on. Shirley and I will always have fond memories and great thanks for that week. It taught us the truth that theology alone cannot teach us. If you could have seen with your eyes that laundry room and seen the pastor and his wife eventually give thanks, you would know there is a God who answers prayer.

The following Sunday morning, with tears streaming down his checks, the pastor explained to the congregation how God had given him that dog because there were things he needed to learn about himself and about the Lord. Now they had renewed hope for themselves and their granddaughter. He said that for the first time they were united in their praise for their granddaughter. I had shared a quote from someone who said, "Children are God's gift to the church to conform their parents (and grandparents) to the image of Christ."

The pastor said, "That's true! That's what the Lord is doing in the life of your pastor and his wife." He publicly thanked the couple that invited us and praised the Lord for us too. When we left, he hugged me and said, "God sent you to me!"

I quote Dr. David Jeremiah, from the June issue of *Turning Points Magazine and Devotional*, p.15: "None of us knows whether today will bring best or worst case scenarios. But in every condition, we *know* that our Redeemer lives, we *know* that He is a great God above all gods, we *know* that all things will turn out for our deliverance and we *know* He is able to keep what we have committed unto Him against that day."

This teaching is the easiest to understand and the hardest to apply. If application is a problem for you, I say, "Join the club!" We can't do it, but *He* can. Praise His Holy Name! Do you have some unwanted bad dog in your life? Praise is the answer. The greater the struggle, the greater is the need for praise. The battle is a barometer of what God wants to do *in* us. *Consider it all joy, my brethren, when you encounter various trials, knowing that the testing of your faith produces endurance, and let endurance have its perfect result, that you may be perfect and complete, lacking nothing.* (James 1:2-4)

Psalm 22:3 declares, *But thou art holy, O thou that inhabitest the praise of Israel.* God inhabits the life that praises Him. Why? Because praise is the purest form of faith! God is pleased when we trust Him, especially when we trust Him when we, in our finite minds, can neither see nor understand how a situation is going to work out, but we choose to trust Him anyway. Praising the Lord in adverse conditions strengthens our faith. That's why Satan hates it so much. Praising God brings us into light that the enemy cannot endure.

When we are praising the Lord, we are focusing, for the most part, on the eternal. When we begin to doubt or question, it is quite often because we are concentrating on what is temporal or visible. What causes us to begin to doubt? We begin to trust in our own efforts, and that allows the enemy to move in and plant more seeds of doubt.

Have you ever noticed when we begin to pray for someone's salvation, they seem to get worse? This can be the enemy trying to get us to focus on the negative, on what's wrong. Our thoughts can be accurate or they can be distorted; either way, praise will bring true light and power. How does praise counter Satan's offense of doubting or questioning? Remember that Satan always engages in subversive warfare; the circumstance we're encountering is never what it seems to be. The deceiver always tries to get us to look at the dark side of people and situations. For example, if the master manipulator can get us to focus on what's wrong with people, it will affect the way we pray. If we choose to focus on what's good about people and about God, it will also affect the way we pray. And the latter is God's way to pray. *Finally brethren, whatever is true, whatever is honorable, whatever is right, whatever is pure, whatever is lovely, whatever is of good repute, if there is any excellence and if anything worthy of praise, let your mind dwell on these things.* (Philippians 4:8)

Counterattacking Through Praise

To further illustrate the power of praise, I'd like to share how this principle of spiritual warfare has enabled me to have victory over my thought life.

I came to Christ from an immoral background. Then, for more than twenty years as a Christian I struggled with my thought life, especially in prayer. Almost every time I would get quiet to pray, I'd feel so ashamed of my past sins, so unworthy to pray, I would stop praying and do something that didn't give me so much trouble. Over those twenty years there were times I would share with other men that I felt I could take into my confidence. They would tell me to read the Word, memorize Scripture, etc. I did that and it helped some, but I was never liberated until I came to realize that the devil would not stop attacking me unless I got on the offensive, to fight spiritually in my thought life. Getting on the offensive means taking whatever spiritual gift God has given me (He has given at least one to every believer), and using it to advance the cause of Christ. To fight spiritually means to take every thought captive to the obedience of Christ to help me obey. Oswald Chambers said, "The golden rule for understanding spiritually is *not* intellect, but *obedience*."[10]

I learned to take Satan's attacks and use them as the basis of praise. If it doesn't cost the enemy to attack me, why should he stop? You see, I have learned how to make the accuser pay when he intrudes into my time with the Lord. I don't make that statement arrogantly because it is God at work. The Word of God teaches that I, as a child of light, do not have to go around stumbling in darkness! When the enemy attacks me with an immoral thought, I will pray something like this:

"Lord, I praise You for allowing the enemy to remind me of what I would be apart from You. Thank You, Lord, for helping me with my thought life. Thank You that those bad thoughts no longer control me. I praise You because greater are You who is in me than he that is in the world." (I John 4:4)

Sometimes when the problem doesn't go away, I have to put feet, so to speak, to my prayers of praise and call or write someone to tell them that I love or appreciate them. Satan never flees from my good intentions. I have to purpose to take action and do whatever I can to bring glory to the Lord Jesus. I know the devil doesn't want me sharing my faith, teaching Bible studies, giving money to the Lord's work, etc. When I am tempted, I take the gift God has given me to serve Him and use it to advance and strengthen the cause of Christ.

For example, I knew my guilt about my thought life and past sins was Satan's attack. To fight off his attacks, first of all I must take every thought captive to the obedience of Christ by praising Him. Secondly, I need to get on the offensive. How could I do that? By actively doing what glorifies the Father. I did this by making a covenant with the Lord that every time the enemy invaded my thought life, I would share Christ with someone.

At the time I was learning this principle, the only thing I knew how to do that the enemy didn't want me doing was to share "The Four Spiritual Laws" (the plan of salvation). I had a special table at the A&W root beer stand that was owned by church members. Anyone who sat at my table got the four laws. I was sharing with everyone that I met. I soon noticed that when people saw me coming, they crossed the street! In fact, my church nicknamed me "G. G. G." –"Go Get'em Gillam!" They thought I had the gift of evangelism, but this was my way of fighting spiritually. When we rely on the Lord and look to Him in prayer, He brings the victory, which strengthens us for the next battle.

A friend of mine was sharing with me that their Bible study group was having a problem with the neighbor's dog barking during their weekly study. It was impossible to concentrate and hard to communicate. He shared that he began to notice that the barking got worse every time the study would get to an important point. In fact, the noise was so bad, they were thinking of canceling or trying to find another place to meet. My friend asked me if I thought it was spiritual battle. I said, "I don't know, but I think I can tell you how we can find out." I reminded him that the Bible says in James 4:7, *Submit therefore to God. Resist the devil and he will flee from you.* I told him, "I think there are times that we need to get on the offensive before the enemy will flee from us." My friend asked how to do that. I asked him, "How does God usually use you? What do you do most effectively in serving the Lord?"

He said, "Teach Bible studies."

"Then I suggest you teach another one. If it is spiritual battle, the devil will back off. Or maybe the Lord wants you to share with your neighbor what your study is all about and how he could be a part of helping people understand the Bible better by keeping his dog quiet."

My friend started another Bible study. Our conversation reminded him that he had been thinking about doing another one even before all the barking started. One week after he started the second study, the dog quit barking. There is a purpose for everything in our lives.

The Holy Spirit may be leading someone to be a missionary or a youth group leader. If my gift is giving, then I give. If my gift is serving, I serve. Whatever the Holy Spirit leads me to do, I purpose to do. *But prove yourselves doers of the word, and not merely hearers who delude themselves.* (James 1:22)

How long do you think the enemy is going to continue to attack me if I end up praising the Lord in and for the attack? If Satan's intrusions into my life motivate me to do more of what I do best for the cause of Christ, he's going to find another place to work!

I know Satan will never completely stop tempting me, but I can get stronger through his tempting. The devil still knocks me down because my flesh is weak. I like to bring attention to myself or take all the credit; but when the accuser attacks me now, I usually get a spirit of expectancy. God's grace is always sufficient to lift me up if I will turn to Him and submit. Then in His power, I'll get up better equipped to serve Him every time. Praise His Holy Name! *Blessed is a man who perseveres under trial; for once he has been approved, he will receive the crown of life, which the Lord has promised to those who love Him.* (James 1:12, also see 13-25)

How do you demoralize an army? By taking away its hope of victory. If we are going to credit God, no matter what, for souls not yet saved and spiritual victories not yet won, why should Satan still fight? There is no reason. No matter what Satan does, if we end up walking closer to the Lord, rejoicing always, the liar may just give up sooner in trying to keep us from praying so much. If we demonstrate by our actions that Satan's attacks just cause us to praise and thank God more and more, he will flee. He must —God tells us he will. (James 4:7)

Reflecting Praise in Adversity: Shirley's Testimony

Reflecting praise in adversity is Gideon's balm for our soul; it is participating in the divine nature of God. How can we do that? How can we learn to apply such a concept?

My Aunt Rose suffered with Parkinson's disease. Her mind was afflicted. She forgot she was related to us; she had long term and short-term memory loss. She knew my name but didn't know I was her niece. She lived with my family when she couldn't live alone any longer. She called me "the lady across the hall." (Our bedroom doors were across from each other.)

We had no intimate family conversations. She didn't remember anyone. She was the caregiver for her parents, never married, and made a home for her father until he passed away. She was uncomfortable having a strange man in the house, always keeping a good distance from my husband. We had been married for 33 years by then, and she knew him well before Parkinson's. Every day she had two questions: "What time is it?" and "What is on the dinner menu?"

She was home alone one night because our daughter had an emergency and was hospitalized. My brother came to take her home with him, but he didn't bring his wife. Aunt Rose wasn't about to go with him and tried to get him out the door by swinging a flyswatter at him. It was hilarious as well as heartbreaking. She would *not* go with him. The next morning, after a good deal of convincing, she did let me take her to my brother's home. However, she knew she had behaved badly and dreaded getting there. She asked repeatedly, "How many miles to his house?" Whenever I had to take her anywhere–the doctor, my brother's, etc.–I would have to prepare her by introducing the idea calmly. I spoke softly, comfortingly, and would sing to her on the way. She was a good sport once we got going.

Eventually she required more help than we were set up to provide and we had to place her in a nursing care facility. I prayed earnestly, knowing that this wasn't just "bad luck." I kept seeking God's purpose for me now that I couldn't care for her–
–what could it be? Aunt Rose was a second mother to my two brothers and me. I knew God's design was a positive one; He meant it for good.

I had recently learned the value and power of reflecting praise, so I put that into practice by each day asking God to remind me of something specific she had done for me in our past that I could bring to light and thank her for. Every day I expressed my gratefulness to her. For example, when I was a kid, she invited me to stay overnight a lot, a great treat for me. She lived in town, at Fort Morgan, Colorado, and we lived in the country. My dad was a farmer. Often I'd get to spend Saturday night with her and we'd go to Sunday school and church the next day. I thanked her for being such a good hostess and for the joy it gave me to look forward to being with her.

In my adult years, she had retired and was always available to help me with our kids. During our move to Bakersfield, California, she and Mom kept the kids and had a delicious chicken dinner waiting for us when we brought the last load. I recalled the details of that day to her and thanked her for going the extra mile. She always looked at me for a few minutes and then would say, "Don't thank me. Thank God!"

Finally, after a couple weeks of this every day, I got the message. I needed to pray with her. Duh! My husband and I teach believers how to make their Bible their prayer book. Here it was—right in front of me. I couldn't see the forest for the trees. So, I tried it.

I read a psalm and prayed, responding to each verse as a dialogue –a conversation with the Lord. When I read a passage that Aunt Rose knew, she said it with me. She had hidden it in her heart. And she prayed about that verse, talking to God as if she wasn't sick at all. I was amazed and astounded! We prayed through several verses, then I began singing praise to God as we do in prayer and worship—and she joined in! Soon she would begin to sing a hymn and tell me to sing too. Her favorite was, "Jesus Loves Me, This I Know."

As she got weaker and could no longer sing with me, I just sang to her, sometimes an hour or two each day. She would relax and smile. Psalm 59:16-17 says, "...*I will sing of your strength, in the morning I will sing of your love; for you are my fortress, my refuge in times of trouble. O my Strength, I sing praise to you; You, O God, are my fortress, my loving God.* (NIV)

What a joyous time! God had opened our line of communication. We spent hours almost every day just singing, praising, reading the Scriptures, and praying. It was so glorious. God gave me a prayer partner like I'd never had. I didn't absorb all that was happening at the time. It was a long while after she died that I realized that her only aim was to glory in the Triune God. Temporal needs were never mentioned. She had no devastating prayer requests. She just focused on the eternal. What a refreshment to hear only prayers of praise to her Lord! I always left that usually "sad place" full of joy and excited to minister, to trust and obey!

Aunt Rose taught me that the eternal side of prayer was the way to go. In contrast, when I spent my prayer time focusing on temporal needs and problems, a natural trait, I was soon depressed and discouraged, even beginning to doubt if God could help. He seemed so small compared to my huge unsolvable needs! I benefitted so much by not dwelling on praying just for her healing. This was her sickness unto death and for the glory of God—not for chastisement!

I saw that since our soul and spirit are eternal, they can always grow and be strengthened, unaffected by what happens to the body or the mind. Our spirit remains healthy when we belong to the family of God and feed it the food of God's Word. Almost a year after our prayer partnership, God took her to her permanent home in glory with Himself, where her beautiful spirit was freed from the prison of her shaky body and crippled mind.

My mother, Aunt Rose's sister, has been my model for applying this principle of praise. When she spoke of her children, loved ones, or anyone, it was with positive remarks. She didn't favor one of us above the other. I didn't fully realize her influence on all of us until summing up this wonderful experience I'd had with Aunt Rose.

As I look back, God's purpose for me in Aunt Rose's affliction was to "Turn my eyes upon Jesus. Look full in His wonderful face, and the things of earth grow strangely dim in the light of His glory and grace!" His plan was to let me see the purpose of prayer—to know Him, to glorify God and enjoy Him forever, every day, in every thought, prayer, communion, and dialogue with Him and with everyone else. I need to have a prayer partner. I cannot do this by myself—I need my Creator Lord to do it in me, through me, and with me.

Chapter 8
All Prayer Leads to Calvary

Viewing prayer as a process of going to Calvary helps to focus and purify our prayers. Let's clarify some terms in regard to this concept.

First, true prayer needs to be offered to the proper object. We must pray to the true God and not to idols or false gods.

Secondly, prayer offered to the proper person must also be offered in the proper way. The proper way is determined by God, not us. "Going to Calvary" is one way of looking at or expressing the proper way to approach God with our prayers.

"Calvary" is the name of the location where Jesus Christ died. The word also refers to that event by referring to the location. "Calvary" is the Latin translation of the Hebrew word "Golgotha," which literally means "the place of a skull." Calvary and the crucifixion of Christ are inseparably linked.

By His life and death, Christ accomplished many important things for us.

1. Jesus is the physical representation of God in the flesh. All that Jesus did showed us what God is like.

> *Philip said to Him, "Lord, show us the Father, and it is enough for us." Jesus said to him, "Have I been so long with you, and yet you have not come to know Me, Philip? He who has seen Me has seen the Father; how can you say, 'Show us the Father'? Do you not believe that I am in the Father, and the Father is in Me?" (John 14:8-10)*

2. The act of Jesus glorifying God is seen in the following example:

> *Jesus spoke these things; and lifting up His eyes to heaven, He said, "Father, the hour has come; glorify Your Son, that the Son may glorify You.* (John 17:1)

3. On the cross at Calvary we see the attributes of God being lived out. The primary attribute we see is God's love.

> *By this the love of God was manifested in us, that God has sent His only begotten Son into the world so that we might live through Him. In this is love, not that we loved God, but that He loved us and sent His Son to be the propitiation for our sins.* (1 John 4:8-11)

His death on the cross also showed that God is a righteous judge by punishing sin.

> *...being justified as a gift by His grace through the redemption which is in Christ Jesus; whom God displayed publicly as a propitiation in His blood through faith. This was to demonstrate His righteousness.* (Rom 3:24-25)

Jesus dying on the cross is the perfect picture and accurate representation of God's love and righteousness.

Prayer is access to God

The first reason we need to come to "Calvary" is that access to God is restricted. Even though God is everywhere at all times, that does not mean we have a hearing with God automatically. Because of the gulf between the righteousness of God and the sinfulness of man, we cannot gain access to the Father, except through Jesus Christ. (John 14:6)

In Hebrews 12:29, God is described as a consuming fire to convey the difficulty in access. No man can look upon God and live, according to Exodus 33:20. Man needs an intermediary to come into God's presence.

Understanding the Old Testament approach to God helps us appreciate what Jesus did for us. The presence of God was symbolized by the Holy of Holies in the tabernacle. Only the High Priest had access to that presence with God, and he was required to carefully and purely enter into God's presence. Hebrews 9:1-24 states that Jesus has entered into the holy presence of God on our behalf.

Confusion arises from the fact that God sees all and knows all. Because of this pervasive presence of God, some think they are automatically heard. The startling words of Jesus in Matthew 7:23 – *I never knew you; Depart from Me, you who practice lawlessness;* show that we can be sadly mistaken about our relationship with God.

1. Salvation gains access to God

No man can come properly into the presence of God without becoming His child. God looks upon the earth and participates in the affairs of men, but the personal relationship we need with God can only come through Jesus Christ.

Man does not have access to the ear of God. It is like a man watching the flight controller up in the tower on an airfield. He can see the controller and the controller controls. But unless that man has a radio, he has no influence on that controller and no access. Salvation gains you access to God to communicate with Him.

Jesus Christ is the only way to gain salvation, according to Acts 4:12. Salvation begins the process of participating with God in His program.

2. Continued access is necessary for service

Even after we are saved and have a special relationship to God by being His children, we still gain access to God based upon what Jesus has done on the cross for us. The way we began our relationship is the way we continue it.

The intercession of Christ is an ongoing process that helps us in our service.

Therefore He is able also to save forever those who draw near to God through Him, since He always lives to make intercession for them. (Hebrews 7:25)

Since access to an all-powerful God is such a special privilege, we could develop a fear to come to God. But we are invited to come to God through Jesus.

Having therefore, brethren, boldness to enter into the holiest by the blood of Jesus, by a new and living way, which he hath consecrated for us, through the veil, that is to say, his flesh; and having an high priest over the house of God; let us draw near with a true heart in full assurance of faith, having our hearts sprinkled from an evil conscience, and our bodies washed with pure water. (Hebrews 10:19-22)

There are times we may incorrectly feel condemned by Satan for sin. We need to know that Christ is in position and determined to help us maintain a proper relationship with God.

Who is the one who condemns? Christ Jesus is He who died, yes, rather who was raised, who is at the right hand of God, who also intercedes for us. (Romans 8:34-35)

Jesus is appearing before God for us. It might be helpful to create a mental picture of Jesus standing before God presenting our case before the Father.

And almost all things are by the law purged with blood; and without shedding of blood is no remission. ... For Christ is not entered into the holy places made with hands, which are the figures of the true; but into heaven itself, now to appear in the presence of God for us. (Hebrews 9:22,24)

With Christ standing at the right-hand side interceding for us, we are now in the proper relationship to participate in God's program.

Our relationship to God and His program

When we are born again and redeemed, we have access to God which we never had before. The question arises, "For what reason do we want access to God?" What are we going to do with our relationship to God?

Our position in Christ in respect to prayer can be discussed from the perspective of three relationships: children, friends, and workers.

1. Children

We are now sons of God, and as children we come to the Father to have our needs met. We cry out to God as our father as we are told to do in Romans 8:14-16. God as our father is our protector. In this sense we come to Him in prayer to seek protection and guidance because we are His children.

For everyone who asks receives, and he who seeks finds, and to him who knocks it will be opened. Or what man is there among you who, when his son asks for a loaf, will give him a stone? Or if he asks for a fish, he will not give him a snake, will he? If you then, being evil, know how to give good gifts to your children, how much more will your Father who is in heaven give what is good to those who ask Him! (Matthew 7:8-11)

We pray to God based upon becoming his children, which happened based upon the death of Christ. Sonship is a positional relationship that continues no matter what. It is irreversible.

Christ cried out for help from the Father in the time of his difficulty:

"Now My soul has become troubled; and what shall I say, 'Father, save Me from this hour'? But for this purpose I came to this hour. Father, glorify Your name." Then a voice came out of heaven: "I have both glorified it, and will glorify it again." So the crowd of people who stood by and heard it were saying that it had thundered; others were saying, "An angel has spoken to Him." (John 12:27-29)

God the Father cannot remove all suffering from his children; some suffering is necessary for our benefit and His glory. Just as Christ entered into great suffering at Calvary, we will likewise have times of going through great suffering.

2. Friends

We also have the ability to become friends of God. Jesus tells us this friendship develops as we are obedient to God's commands.

You are my friends if you do what I command. No longer do I call you slaves, for the slave does not know what his master is doing; but I have called you friends, for all things that I have heard from My Father I have made known to you. (John 15:14-15)

But we should not just sit around as Jesus' friends, nor do we merely bask in the glory of being His children. Our purpose is to bring glory to God in the same way as Christ—by obedience. We do work for and with God.

3. Co-workers

Co-laborer describes our relationship to God in light of our activity. God works and we are to work, just as Jesus did with His father. As 1 Corinthians 3:9 says, ... *for we are God's fellow workers*. But do not ever forget this relationship is possible because of Calvary.

How much more will the blood of Christ who through the eternal Spirit offered Himself without blemish to God, cleanse your conscience from dead works to serve the living God? (Hebrews 9:14)

God has predetermined the works he wants us to do.

For we are His workmanship, created in Christ Jesus for good works, which God prepared beforehand, that we should walk in them. (Ephesians 2:10)

Our three relationships to God –children, friends, and fellow workers –all find a common ground in what Christ did at the cross for us. All require proper communication in prayer with God. We need to know how to ask God for things.

The Art of Asking

Our prayers need to move beyond avoiding sins and removing discomfort to aligning our hearts with Jesus Christ.

What do we ask for? What are proper requests?

A primary prayer should be to gain wisdom, to see things the way God does and to act in conformity to God's will. If we do not have full insight, we still want to have attitudes and actions in conformity with God. How do we receive insight? How do we determine which good works to do?

1. The act of asking glorifies God no matter what the answer is.

The very act of praying and seeking God brings God glory because in our asking we are acknowledging that God is our provider; all that we need and want comes from Him. Coming to Him demonstrates our humility in contrast to His greatness, as well as faith in His goodness, according to Hebrews 11:6.

2. Asking in Jesus' name

And whatever you ask in My name, that will I do, that the Father may be glorified in the Son. If you ask Me anything in My name, I will do it. (John 14:13,14)

A name is the representation of a person's being. Some names contain descriptions in them. Calling someone Red or Whitey designates a physical feature as well as represents the person. God's names and Jesus' names are descriptive.

When we pray in Jesus' name we are actually praying based upon who Jesus is. "Jesus" is translated as "Jehovah saves." The name Christ means the anointed one, or the specially appointed one.[11]

The greatest act of God's program of redemption was the crucifixion of Jesus Christ. This is where Jesus acted out his name and saved us on the cross. The crucifixion and resurrection manifested and glorified both God and the Son.

Our understanding of salvation needs to go beyond the mere fact that we do not have to go to hell and now are headed for heaven. Salvation has changed our relationship as well as our destiny. We now have the ability to participate with God in the advancement of God's goals. We appreciate this most when we accurately understand and remember what our relationship to God was before we were saved.

Asking according to the name and nature of Christ brings us joy as we participate with God.

Until now you have asked for nothing in My name; ask, and you will receive, that your joy may be made full. (John 16:24)

3. Asking for things and being denied

Asking and receiving a denial may be a disappointment but it is not a sin. We are not expected to always ask for the right things. But we are expected to graciously receive answers we do not want. Right before going to Calvary, Jesus asked that He be spared from it.

And He went a little beyond them, and fell on His face and prayed, saying, "My Father, if it is possible, let this cup pass from Me; yet not as I will, but as You will." (Matt 26:39-40)

Paul prayed for his thorn in the flesh to depart, and when he was denied his request, he gloried in the refusal.

Concerning this I implored the Lord three times that it might leave me. And He has said to me, "My grace is sufficient for you, for power is perfected in weakness." Most gladly, therefore, I will rather boast about my weaknesses, so that the power of Christ may dwell in me. (2 Cor 12:8-10)

Paul did receive a refusal and a reason for the refusal. We do not always receive an immediate reason for a denial. But responding correctly to a refusal brings great glory to God when we graciously accept a "no" answer.

Asking when we are in trouble acknowledges the power and greatness of God.

In my distress I called upon the LORD,
And cried to my God for help;
He heard my voice out of His temple,
And my cry for help before Him came into His ears.
(Psalm 18:6)

This poor man cried, and the LORD heard him
And saved him out of all his troubles.
The angel of the LORD encamps around those who fear Him, and rescues them.

O taste and see that the LORD is good;
How blessed is the man who takes refuge in Him!
(Psalm 34:6-8)

4. Asking for seemingly insignificant requests

From a human perspective the first recorded miracle performed by Jesus seems hardly necessary for the advancement of the kingdom. How important was it to have more wine at a wedding compared to raising Lazarus from the dead?

Are not five sparrows sold for two cents? Yet not one of them is forgotten before God. Indeed, the very hairs of your head are all numbered. Do not fear; you are more valuable than many sparrows. (Luke 12:6-7)

You are not going to wear God out with your requests as if they will overload him with too much detail. God meets many needs that are in some senses trivial. He is always working from an eternal perspective and from a spiritual vantage point.

If you abide in Me, and My words abide in you , ask whatever you will, and it shall be done for you. By this is My Father glorified, that you bear much fruit, and so prove to be My disciples. (John 15:7, 8)

Our prayers for physical things are still to advance spiritual objectives and need to find a rationale in God's nature. But God is also a father, and fathers like to do good things for their children as we saw in Matt 7:8-11.

Peter is an example of pushing the envelope with requests from God.

Peter wanted to walk on water. Peter wanted to build three tabernacles on the Mount for Moses, Elijah, and Jesus. The first request was granted, the second did not even receive consideration.

The real issue of significance is motive; why are we asking for something? The same request may find its ground in spiritual or carnal motives. For example, is it right for a mother to ask for parking place close to the store she is going to?

If she is seeking the parking place only because she wants it for her own convenience and comfort, she may not get it. However, if she is asking for it based on the health and safety needs of infant children or an elderly passenger, she is praying on a more spiritual basis.

In the case of being denied, her right response could be something like, "Thank you, Lord, for giving me some additional exercise; it's good for me."

The problem arises when our hearts and prayers become preoccupied with meeting our own fleshly needs.

You ask and do not receive because you ask with wrong motives, so that you may spend it on your pleasures. (James 4:3)

Some requests, if answered, would make us more worldly. The typical prayer for a bright shiny new fast car is hard to justify and so is land or a vacation home in the country. Focusing on a car beyond moving from point A to point B runs the risk of a worldly desire. Yes, we all know that for others' sake we need a dependable car to be good stewards; but splashy color, high horsepower, sun roofs, and leather interiors are more status symbols than functional requirements.

You adulterers and adulteresses, do you not know that friendship with the world is hostility toward God? Therefore whoever wishes to be a friend of the world makes himself an enemy of God. (James 4:4)

Worldliness is taking care of your flesh first instead of meeting needs of others.

Self preservation is the first law of physical life.
Self-sacrifice is the first law of spiritual life.

Meditating on all that Christ did on Calvary and all that it accomplished for us helps to straighten out our thinking and refine our prayers for God's glory and other's benefit.

Calvary provides a guide to fervency.
Understanding Calvary will help us correctly understand our fervency when praying.

As Oswald Chambers so deftly stated it:
> When we pray relying on the Holy Spirit, He will always bring us back to this one point: we are not heard because we are in earnest, or because we need to be heard, or because we will perish if we are not heard; we are heard only on the ground of the Atonement of our Lord.[12]

> We tend nowadays to worship prayer. We stress nights of prayer and the difficulty and cost of prayer. It is not prayer that is strenuous, but the overcoming of our own laziness. If we make the basis of prayer our effort and agony, we mistake the basis of prayer. The basis of

prayer is not what it costs us, but what it cost God to enable us to pray.[13]

A summary

The essence of prayer is to stay in communication with God so we can accomplish His goals to bring glory to Him. Every prayer needs to have an eternal perspective. At Calvary we see all the eternal perspectives manifested as Jesus died to save sinners and provide the way to make them holy.

Spiritual prayers can include physical needs, but any prayer that primarily feeds our selfish flesh is suspect as far as being "Calvary-based" prayer. Prayers for safety or restoration from sickness are allowed and many times answered, but spiritual advancement is most important.

Chapter 9
A Brief Look at Faith

What would a book on prayer be without a word about faith? Biblical prayer is the purest form of faith because it is founded on the Word of God. Faith has to have an object, and as Christians, the object of our faith is God as He has revealed Himself in His Word. Prayer without faith is not prayer at all from God's perspective. Faith without prayer is an oxymoron.

When Christians talk about faith, the conversation will often lead to the man who truly lived it, George Mueller. He was a man of great faith and an anointed prayer warrior. I highly recommend that you read about this man of God. I am including here an excerpt written by him that is only a shadow of what he lived for the glory of God.

"Real Faith" by George Mueller

Faith is the substance of things hoped for, the evidence of things not seen. Through faith we understand that the worlds were framed by the Word of God, so that things which are seen were not made of things which do appear, (Hebrews 11:1,3).

I read in God's Word, *Cast thy burden upon the Lord, and He shall sustain thee,* (Psalm 55:22).

Day by day I do it, and have been doing it now for fifty-one years. I have lacked nothing—absolutely nothing. Often I have had trials, difficulties and an empty purse, but receipts for the Lord's work in half a century have aggregated hundreds of thousands of dollars. To the glory of God I say this.

Often I am asked, "What is faith? How may it be increased? What characterizes its growth?" These points I will endeavor to illustrate by some of the experiences which, by the grace of God, have come to me personally in the exercise of belief in His promises revealed in His Word.

First: What is faith? In the simplest manner in which I am able to express it, I answer: Faith is the assurance that the thing which God has said in His Word is true, and that God will act according to what He has said in His Word. This assurance, this reliance on God's Word, this confidence is faith.

Viewing the matter negatively, we may say that faith is not a matter of impressions, nor of probabilities, nor of appearance. Impressions come from human reasoning which at best is untrustworthy. Faith, on the other hand, is based upon the impregnable Word of God. It is not impression, strong or weak, that will make any difference. We have to do with the written Word. We have to rely on the written Word, and not on ourselves or our impressions.

Probabilities are not to be taken into account. Many people are willing to believe regarding those things that seem probable to them. Faith has nothing to do with probabilities. The province of faith begins where probabilities cease and sight and sense fail.

A great many of God's children are cast down and lament their want of faith. They write to me and say that they have no impressions, no feeling, they see no probability that the thing they wish will come to pass (Luke 18:27). Appearances are not to be confused with faith. The question rather, is this: Has God spoken in His Word concerning this matter? If he has, that is the ground for faith. It is because there is so much dependence upon impressions, probabilities, appearances, and similar unimportant issues that we have so little blessing among us. All these things must be abandoned. The naked Word of God is what we are to depend upon. This is enough for us.

And now, my beloved friends, you are in great need to ask yourselves whether you are in the habit of thus confiding in your inmost soul, in what God has said, and whether you are in earnest in seeking to find whether the thing you want is in accordance with what He has said in His Word. If it is, the object you seek is sure of procurement. It is as certain as is the fact that you were able to confide in Him.

Secondly: How faith may be increased. The increase of faith is the work of God in the human heart. God delights to increase the faith of His children. By this means God is glorified before an ungodly world and the powers of darkness. Furthermore, this confidence that His children show in Him in times of trial, discouragement, pain and sorrow gives great encouragement to other Christians. God delights to do good to others through them that they themselves, through the exercise of faith, may obtain an increase of it. Difficulties, limitations, hindrances, bereavements and losses, though we shrink exceedingly from them, are the very agencies that God uses to cause us to grow. As an infant has its limbs developed by means of exercise and nourishment until ultimately they possess the power of a man's, so in a spiritual sense, is the Christian made strong by adversity. I am not one who believes that we can attain to strong faith instantly, any more that I would affirm that a weak infant can spring into manhood at once. Our faith which is feeble at first, is strengthened more and more by use.

Again, the increase of faith is dependent upon the individual's attitude toward the methods God uses for this purpose. Instead of wanting no trials before victory and no exercise of patience, the child of God must be willing to take these things from His hands as means of expanding his Christian life. Trials, difficulties, obstacles, griefs, necessities—all are the very food of faith.

I get letters from so many of God's dear children who say, "Dear Brother Mueller: I'm writing this because I am so weak and feeble in faith." Just so surely as we ask to have our faith strengthened, we must feel a willingness to take from God's hand the means for strengthening it. We must allow Him to educate us through trials and bereavements and troubles. It is through trials that faith is exercised and developed more and more. God affectionately permits difficulties, that He may develop unceasingly that which He is willing to do for us, and to this end we should not shrink. If He gives us sorrow and hindrances and losses and afflictions, we should take them out of His hands as evidences of His love and care for us in developing more and more that faith which He is seeking to strengthen in us.

Thirdly: What characterizes growing faith? Faith grows as one acquaints himself with God as He has revealed Himself in the Scriptures. We must not content ourselves with the notions that people have about God, but diligently seek to know exactly what He has disclosed regarding Himself. We dare not be satisfied to take the ideas which the church and many professing Christians have of God, but we must come to the very fountain of knowledge, the revelation the Lord Has made of Himself in His written Word.

Here one is to pause often, to meditate and to adore. Here one is to drink deeply if faith is to flourish. There can be no substitute for the study of the Scriptures.

Again, faith grows as the Person of Christ is known and appreciated. As we read the Word, we shall learn not only of the power, wisdom, justice and holiness of our God, but also of His gentleness, pity, beauty, and bounty—all embodied in our Saviour. More and more we shall observe that God is the Lovable One. Is He this to you? If He is not, you are not acquainted with Him. Oh, seek to say in your inmost heart that He is the One altogether lovely! The result will be that you will confide in Him unreservedly, at all times and in all circumstances. Though He slay you, yet, like Job, you will trust in Him. Turn and read the ninth Psalm. With your very own eyes look at the ninth and tenth verses, *"The Lord also will be a refuge for the oppressed, a refuge in times of trouble. And they that know thy name will put their trust in thee, for thou, Lord, has not forsaken them that seek thee."* We who learn to see God as He has portrayed Himself in His Word are so satisfied with Him, and in His dealings with us, that we perceive also that everything is for our good. On this account it is deeply important for usefulness and for our growth in faith that we get correct ideas of God from the fountain of truth contained in His Word. In the exercise of our faith, and in studying God in His Word, our faith grows. I say this deliberately, advisedly, and tens of thousands of God's tried children will say the same thing.

The Church of God is not aroused to see God as the beautiful and lovable One He is, and hence the littleness of blessedness. Oh, beloved brothers and sisters in Christ, seek to learn for yourselves, for I cannot tell you the blessedness! In the darkest moments I am able to confide in Him, for I know what a beautiful and kind and lovable Being He is, and, if it be the will of God to put us in the furnace, let Him do it, that so we may acquaint ourselves with Him as He will reveal Himself, and that we may know Him better. We come then to the conclusion that God is a loveable Being, and we are satisfied with Him, and say, "He is my Father, let Him do as He pleases." He who has this confidence, founded as it must be on the written and the living Word, will experience growing faith.

When I first began to allow God to deal with me, relying on Him, taking Him at His Word, and set out fifty years ago simply relying on Him for my self, family, taxes, traveling expenses and every other need, I rested on the simple promises I found in the sixth chapter of Matthew, *I say unto you, take no thought for your life, what ye shall eat, or what ye shall drink not yet for your body, what ye shall put on. Is not the life more than meat, and the body than raiment? ...If God so clothe the grass of the field which today is, and tomorrow is cast into the oven, shall he not much more clothe you, O ye of little faith? Therefore take no thought, saying, what shall we eat? Or, What shall we drink? Or, Wherewithal shall we be clothed?—for your heavenly Father knoweth that ye have need of all these things. But seek ye first the kingdom of God and His righteousness; and all these things shall be added unto you,* Matthew 6:25-33. I believed the Word, I rested on it and practiced it. I took God at His Word. A stranger, a foreigner in England, I knew several languages and might have used them perhaps as a means of remunerative employment, but I had consecrated myself to labor for the Lord. I put my reliance in the God who has promised, and He has acted according to His Word. I've lacked nothing—nothing. I have had my trials and difficulties, and my purse empty, but my receipts have aggregated. I have received thousands and thousands of dollars, while the work has gone on these fifty-one years. Then, with regard to my pastoral work, for the past fifty-one years I have had great difficulties, great trials, and perplexities. There will always be difficulties, always trials. But God has sustained me out of them and the work has gone on.

Now, this is not, as some have said, because I am a man of great mental power, or endowed with energy and perseverance—these are not the reasons. It is because I have confided in God; because I have sought God, and He has cared for the Institution, which under His direction, has over one hundred schools, with masters and mistresses and other departments (in addition to the orphanage). The difficulties encountered in this undertaking have been gigantic. But I read they that put their trust in the Lord shall not be ashamed—I read and believed. God has upheld me.

Nearly twenty years ago a beloved brother from America came to see me. He expected to find an old man helpless and decrepit, bowed down with burdens. He marveled that I did not look old. "How is this?" he asked. "How do you keep so young under the load you are carrying?" "My dear brother," I replied, "I have always rolled the burden on the Lord. I do not carry one-hundredth part of it."

By His grace, that is the secret of true restfulness. And now in my seventy-sixth year, I have physical strength and mental vigor for as much work as when I was a young man in the university studying and preparing Latin orations. I am just as vigorous as at that time. How comes this? Because in the last half-century of labor I've been able with the simplicity of a child, to rely upon God. I have had my trials, but I have laid hold upon God, and so it has come to pass that I have been sustained. It is not only permission, but positive command that He gives, to cast the burdens upon Him. Oh, let us do it! My beloved brothers and sisters in Christ, *Cast thy burden upon the Lord and He shall sustain thee,* (Psalm 55:22). Day by day I do it. This morning sixty matters in connection with the church of which I am pastor, I brought before the Lord, and thus it is, day by day I do it, and year by year: ten years, thirty years, fifty years. With all earnestness I invite you, beloved brothers and sisters in Christ, to come with your burdens, with the problems of your business or profession or household—come to God in faith and you will find help.

Many persons suppose it is only about money that I trust the Lord in prayer. I do bring this money question to Him, but it is only one of many matters of which I speak to God and find that He answers. Often I have perplexity in finding persons of ability and fitness for the various posts that I must supply. Sometimes weeks and months pass, and day by day, day by day, I bring the matter before the Lord, and invariably He helps. It is so also about the conversion of unsaved persons; sooner or later prayer on their behalf is turned to praise. Prayer prevails also in the needs of our sending our tracts and books and missionary funds. After a while, God shows us His answer. We are never left; we are never confounded.

Do not, however, expect to obtain full faith at once. All such things as jumping into full exercise of faith in such things, I discountenance. I do not believe in it. I do not believe in it, I do NOT believe in it and wish you plainly to understand I do not believe in it. All such things go on in a natural way. The little I did obtain I did not obtain all at once. All this I say particularly, because letters come to me full of questions from those who seek to have their faith strengthened. Begin over again, staying your soul on the Word of God, and you will have an increase of you faith as you exercise it.

One thing more. Some say, "Oh, I shall never have the gift of faith Mr. Mueller has got." This is a mistake—it is the greatest error—there is not a particle of truth in it. What little faith I have is the grace of faith, not the gift. My faith is the same kind of faith that all God's children have had. It is the same kind that Simon Peter had, and all Christians may obtain the like faith. My faith is their faith, though there be more of it because my faith has been a little more developed by exercise than theirs; but their faith is precisely the faith I exercise, only, with regard to degree, mine may be more strongly exercised. Mark this concerning the grace of faith, it has to do with the written Word of God; it is always accompanied by love, and it eventuates in spiritual power—ability to command even devils in the name of the Lord. That faith any Christian may enjoy. It is not a gift bestowed once for all; but is a day by day development wrought in the life of the Spirit of God.

Now, my beloved brothers and sisters, begin in a little way. At first, I was able to trust the Lord for ten dollars, then for a hundred dollars, then for a thousand dollars, then for one hundred thousand dollars, and now, with the greatest ease, I could trust Him for millions of dollars if there were occasion for it. But first, I should quietly, carefully, deliberately examine and see whether what I was trusting for was something in accordance with His promises in His written Word. If I found it was, the amount of difficulties would be no hindrance to my trust.

Fifty-one years, and God has never failed me! Trust Him for yourselves and find how true to His Word He is.

The quality and source of George Mueller's faith is also vividly exemplified in his response to a problem-filled situation in 1843 as we see here:

> "I had a secret satisfaction in the greatness of the difficulties which were in the way. So far from being cast down on account of them, they delighted my soul; for I only desired to do the will of the Lord in this matter—the greater the obstacles, the more abundantly plain the proof, that I had come to a right judgment, if they were removed by prayer—I did nothing but pray. Prayer and faith, the universal remedies against every want and every difficulty; and the nourishment of prayer and faith, God's holy Word, helped me over all the difficulties."[14]

In the Prayer Enrichment Seminar I often ask, "How many pray for more faith? A lot of hands go up. Then I ask, "How many pray for more patience?" More hands go up. Then I ask, "Why are some of you smiling?" The smiles come because some understand that when you pray for more faith and more patience, you get trials and tribulation. That's true. Did you hear that come through in Mr. Mueller's testimony or have you experienced that yourself? It didn't take me long as a young Christian to learn not to pray for more faith or more patience.

Then I ask the class, "If I could share with you how you can pray and receive more faith and patience without tribulation, would you be interested?" Every hand goes up. That is what I am endeavoring to do in this writing.

We need to go back to the "gaze and glance" principle. For example, let's say you have a burden for your child to come to know the Lord. We have learned that the first response is not to pray to change the child. Instead you ask the Lord to *teach* you to pray for the child's salvation. The Lord seems to impress you to think about what the most positive things are that you see in the child. Is he kind, does he have a good mind, etc.? Then you praise the Lord for what you know and believe is true of the unsaved child. This is an act of obedience. God is pleased and blesses you with His love for this child. As a result of your obedience to the known will of God, your faith is strengthened and you can have patience while God does His perfect work.

Now let's say you just lost your job through no fault of your own. You have bills to pay. Going back again to the "gaze and glance," you glance at your need and see the problem. But instead of asking for more faith, you purpose to apply the faith you already have; you believe that God is sovereign and that He loves you. You praise Him by faith for being your Provider. You see, the key to more faith and more patience is obedience and trust. Your prayer is, "Lord, please help me to trust in You in this situation and, Lord, empower me to obey You."

"Trust and obey, for there is no other way to be happy in Jesus, but to trust and obey."

I don't believe that praying for more faith or more patience is necessarily wrong; I just think there is a better way to be consistently more effective. Faith is like a muscle; it has to be exercised to get stronger. To each man who is born again, God has given a measure of faith (Romans 12:3). When I pray according to my faith (we are never asked to pray according to someone else's faith), where my faith and God's will intersect, God has obligated Himself to answer my prayer, (Romans 1:17). I am never asked to pray beyond my faith (Matthew 9:29; 17:20; 21:21-22; Luke 17:5-6). When God answers my prayer of faith, my faith is increased. My faith is strengthened by my obedience to use the faith given me (Hebrews 11). It seems to me that to ask for more faith without using the faith I have is asking God to bless me with power I'm not using. In reality I am "asking" God to increase my adversities so that I will use what I have (Colossians 3:6, including 3:1-11).

Spiritual understanding does not come from intellect, but from obedience. When I ask the Lord for help to walk uprightly in my situation rather than asking Him to remove it, I am exercising my faith and God is pleased. Faith will grow when exercised as surely as water makes the crop grow. Let's base our prayer on Psalm 119:18: *Lord, open my eyes that I may behold the wonders of Your beautiful Word.* The promises of the Living Word are where our faith is grounded. How good He is!

Chapter 10
Prayer Partners: AKA Back to Back

We live in an unprecedented time in history. Dr. Charles Swindoll from Dallas Theological Seminary has said, "We are presently facing a very great opportunity brilliantly disguised as a nearly impossible situation." There has never been a time when people need each other more. Why is that? It's because God has brought us to the end of ourselves as a society. We have no humanly workable answers, but prayer works!

Now I know that the Lord saves His anointed; He will answer him from His Holy heaven, with the saving strength of His right hand. (Psalm 20:6)

More effective communication with God will reduce the number of failures in individual Christian lives, in Christian families and the local church. We know biblically that the strength of the family unit is the strength of the church and of the nation. Jesus told us that *no city or house divided against itself will stand.* (Matthew 12:23) What we are seeing across all of society is fragmentation and schism. God's desire is for true unity found in Him based on His Word.

Praying with a prayer partner is a biblical way to gain power and effectiveness in prayer. It is difficult to fulfill God's call without a commitment to each other of prayer.

*Two can accomplish more than twice as much as one, for the results can be much better. If one falls, the other pulls him up; but if a man falls when he is alone, he's in trouble. Also, on a cold night, two under the same blanket gain warmth from each other, but how can one be warm alone? And one standing alone can be attacked and defeated, but two can stand **back to back** and conquer;*

three is even better, for a triple-braided cord is not easily broken. (Ecclesiastes 4:9-12, The Living Bible)

Do you have an intimate personal prayer partner? If not, why not? I have asked these questions wherever I've gone and found that no more than one in 100 Christians have prayer partners. I've asked older Christians who do have prayer partners how long they've had them. Four to five years is the regular reply. Then I ask how long they've been Christians. Often they'll say 25 or 30 years. Next, I ask if they would ever be without a prayer partner again. The answer is always no. Interesting answer. If mature Christians regularly find having a prayer partner to be a valuable asset in their Christian walk, what are some of the factors that hold the rest of us back from seeking that benefit?

One day I asked a pastor if he had anyone praying for him. He said that if he were to publicly ask someone in his church to pray for him, it would be all over town the next day that he had a personal problem. That is so sad, but probably true in some churches (Thankfully, not in all of them!) Fear of gossip has kept many from having prayer partners.

Others simply have an inaccurate view of prayer and prayer partners. They may be Christians, but they've never been taught how to pray from Scripture, or they've never understood that it's often more effective to pray *with* someone rather than just *for* them. After all, Scripture teaches us that God did not create us to fulfill His purpose on earth by ourselves. He has not created one soul to do it alone. ...*It is not good for the man to be alone*... (Genesis 2:18).

Some others are open to having a prayer partner, but their motive is selfish—it's to get things from God without expending as much personal effort. Such was the case when a lady called me to ask prayer for her husband. She gave a lot of details. After listening for some time, I interrupted and asked if we could pray together right then on the phone. She was in a hurry and wasn't comfortable praying with others and hung up. I did pray, but primarily for her walk with the Lord.

In another situation, a fellow asked for prayer while handing me a couple 8 1/2" X 11" sheets of paper filled with requests to pray for his wife who had left him. The list was focused on changing *her*, such as, "pray she'll not sleep until she repents and comes home to the children and me," etc. Nothing on the list was asking God to help him see his circumstances from the Lord's perspective. I told him I couldn't comfortably pray the way he asked, but I asked if he'd be interested to meet with me and pray together for his relationship to the Lord. He said that would be good, but it never did happen.

Has something like this happened to you? I have found it helpful to teach such people the biblical principle of praying in unity *with* other Christians, using Scripture as a basis for our prayers. Here's an example of a scripture from which to pray, from 1 Peter 3:15: *But sanctify Christ as Lord in your hearts, always being ready to make a defense to every one who asks you to give an account for the hope that is in you, yet with gentleness and reverence.*

Using this passage, you could pray something like this: "Father God, I pray that Shirley will set apart Christ as Lord in her heart, always ready to make a defense to every one who asks her why she has hope and to tell them about it gently and respectfully. Amen."

The Word of God disarms the enemy from trying to get us to pray for each other from wrong motives.

If I tell a person who is in trouble that I'll pray for them, they may be apprehensive because they don't know how much I know. They sometimes assume I'm going to pray to change them, and they just want to get their need met without changing their lifestyle. We are commanded to pray even if we can't get agreement, but what I want to convey is that if we can enter into a dialogue and achieve unity about how to pray, we can often pray much more effectively.

There is a practice in prayer in some churches that isn't scriptural: it's taking unspoken prayer requests. That practice is a hindrance to praying in unity for true needs. I find no biblical basis for unspoken requests, but in researching church history, I believe it started during the First Great Awakening. People would stand up in church and share inappropriate things that caused others to stumble. To avoid this, leaders started taking unspoken requests. Their motive probably was good, but they didn't realize they were teaching Christians how to get others to do their praying for them, giving the false impression they could get their need met without getting right with God.

This was made clear to me a number years ago when a man in our church who was blatantly living in immorality asked me to pray for him to find a job. When I asked him about his relationship with the Lord, he walked away. In the service, the pastor asked if there were any unspoken requests. Guess whose hand went up! His request was likely not for repentance.

After hearing sound teaching on spiritual defilement, I was shaken to realize I was being defiled in prayer meetings. Information was shared that never should have been. Once in a Sunday school class a lady who was burdened asked us to pray for her daughter. Her request was out of line. When I cautioned her, she said, "We just let it all hang out!" Yes, we all were defiled. When you "let it all hang out," perhaps you go home feeling better for a while, but nothing has changed and the Lord is not glorified.

What should we do in such cases? The answer is not to go the route of "unspoken requests." There are times I need others to pray for me but wouldn't be comfortable sharing the details that might cause them to stumble. If I give them a relevant Scripture such as Colossians 1:9 or Ephesians 1:15–19, instead of gory details, and ask them to pray for my spirit, everyone is blessed and the Lord is glorified.

When I have told people that I would pray a specific passage of Scripture (for example, Ephesians 1:15-19) for them during the week, their response is usually positive or neutral.

"Oh," they ask, "what does that say?"

"It says to pray for the eyes of your heart to be enlightened, that you may know the hope of your calling." I reply.

"Oh, that sounds like a blessing," they answer, "Don't miss a day!"

How about you? Is your view of prayer or prayer partners based on some negative experience? On those distraction-filled moments in the past when you asked God for a wish list of things and signed off? Is it based on habits of praying just in a crisis or sickness; or is it on God's faithfulness as recorded in the Bible? The former is the way the world prays. The latter is the way the Holy Spirit leads us to pray when we abide in Him and His words abide in us (see John 15:7).

Then we can expect to be effective.

God's purpose for prayer partners is not to help us to beg Him for things, although He does often bestow blessings, but to give both partners an eternal view into His ways of conforming us into His image. He has not given all of His gifts to any one of us, but to each one He has given at least one unique gift (Ephesians 4:1-16). Because this is true, we need each other.

Prayer partners are not there just to help us get out of trouble, but to help us to get to know God in a fuller way than we could on our own. Everything that touches our lives is allowed or created by God so that we may be conformed to His likeness (Romans 8:29). Thus, when we commit ourselves to a prayer partner, we are bringing more gifts than just our own to bear on the circumstances, and we can expect to grow spiritually (see John 15:1-8). Of course, our own gifts are adequate when we pray in the closet. The principle isn't either/or, but both; I must pray in my closet and with others to be the person God would have me to be.

When we recognize a need for a prayer partner in our life, God has already prepared one who is in our sphere of influence who also has a need to pray with someone. When we ask the Lord to show us who this might be, He will do it. He will lead us into all truth (John 16:13). God didn't create the fish and toss them on the ground until He created the ocean. No, He created everything the fish needed before He created the fish. The same is true for us.

I had a prayer partnership with a man I greatly admired for both his spirituality and expertise in the biblical approach to finances. When I needed prayer for money matters, I wanted to pray with him. He knew me and knew that I am an impulsive spender. I know God brought this man into my life to help me pray more effectively about finances. Relationships are to build one another up in the Lord, and give us the freedom to confront each other when necessary. As I pray with my friend on a regular basis, even if it's just once a month, it gives me an enlightened prayer partner when I am in trouble financially. More importantly, he feels free to question me about other crucial matters before we pray about my finances, such as, "Have you considered your attitude toward your son lately?" Maybe there's something that I haven't acknowledged, so I confess it and go to prayer with the confidence that God will hear and answer.

Sometimes my friend realizes in our preparation time that he needs to take care of something. Rarely does God put people together to meet the needs of only one person.

I didn't pray only with him, however. When it came to my struggles with relationships, God provided another man for me who was a "people" person, a man who saw the good in everybody and would even have forgiven a telephone marketer who interrupted his Thanksgiving dinner. Being on a committee with him, however, was a trial because he was always late. If the meeting was at 7:00, we'd try tricking him by saying the meeting was at 6:00, hoping to see him by 7:30! I discovered the reason he was late was because he was meeting with others and was so sensitive to their needs that time was of no concern. That was great when I was with him, but not so great when I was waiting for him. The point is, we all have blind spots. One reason God made us that way was to prevent us from being self-sufficient, resulting in arrogance.

One may have a gift of giving, but not the wisdom to give wisely. Another may be an exhorter, but without compassion, and his gift is not used effectively. God enabled my first real prayer partner to remind me to look for the positive traits in others. He was a people person; I am a pusher. God drew us both closer to Himself by showing us how much we needed each other. He made it clear that we could not get the job done independently.

God allows needs in our lives to help us realize His strength. Sometimes He will bring a calamity into our lives to strengthen a weakness in order to bless in a yet unknown area. God brought a "spiritual basket case" into my life. Working with her seemed like such a waste of time. But several years later, because of our ministry in her life, the Lord used this person to meet needs in my son's life that we could not. We are grateful for her to this day. Two, or three or four, are better than one!

I had been a Christian 25 years before I had a prayer partner. Oh, I'd heard of Christians with prayer partners and had even known a few, but I always told myself it was because they were in serious trouble or going through a major crisis. I grew up independent with a capital *I*; the Lord had to work hard to convince me of my need of Him and others.

I was born in 1929. I am the middle child of seven and was raised on the "wrong side of the tracks," so I learned early how to take care of myself. I was "street smart." I began working for pay when I was nine. At sixteen I left home, not willing to submit to my father's wishes. In high school I wasn't interested in academics but did manage to graduate from high school, a first in my family.

When I turned 22, my bride Shirley and I received Christ through the efforts of a Berean missionary. He came to tell us about Shirley's father giving his life to the Lord just before dying of cancer. His wish was for his children to follow him into the family of God. Shirley responded eagerly to the Gospel. I was agreeable but didn't sense the need to make a commitment because I thought I was doing great without a "crutch."

A few months later when I was driving on a lonely stretch of road between Scottsbluff and Chadron, Nebraska, I was convicted that I was lost and would spend eternity in hell. I stopped the car, got out alongside the dirt road, knelt and asked God to forgive my sins and come into my life. I experienced His peace immediately. I knew for sure that I would spend eternity with God. It was a beginning, but Shirley and I remained spiritually immature for twenty years. During that time the Lord blessed us with four children, and I became successful in business. I grew more independent and self-sufficient.

When I was 41, our pastor in Blythe, California, prodded us to attend a LIFE (Lay Institute For Evangelism), with Campus

Crusade for Christ in San Bernardino, California. What an eye opener! *Behold, all things became new*! I responded to God's call and we were accepted on their staff. That required raising my own support. Whoa, not me! I'm not going to beg people for money!

The Lord went to work on me. I soon learned I could not do all things. I had to do a lot of praying. I remember Lew Bishop and how he would put his arm over my shoulder and pray for me. Often he just listened to me tell him over and over how it wouldn't work. He would smile and pray some more.

Much of what I have to share with you is a result of what God taught me during that very difficult time of raising my support. It brought me to the end of myself. One person would say, "Gil, when you come to the end of your rope, just tie a knot and hang on." Another would say, "Gil, what you need to do is let go and let God!" Between letting go and hanging on, I was a mess. It was through prayer with many prayer partners that I learned when to hang on and when to let go.

One of Satan's ploys is to keep Christians isolated. But even the world teaches us that if our kids are spending a lot of time alone, it's a sign for us as parents that things may not be going well for them. But if one has not been intimate with the Lord, it's hard, if not impossible, to be intimate with others. Self-sufficiency has been the consistent pathway for some of us.

Doesn't common sense tell us we ought to have a prayer partner? If you were a firefighter, policeman, soldier, athlete or wilderness camper, would you deny the value of the buddy system? Look at Alcoholics Anonymous; without the members' commitment to one another, AA wouldn't exist. Most of us were taught to never swim alone, yet when we try to live the Christian life on our own, we are swimming alone without a lifeguard.

More importantly, Scripture itself suggests that we ought to have prayer partners. One pertinent passage is Hebrews 10:25: *And let us consider how to stimulate one another to love and good deeds, not forsaking our own assembling together, as is the habit of some, but encouraging one another; and all the more, as you see the day drawing near.*

I'm convinced that it is very encouraging for Christians to have a sincere ongoing commitment to pray with one another. Several logs burn brightly together; but put one aside on the cold hearth and the fire goes out.

In Ephesians 6:18, we are commanded to pray for one another. It is not just the Apostle Paul's opinion: *With all prayer and petition pray at all times in the Spirit, and with this in view, be on the alert with all perseverance and petition for all the saints.* (New American Standard Version)

Numerous passages of Scripture directly and indirectly suggest the principle of prayer partnership. A pastor friend of mine counted 34 "one another" verses in the New Testament. They teach us to love one another, pray for one another, confess sin to one another, bear one another's burdens, encourage one another, submit to one another, forgive one another, and be devoted to one another. Growing in faith and obeying the commands most often occurs in prayer with other believers. We can develop every fruit of the Spirit by praying together. If we're not open to change in each of these avenues, we are not being conformed to the image of Christ (see 2 Peter 1:3-21).

In his ministry on earth, Jesus seemed to stress the importance of partnership. How did He send out His disciples? Two by two! Mark 6:7 reads, *And He summoned the twelve and began to send them out in pairs.*

We've already noted that the great majority of Christians don't have prayer partners. Why is this so? Well, first, we're not praying people by nature unless we are in trouble. Second, it is against our human nature to be transparent with other people; the cost of overcoming our fear, pride, shyness, and reluctance to become involved is just too high. Third, many of us may have already thrown in the towel on prayer partnership because of a distorted view of Matthew 18:19, which says, *Again I say to you, that if two of you agree on earth about anything that they may ask, it shall be done for them by My Father who is in heaven.*

A lot of us have taken that to mean that as long as two or more of us can agree on a new car for you or me, God is obligated to deliver one. It's amazing how we think we can manipulate God with this verse. When a shiny, new Cadillac doesn't show up in our driveway, we figure that praying with a partner is pointless and we give up.

But perhaps the most overlooked reason for people not having prayer partners is that prayer is spiritual battle. Some people think that spiritual battle is casting out demons or binding the enemy. But the enemy is more concerned about keeping Christians from praying. Satan doesn't want us praying, especially together (Matthew 18:19). He knows that when we pray in unity with others, we will pray more often and more effectively, and when that happens, demons are cast out and the enemy is bound.

The principle of relationship with God is better understood and experienced when we have prayer partners with whom we also must work to build relationships. Now I know what some of you might be saying: "Hold on here. Prayer is mentioned all through the Scriptures, but *prayer partner* is never mentioned." You're right, but that shouldn't bother us, because the principle is certainly taught. The word *trinity* is not used in the Bible either, but we believe in the Trinity because the principle is scripturally derived. So is the concept of prayer partners.

Did Jesus have prayer partners? Yes, He did. They were His disciples. Of the twelve, Peter, James, and John were closest to Jesus. Of these three, John was the most intimate one. If the Son of God had prayer partners, how much more should we?

Did Moses have a prayer partner? Absolutely. One was Aaron, his brother. In the battle of Amalek, he had two prayer partners; Aaron and Hur joined him on the top of the hill to intercede for Joshua so that he could defeat the enemy (Exodus 17:8-13).

Did the Apostle Paul have prayer partners? Yes. Ananias, Barnabas, Silas, and Timothy were his prayer partners at different stages in his life. In fact, I have not discovered one godly man or woman in history who did not pray in unity with a partner at some point. Anyone without a prayer partner is saying, "I can do whatever God wants of me on my own." And the person who believes that is not only deceived, but is also robbing someone else of a blessing.

The Bible teaches that a multiplication factor is at work when Christians are united. Praying together increases the potential for unity and helps assure that the desired result will be achieved. Observe what the Bible has to say about this multiplication factor:

One witness is not enough to convict a man accused of any crime or offense he may have committed. A matter must be established by the testimony of two or three witnesses. (Deuteronomy 19:15, NIV)

Five of you will chase a hundred, and a hundred of you will chase ten thousand, and your enemies will fall before you by the sword. (Leviticus 26:8)

You would think that if five put one hundred to flight— one to twenty–a hundred would put two thousand to flight. God is confirming the principle of synergy. Webster's Dictionary defines synergy as "the combined effect in which the action produced is greater than the sum of the effects taken independently." That's a mouthful! A simpler definition is 1 + 1 can equal 6 or even 8! Synergy also describes the effect of two believers united in prayer. Working together is always better than working alone. Having a partner always helps.

For example, I have to move a huge timber 100 yards. If I have the strength to pick up one end, I could walk six or eight feet with it, put it down, pick up the other end and do the same. I could eventually catwalk the timber, so to speak, 100 yards. But if I had a friend of the same strength and mind to help me, we could move that timber many times faster than I could by myself. But it wouldn't help if he picked up the other end and went in the opposite direction. After all, *do two walk together unless they have agreed to do so?* (Amos 3:3, *NIV*)

Remember the old story about the three boys walking along the railroad tracks? They could only walk the tracks for a few feet before losing their balance. After a while, two of the boys got together and bet the third that they could walk the track for a quarter of a mile without falling off. A pretty safe bet since none of them had successfully done it all morning. The other two got on the track, reached across, took each other's hand and stayed on the track as long as they liked with no problem! That's synergism.

Now, let's look again at Ecclesiastes 4:9-10 (*NAS*), in the light of the value of partnership: *Two are better than one because they have a good return for their labor. For if either of them falls, the one will lift up his companion. But woe to the one who falls when there is not another to lift him up.* Here the Bible is talking about synergy.

Ray Stedman, who was a great pastor and Bible teacher at Peninsula Bible Church in Palo Alto, California, said that the word "woe" is a devastating term that would have been used if your throat were cut from ear to ear. Woe! It means there is no hope when you are down and have no one to lift you up. But when two are working together, there is hope.

Look at how *The Living Bible* paraphrases Ecclesiastes 4:12: *And one standing alone can be attacked and defeated but two can stand **back-to-back** and conquer.* We all have blind spots, but when two men put their backs together, they are ready for battle. It's like a tag team in wrestling. They now have 360 degree vision rather than only 180. I can't get between Satan and myself, but if you are my prayer partner, you can step between Satan and me until I get a breath or until he is defeated!

We all need a prayer partner who's not wishy-washy or prone to pride about being your prayer partner so he'll look good, or one who's a sunshine patriot and will leave you when the battle heats up. We need the kind of person we're told about in Exodus 32:9-14. In those verses, God told Moses to stop praying for his people. It's the only time in Scripture that God told anyone to stop praying. Because of their disobedience, God was going to destroy the Israelites, and He told Moses that if he would stop praying for them, He would multiply Moses' descendants until they became a great nation. But in verse 32, Moses said something astounding: *But now, if Thou wilt, forgive their sin—and if not, please blot me out from Thy book which Thou hast written!*

Boy, we're certainly not there! But Paul suggested a similar self-sacrifice in Romans 9:3: *For I could wish that I myself were accursed, separated from Christ for the sake of my brethren, my kinsmen according to the flesh.* By comparison, it's a relief to know that we're only asked to lay down our lives, not our souls, for our brother. 1 John 3:16 states, *We know love by this, that He laid down His life for us; and we ought to lay down our lives for the brethren.*

Dying to self, seeing others as more important than myself, is at the heart of true prayer partnership, and it's a principle that Moses and Paul knew and practiced. They were aware of the fact that the cause of Christ is set back if we as believers are not committed to each other. But that commitment is a rare quality. As Ezekiel 22:30 says, *And I searched for a man among them who should build up the wall and* **stand in the gap** *before Me for the land, that I should not destroy it; but I found no one.*

Do you have someone who would be willing to stand in the gap for you, who loves you enough to lay down his or her life for you? God has that person out there for you if you are willing to become totally vulnerable and transparent in a prayer partnership. Perhaps you have been involved in a ministry, and its effectiveness has provoked Satan to attack you and cause you to sin in an area where you know you are weak. Do you have a person who would say, "God, charge the consequences of that sin to me, and if he sins unto death, take my life first"? In my opinion, no Christian can say that unless he is a committed, praying child of God. It's a dangerous prayer. None of us knows if or when God would take us up on our offer.

When I was with Campus Crusade for Christ in the 1970's, my wife and I knew a devout young staff member who prayed that if the Lord would bring her parents to Himself at the cost of her life, she was willing to die. She lost her life in a flash flood in the Big Thompson Canyon in Colorado a few months after her prayer. Her parents, without knowing about her prayer, came to Christ at her funeral.

I'm not saying that in every case God requires a commitment unto physical death from His children, but we are called to die to self (Mark 8:34). For some people, dying physically might seem easier than giving up our own desires and priorities. Having a prayer partner in the biblical meaning of the term is a first step in this direction because it requires us to be willing to set aside our own tasks to make ourselves available to a brother or sister in Christ.

Several years ago, the truth of sacrificial commitment was quite new to me, but God gave me an opportunity to see it applied in a life-transforming way. While running one Sunday morning before church, I saw a young black man in the park. He must have slept there and was wet, cold, and hungry. I stopped to talk with him about his situation and soon led him in a prayer of repentance and acceptance of Christ! Well now, I just couldn't leave him in the park, so I took him home. He took a bath, had breakfast, put on some of my clothes, and we went to church.

I didn't hear much of the message. My mind was on this young man. How was I going to be the Good Samaritan? I didn't know what to do, so I began to pray and a thought came to me about a black pastor friend of mine, Rev. Charles Johnson, who worked in a difficult neighborhood. He would know better how to follow up with a hard case than I did. His church was only about thirty minutes away. I had done a Prayer Enrichment Seminar there earlier.

If we hurried, we could go to his church and get his counsel about what to do next. My wife thought it was a good idea too, so we rushed to Paradise Avenue Baptist Church, Oakland, California. When we arrived, the music was playing and Pastor Charles was just giving the invitation to come forward to receive Christ. Soon a lady came forward who was obviously right off the street, dressed in prostitute fashion. As the pastor questioned her, she indicated her desire to become a Christian and prayed with him. At the conclusion of their prayers, Pastor Charles turned to the congregation and shared the story from Exodus 17:

8-16 of Moses on the hill at the battle with Amalek. You know the story—as long as Moses kept his hands up in prayer, Israel won the battle: when Moses stopped praying, the Israelites started losing. Remember Exodus 32:32, *"But now, if You will, forgive their sin--and if not, please blot me out from Your book which You have written!"*

He began to expound on this Bible story as only a good black pastor can! Then he explained that this assembled family of God had a brand new sister in Christ, prone to sin, and that she wouldn't make it on her own. She needed partners to support her in the spiritual battle that was about to begin in her life. He asked the Lord for a lady to come forward and commit herself to the Lord and to this babe in Christ as Moses did for the Israelites.

Boy, I was sure glad I wasn't a member of that church that day! But I'll never forget what took place in the next few moments. It permanently changed my life and my family. I was thinking to myself, "I might, maybe, go forward for Billy Graham, but for this lady?" Finally one lady came forward rather hesitantly. Pastor Charles asked her if she was absolutely certain that she would spend eternity with the Lord. She immediately said, "Yes!" Then he asked, "Do you have any unconfessed sin in your life? Would you be willing, with God's help, to walk uprightly for the next ninety days in order to pray for and with this lady? And if she sins and can't handle the consequences of the sin, are you willing for God to charge those consequences to you? And if she sins unto death, that God will take you first?"

Let me tell you it got mighty quiet! After a few moments she said, "Well, I've given my life to Christ. I have told the Lord He could do anything He wanted with my life. I see this as being in His hands, so, yes, I will."

Then the pastor turned again to the congregation and said, "We have one on her right and now we need one for her left!" I thought, "Brother, you were lucky under those conditions to get one. Now you're going for two?"

No one responded. Pastor said, "Let's pray. We are doing business with God." After a few more moments that seemed like an eternity to me, another lady came forward with fear and trembling, tears streaming down her checks. She said, "I don't fully understand all this and I don't want to be here, but *I brought this lady this morning!*" The pastor went through the same questions with her. When Pastor Charles asked if she had any unconfessed sin in her life, she responded with, "I took care of that on the way up here!"

The pastor led the congregation in a prayer of commitment. Then the one who brought her took the new convert's shoulder with both hands and shook her and said with emphasis, *"And you're going to do what I say!"* Everyone knew she meant business. Now with these two prayer partners, the young woman had a fighting chance.

I sat there somewhat stunned as I thought about the twenty-some years I had watched people go forward to rededicate their lives or to receive Christ, and, knowing something of their lifestyles, thinking to myself, 'I sure hope they make it this time.' Today I know full well they won't persevere in the Christian life unless someone comes alongside to hold them up. For the past twenty years in the prayer ministry I've endeavored to apply this principle, first in my family and then with anyone who desired to walk closer to the Lord or who was in serious trouble. Without the commitment of the righteous to one another, the enemy will always get the victory. I don't believe God always requires commitment unto death, but I do believe He does at times when the battle is of an eternal nature.

Oh, by the way, about that young man we took to Charles' church– After the service, Pastor Charles talked with him for about three minutes and saw right through him. He was a felon and not about to become a child of God. He was, as they say, shinning us on. It was his practice to take Christians for all he could. I believe God used this young man to get *me* to Charles' church that Sunday morning that I might learn a very valuable lesson about biblical prayer.

How can we know if we have enough prayer partners? We know by what God is doing *in* us, not *for* or *through* us. I may be praying for a loved one's salvation, for example, and may have numerous prayer partners praying with me and yet never physically see the loved one come to Christ. When praying without seeing the results discourages us, we are not focusing on God and need either more prayer partners or more time in prayer with the partners we have to help us keep a proper perspective on God's ways and purposes.

Perhaps we are out of harmony with God's timing. However, if I know my praying has drawn me closer to the Lord and made me more sensitive to His will for my life, if the fruit of the Spirit is increasing in me, I can have confidence I'm in harmony with God and I'm winning. My blind spots, frustrations, and fears are covered, and I have assurance that God has heard my prayer and that the problem I've addressed to Him will be met in His own time.

The number of prayer partners we need for any given battle is in God's hands. It is determined by God's plan for conforming us to the image of Christ. If I'm dying of leukemia, yet have peace and confidence that God is using the affliction for His glory, and I am manifesting the fruit of the Spirit, the number of prayer partners I have is sufficient. God has obligated Himself to lead and guide each one of us if we seek Him with all our heart. His eternal fruit in our lives will tell us how we are doing.

God often leads different prayer partners into our lives for different situations. He didn't use Peter the same way He used Paul, and He doesn't use one person in our life exactly the way He uses another.

Because intimacy with God and our prayer partners is based on building relationships, we should not overlook the most important relationships God has already established in our lives–relationships with family members. Being partners in prayer with born-again family members should be our normal practice, but God may desire to draw us even closer together through praying in dedicated partnership for special needs at various times.

The Husband-Wife Prayer Team

Now I want to address God's most powerful and biblical prayer team; a husband and wife functioning in spiritual unity. God's Word says in Genesis 2:24: *For this cause a man shall leave his father and his mother, and shall cleave to his wife; and they shall become one flesh.* This is only fully possible in a spiritual sense through the Word of God and prayer. The Apostle Peter records for us in 1 Peter 3:7, *You husbands likewise, live with your wives in an understanding way, as with a weaker vessel, since she is a woman; and grant her honor as a fellow-heir of the grace of life, so that your prayers may not be hindered.*

Tell me, how could a Christian man live with his Christian wife in an understanding way if he were not praying with her? Men, God's Word says your prayers are hindered if you are not praying with your wife. For several years, I was teaching classes on prayer and would travel far to pray with a spiritual giant but

> *Magnificent Marriages Magnify our Maker's Majesty*
> Rev. David Breeden

wouldn't walk across the room to pray with my wife. I was most uncomfortable praying with my wife, as she was with me.

Before I fully understood this command, if you would have asked me if I prayed with my wife, I would have said, "Yes, of course. I'm a Christian. We pray at meal time, we pray when the church is in trouble, or when the kids are in trouble." But this kind of praying never helped me live with my wife in an understanding way. But what did it matter? Women don't understand themselves. Men don't even understand themselves, as far as that goes. This, of course, was merely a self-justification.

I discovered one of the reasons I was uncomfortable praying with her was that I didn't know how. Shirley says she didn't either, back then. We were embarrassed. Praying is the most intimate act a husband and wife can do together, far more intimate than physical sexual pleasures. A guy will quickly pursue sex but shy away from praying; praying is too personal.

Our old habit of praying "together" was to pray AT each other. If I couldn't get her attention some other way, I would say, "Let's pray!" Then in prayer, I would give her a message from my flesh, "Lord, if Shirley would just change, I could be a good Christian husband." Can you understand why she didn't want to pray with me?

Sometimes we would agree together to tell God on our kids: "Lord, we could be good Christian parents if You hadn't given us these kids!" Someone has said that children are God's gift to the church to conform their parents to the image of Christ. It's true!

When Shirley and I learned to pray together from the Bible, we truly began to live with each other in an understanding way – most of the time! I will always be grateful to

> *There is no estate to which Satan is more opposed than to marriage.*
>
> Martin Luther

God for empowering us to pray together. Whatever spiritual ground we have taken, we owe it to the Lord as He taught us to pray together.

When I teach this to others, it is very revealing how foreign this concept is. As a result we have developed material to help couples learn to pray together. We call our booklet *Joint Heirs*. (See appendix for availability.) The following is a passage from page three of *Joint Heirs*:

> 'Couples have shared that they would appreciate a few suggestions on how to get started praying together. If you do have a problem praying together, it may be helpful to openly discuss the benefits of such praying. There is no power on the face of the earth as great as a husband and wife praying together in unity to move the hands of God.
>
> As a couple, begin your prayer time by thanking God for each other, using Scripture as your base. It is very helpful to use the Word as you pray. This keeps your focus on the Lord and His Word and not on each other. It is not helpful to focus on your mate's negative traits; in fact, such a focus will hinder your prayers (see 1 Peter 3:7).
>
> To illustrate, we shall use Psalm 100. The husband should start by reading the first verse out loud, *Shout for joy to the Lord, all the earth.* Pause for a moment and look for an attribute of God in that verse. Your prayer might be, "Lord, I praise You for being a God of joy. You are a God that brings joy. Joy to the world, the Lord has come!" Try to keep your prayer short. The longer you make your prayers, the harder it is for your mate to stay in the same spirit with you. After your prayer, ask yourself, "Do I see this attribute in my mate?" If so, pray

something like this, "Lord, I praise You for Your joy I see in Jane (my wife). Thank You for the joy You have brought into my life through her."

The wife will read verse two out loud, looking again for an attribute of the Lord to praise Him for and to thank Him when that attribute is visible in her husband. *Serve the Lord with gladness, come before Him with joyful songs.* Pause for a moment to reflect. Then her prayer may be, "Father, I praise You for being the source of gladness and joy and that You allows us to come before You with songs of praise." Pause for a moment in case your mate would like to add something. If not, you might add a petition or a confession as the Holy Spirit leads you, "Lord, forgive me for serving You with a negative attitude."

Continue through Psalm 100, alternating the verses between the two of you and personalizing them as the Lord leads.'

Another help is *The Ulti-Mate Adventure.* It is designed to guide couples to spend two to three days in intimate prayer and discussion. We believe God led us to put it together because of our experience with a number of other ministries, including Marriage Encounter, Marriage Enrichment, the Abundant Life Conferences, etc. We found that the ongoing results of these outreaches were often short-lived. For example, we helped a couple go to one of these retreats and they were really blessed, but six months later they divorced, partly because after the retreat they were more knowledgeable about what they were not experiencing, but were unequipped to sustain it. Many of these marriage ministries are very good, but often very limited in the result of the partners becoming one because Biblical prayer together is not taught.

I remember Coach Bill McCartney, founder of Promise Keepers, telling men they must pray with their wives, but no training was given on how to do that. I am not sharing this to be critical. I know Promise Keepers has helped a lot of men get right with the Lord; however, the fruit has not always remained and multiplied. The same thing happened in my own ministry before Shirley and I learned to pray together from Scripture. I don't mean to say that now we have arrived, not by a long shot, but I can assure you that we are on the right road now, going in the right direction. To God be the glory!

Remember, 1 Peter 3:7 is a command, not just a good idea. We must understand from Scripture that wives are husbands' completers, **not** competitors. Jack Taylor, a well known Baptist preacher and conference speaker, has said, "There is an unstruck cord in the symphony of life that will never be sounded apart from a husband and wife praying intimately together."

God created marriage for at least three purposes. By His design, a married couple should:

- Reflect God's image by being one as the Triune God is one.
- Reproduce a godly heritage.
- Overcome together (in oneness) in spiritual warfare against Satan.

The Christian life is a spiritual battle. When a husband and wife function as "two... who agree about anything they ask," as described in Matthew 18:19, Satan knows God has won. For that reason, the enemy will do anything he can to keep husband and wife from praying together. Satan will make you feel better for a while or give you extra money if that's what it takes to keep a husband and wife from praying together from Scripture for their walk with the Lord.

Remember, our bodies are the Lord's. Read this foundational passage about God's design for marriage. In 1 Corinthians 6:12 through 7:7 Paul wrote:

All things are lawful for me, but not all things are profitable. All things are lawful for me, but I will not be mastered by anything. Food is for the stomach, and the stomach is for food; but God will do away with both of them. Yet the body is not for immorality, but for the Lord; and the Lord is for the body. Now God has not only raised the Lord, but will also raise us up through His power. Do you not know that your bodies are members of Christ? Shall I then take away the members of Christ and make them members of a harlot? May it never be! Or do you not know that the one who joins himself to a harlot is one body with her? For He says, "THE TWO WILL BECOME ONE FLESH." But the one who joins himself to the Lord is one spirit with Him. Flee immorality. Every other sin that a man commits is outside the body, but the immoral man sins against his own body. Or do you not know that your body is a temple of the Holy Spirit who is in you, whom you have from God, and that you are not your own? For you have been bought with a price: therefore glorify God in your body. Now concerning the things about which you wrote, it is good for a man not to touch a woman. But because of immoralities, let each man have his own wife, and let each woman have her own husband. Let the husband fulfill his duty to his wife, and likewise also the wife to her husband. The wife does not have authority over her own body, but the husband does; and likewise also the husband does not have authority over his own

> *body, but the wife does. Stop depriving one another, except by agreement for a time that you may devote yourselves to prayer, and come together again lest Satan tempt you because of your lack of self-control. But this I say by way of concession, not of command. Yet I wish that all men were even as I myself am. However, each man has his own gift from God, one in this manner, and another in that.*

Shirley and I came from an immoral background. For more than twenty years as a Christian I struggled with my thought life. Some spiritual exercises, such as memorizing and meditating on Scripture, would help temporarily. I tell you today that I was never liberated until Shirley and I committed ourselves to pray together from the Bible. My thoughts of sexual pleasures have been fully lived out with her since we developed oneness of spirit through prayer. Thank you, Lord.

In all of the marriage conferences we attended over the years, not one taught us or even suggested that a fulfilled sex life was a God-ordained blessing of a husband and wife praying together in unity of body, soul, and spirit. Almost all of them mentioned that husbands and wives should pray together, but we were never taught how. No one taught us that a fulfilled sex life begins with a fulfilled prayer life. Men, if that doesn't motivate you to start praying with your wife, there is no hope for you.

Our culture is obsessed with sinful and perverted sexual unions. Why is that? I believe it is because the Bible teaches that God has ordained the marriage union to be to His glory. Physical acts outside the purity of marriage are an abomination to God, and can even be an abomination to Him when a married couple's hearts are full of sin. When the Spirit of God is grieved or quenched by sin, our flesh can never ever be at peace nor can it ever be fulfilled. Read and pray through 1 Corinthians 6:12–7:7 with your mate and ask, "Is our love life pleasing to the Lord?" If you believe it could be better, consider going on an *Ulti-Mate Adventure*.

What is *The Ulti-Mate Adventure*? It is field-tested personal retreat material to help Christian couples experience the entirety of what God has predestined for them. Almost every married couple would agree that marriage takes work to make it fulfilling. Couples need to take time out periodically to be alone with each other to reflect, evaluate, and plan for further growth and fulfillment in their relationship. It takes lots of listening and interaction to bring harmony to a marriage, and it takes vision and planning to give it direction and purpose.

The Ulti-Mate Adventure is designed to help you communicate clearly with your spouse as well as give you a chance to get away together for a weekend to relax and be refreshed by each other's company. These workbooks have specific questions and guidelines for discussion and also include a goal sheet and timetable so that you can define what you think is important for your marriage and measure your success in achieving your goals.

It takes time to get to the deep needs on your heart. That's why we suggest two to three days for this exercise. Some of the questions in our outline opened communication in areas of our own lives that previously had not been talked about, plus the uninterrupted time to be with each other was great. It solidified our marriage, freeing us to come to a new depth of love and appreciation for each other. The program works when you schedule time away every year, every six months, or even every quarter, depending on your ministry. Just one time is not enough, as with confession and filling of the Holy Spirit.

Jeff and Judy Myers, who have been on staff at Los Gatos Christian Church in California, gave this testimony: "Marriage is not necessarily choosing the right person, but getting to know the person you've chosen. Communication in prayer is the only way to do that."

If you and your spouse were to consider going on a personal prayer retreat together, which of the following would be the greatest hindrance to going?

> Time
> Place
> Money
> Babysitting

If you agree that it is God's will to go on a marriage building retreat, start thanking Him now for His provision and pray, claiming Proverbs 16:3 as your own promise: *Roll your works upon the Lord—commit and trust them wholly to Him; [He will cause your thoughts to become agreeable to His will, and] so shall you plans be established and succeed.* (Amplified Bible)

Set the date! The Ulti-Mate Adventure retreat will enable you to:

> Know God, as a couple.
> Conduct your own prayer and planning weekend.
> Become one in finding solutions to your needs.
> Enhance your prayer life together.
> Renew romance and desire for each other.

These goals can never be a reality apart from husbands and wives praying together from Scripture in unity. I remember hearing well-known Christian speaker Josh McDowell, say at a confernce, "Book after book has been written, counseling services and divorce clinics have sprung up coast to coast. Like a fleet of ambulances at the bottom of a treacherous hill, they wait for the next divorce victims to come tumbling down. Then rush them off to the "hospital" where counselors, pastors, friends and relatives try desperately to save the marriage."

It has been said that by the time a couple seeks a counselor, it's already too late. Counseling can save only one out of ten marriages, on average. What is the solution? Biblical prayer with your mate! Unity through biblical prayer can save any marriage if both partners are committed to success. But it is even better to begin early and build marriages on a solid foundation from the start. Biblical prayer is the foundation for an impenetrable wall at the top, preventing a fall down that treacherous hill of damaged and broken marriages.

Guidelines for Prayer Partners

1. When you begin to understand the biblical basis for a prayer partner, the Holy Spirit is at work in you. Ask Him to show you who He has prepared for you. As Psalm 37:4,5 says, *Delight yourself in the LORD; and He will give you the desires of your heart. Commit your way to the LORD, trust also in Him, and He will do it.*

2. If you are facing a difficult problem, do not ask your partner to pray primarily for the problem to be removed. It is often more profitable to pray for your spirit to be strengthened. Proverbs 18:14 says, *The spirit of a man can endure his sickness, but a broken spirit who can bear?* Seek prayer for your walk with the Lord in the situation, claiming such verses as Ephesians 1:15-19; 3:14-19 and Colossians 1:9.

3. If you don't know how to pray about a particular problem, simply praise God for who He is, using the Psalms and other portions of Scripture as a praise guide for two weeks or a month. Delight yourself in the Lord as you praise Him for the attributes you notice. He will teach you how to pray. Also you may consider not asking Him for anything. Instead, pray through the 31-day project of "The 10 Facets of God's Love" in the appendix. Do as it says in Psalm 37:7a: *Be still before the Lord and wait patiently for Him.*

4. Be wise in how much information you share with your prayer partners. Don't cause them to stumble or put an added burden on them to keep a secret. If you are unsure, then only share what you would want anyone to know. Always share a Scripture relative to your request. Your partner(s) can pray effectively and powerfully for you without knowing all the details. The verse you claim for yourself will bless your partner as well. *... he who is trustworthy in spirit keeps a thing covered.* (Proverbs 11:13b)

5. If you are married, you should not share intimate information with a prayer partner that you are not telling your mate. Never share negative information about your mate, Christian or not. *However, let each of you love his wife as himself, and let the wife see that she respects her husband.* (Ephesians 5:33)

6. If you are separated or having financial problems, don't look for a partner who is in the same circumstances. Look for a person in your sphere of influence who is spiritually stronger than you are in the area of your need. *If they fall, one will lift up his fellow...* (Ecclesiastes 4:10)

7. You can begin by exchanging verses and requests with another believer for a week or two. Always try to share a Scripture promise that is relevant to your need and ask you prayer partner to do the same. *Your testimonies are my delight: they are my counselors.* (Psalm 11:24)

8. Almost all prayer leads to an action. Ask the Lord to make you sensitive to His leading and empower you to obey. Psalm 25:4-5 is a good prayer. It tells us what our heart's cry should be: *Make me know Thy ways, O LORD; teach me Thy paths. Lead me in Thy truth and teach me, for Thou art the God of my salvation; for Thee I wait all the day.*

9. Become a prayer partner with your mate, your first and foremost prayer partner. As you pray together, you will grow closer to each other and closer to God. *Likewise, husbands, live with your wives in an understanding way... since they are heirs with you of the grace of life, that your prayers be not hindered.* (I Peter 3:7)

10. Become a prayer partner with your parents, if possible. If you are a parent, pray with your children. Seek prayer partners among those who know you best. *Honor your father and mother* (the first command with a promise), *that it may be well with you, and that you may live long on the earth.* (Ephesians 6:2,3)

11. If you are a Sunday school or Bible study teacher, a choir or education director, etc, ask the group to pray with you for that group. Build prayer support with those you serve. *Remember your leaders, those who spoke to you the Word of God...* (Hebrews 13:7)

12. Attend prayer meetings. Make it a point to be a part of a prayer group.: *For where two or three are gathered in my name, there am I among them.* (Matthew 18:20)

13. Attend classes on prayer. Read books on prayer. Set a goal to get your "Ph.D. in prayer!" *"Lord, teach us to pray..."* (Luke 11:1)

Chapter 11
Prayer: Who Hears? Who Answers?

One of my favorite sayings is, "Prayer without purity is function without effect."

Just what does that mean? It means God does not hear the prayer of a sinner. *If I regard wickedness in my heart, the Lord will not hear* (Psalm 66:18). *We know that God does not hear sinners, but if anyone is God-fearing, and does His will, He hears him* (John 9:31). (See also 2 Chronicles 7:14; Job 17:8-9; Psalm 18:41; 24:3-4; 80:4, Proverbs 1:28; 15:8,29; 21:13; 28:9: Isaiah 1:15; 59:2; Micah 3:4; 1 Peter 3:12; Matthew 7:15-23.)

When I first became aware of the truth that God does not hear the prayers of a sinner, I resisted it. The idea seemed to go against my view of God. I was raised with the idea that "God answers prayer – period!" I always assumed that meant prayers of anyone, anytime, for anything. It is true that God hears and answers prayer, but it's been said that any truth taken out of balance leads to heresy.

The statement "God answers prayer" is incomplete because God is *committed* to answer only the prayers of the righteous. *The effective prayer of a **righteous** man can accomplish much (*James 5:16b). However, the prayer of an unrighteous man accomplishes nothing of eternal value. God has only committed Himself to answer the prayers of His obedient children. (See also Job 35:12-13 and James 4:3.) He is not obligated to answer the prayer of the unrighteous, except for a prayer of repentance. You and I can't get bad enough for God not to hear our prayer as a repentant sinner. Praise God!

As I thought about the truth of these verses, I was plagued by the question of how my prayers were answered both when I was a non-Christian and when I was knowingly out of fellowship with the Lord. From God's perspective, until a person calls on the name of the Lord for salvation, that person has no prayer life —that is, no communion/communication with the Lord. Our power in prayer is based on our intimate relationship to the Father, through Jesus Christ. This relationship began through Christ's death on Calvary and is sustained through the work done at Calvary. As Charles Haddon Spurgeon stated it, "We will misread Calvary if we fail to see the necessity of the cross in relationship to prayer."

There was a time when I was knowingly out of fellowship with God and in trouble financially. I prayed for a specific amount of money and I got it! When I shared this example with a friend, I tried to convince him that God might answer my prayer even when I am in sin; after all, we are all sinners. My question to my friend was, "How would you explain this answer to prayer?"

He answered, "Could it be that God has blessed you with loved ones and friends who are walking close to the Lord and are praying for you?" As a result of our conversation, it dawned on me that perhaps that was one explanation. I now know that this explanation accounts for many of the inconsistencies in my prayer life.

A bumper sticker that I like says, "If you don't know Jesus, you don't have a prayer." Is that true? Yes, it is, according to 1 Timothy 2:5: *For there is one God and one mediator between God and men, the man Christ Jesus.*

But what about the answered prayer that I had experienced before I became a Christian? I know of some who might have been praying for me. The seeming answers to my prayers could have been the answers to the prayers of others who were in a right relationship to God. Or they could have been the blessings of God's common grace to all mankind. God blesses whomever He pleases. Matthew 5:44-45 reminds us to *love your enemies, and pray for those that persecute you; in order that you may be the sons of your Father who is in heaven; for He causes the sun to rise on the evil and the good, and sends rain on the righteous and the unrighteous.* We must be careful that we don't take a blessing and automatically consider it an answer to prayer. Why? Because a blessing of God's common grace does not constitute an answer to prayer. The Bible says that *God hears the prayers of the righteous* (Proverbs 15:29).

I am sure prayer will always seem in some ways to be a mystery. In order to know and understand all the mysteries about prayer, one would need to know and understand all the mysteries of God. As a finite person, I know that my knowledge of and experiences with God in this life are limited. I also know there is much more to prayer than what I am currently experiencing. But I am certain of one thing, that God does not hear the prayers of an unrepentant sinner; He hears the prayers of the righteous. The joy in my experience of knowing God will always be in direct proportion to my willingness to have God search my heart. In Matthew 6:33 we read, *but seek first the kingdom of God and His righteousness, and all these things shall be added to you.*

Search me, O God, and know my heart; try me and know my anxious thoughts; and see if there be any hurtful way in me, and lead me into the everlasting way (Psalm 139:23-24). This was the sincere prayer of the psalmist's heart. Oswald Chambers in his daily devotional says, "Only a fool or a sincere Christian would pray that prayer." [15]Why is that? Because God hears and answers that prayer 10,000 times out of 10,000. And the answer to that prayer means that God will purge what is sinful and worthless from our lives. Biblical prayer will always reveal every secret sin. That's a promise of God.

Righteousness is the basis of an effective prayer life. By righteousness, I mean that the pray-er is a child of God, has no unconfessed revealed sin, and has a real desire and commitment to walk obediently with God. That's what I call "being on praying ground." Praying ground is the ground that Christ took at Calvary. His finished work secures for us salvation, cleansing, and filling of the Holy Spirit, which in turn give us the confidence to ask for things in God's will and know that they *will be done unto us* (John 15:7). This concept is covered thoroughly in the chapter on Calvary-Based Prayer.

In the Old Testament, the high priest who went into the presence of God with sin in his life met instant death. God provided the way for His people to come to Him, but they were required to obey His instructions. The same thing is true in the New Testament. Attempting to come to the Father with known sin in our lives is death to our communication with God. God is the same yesterday, today, and forever. (See Hebrews 13:8, Psalm 102:27 and Malachi 3:6.) Not knowing for sure that we are on praying ground means for believers that we no longer have confidence in communicating with the Father. Our confidence in prayer is limited to repentance.

Another possibility, however, still remains. Could the answer to my prayer for financial aid have come from a source other than God? I am presently persuaded that prayer not based on Christ's righteousness gives Satan an opportunity to falsify or counterfeit an answer to a prayer that God does not hear. In my opinion, this is especially true when the prayers are for temporal needs, that is, for physical or material needs in the here and now. When our prayers are in the eternal realm of the spiritual, it is much more difficult for the enemy to deceive us.

The basis of my thinking is the known, revealed attributes of God and the known, revealed attributes of Satan. The devil is the adversary, accuser of the brethren, Beelzebub, deceiver of the whole world, father of lies, god of this world, prince of this world, prince of the power of the air, the tempter, a fallen angelic being, a spirit being mightier than humans –but he is not God, and God has put limits on his operations.

Perhaps we need to be reminded of 2 Corinthians 11:14-15: *... no wonder, for even Satan disguises himself as an angel of light, therefore it is not surprising if his servants also disguise themselves as servants of righteousness; whose end shall be according to their deeds.* In 1 Peter 5:8, we read, *Be of sober spirit, be on the alert. Your adversary, the devil, prowls about like a roaring lion, seeking someone to devour.* Satan is not omnipresent, but he does have many fallen angels working for him. Not all theologians agree whether or not Satan can hear our prayers. There would seem to be no reason why he or his agents could not at least hear audible prayers. To me it really doesn't matter in this sense: if we are in the Spirit, he cannot devour us, but if we have known sin in our lives, he knows exactly how we are praying because of his millennia of experience with fallen mankind.

In 2 Thessalonians 2:1-4 Paul writes to believers about the second coming of Christ: *Now we request you, brethren, with regard to the coming of our Lord Jesus Christ, and our gathering together in Him, that you may not be quickly shaken from your composure or be disturbed either by a spirit or by a letter* [or by answered prayer not based on righteousness, my thought added] *to the effect that the day of the Lord has come. Let no one in any way deceive you* [even by prayer, my thought], *for it will not come unless the apostasy comes first, and the man of lawlessness is revealed, the son of destruction, who opposes and exalts himself above every so-called god or object of worship, so that he takes his seat in the temple of God, displaying himself as being God.* This deceiver falsifies and counterfeits everything he can about God, including all things associated with the worship of God.

Verse 7 goes on to say, *for the mystery of lawlessness is **already** at work* [emphasis added]. Verses 9 and 10 go on, *that is, the one whose coming is in accord with the activity of Satan, with all power and signs and false wonders, and with all the deception of wickedness for those who perish, because they did not receive the love of the truth so as to be saved.* If we do not love God's truth, we will buy any lie of Satan.

We have a subtle adversary who will sometimes promote error even by means of the words of Scripture, as he did when he tempted Christ in the wilderness. It would be foolish of us to exclude the deceiver from distorting the doctrine of biblical prayer. Our enemy would like us to believe that God hears and answers all prayer regardless of the spiritual condition of the pray-er. For example, the world says it does not matter how you live your life; when you get into trouble, just call on the man upstairs. He will hear and answer because he is loving and kind. This falsehood is right out of the pit. It makes God over into man's image, making Him no better than a delivery boy who does whatever we want.

The *Wycliffe Bible Commentary* states, "Antichrist has his coming as Christ has His. Satan's working (power in operation) is Antichrist's dynamic (cf. Revelation 13:2). His coming reveals itself in all power (to work miracles) and signs (significant, meaningful miracles) and wonders (amazing their observers). In the Greek, lying seems to apply to all three; the miracles are steeped in falsehood."[16]

How are these signs and wonders brought about? Probably by prayer! Why do I say that? Because that is the way Jesus worked on earth—through prayer in communion with His Father.

Many cults are based on some type of meditation and prayer. They think they are praying to God, but Scripture confirms that any activity associated with false worship is due to demons (I Corinthians 10:20). Do you think Satan can meet needs? He said he could meet Jesus' needs in the wilderness. If you think he can't, you should check out what the cults are doing. How long do you think people would be in a cult if they weren't convinced of having answers to their prayers? How long could Satan keep a believer defeated if he didn't mess with his prayer life?

God has given Satan power to deceive people who *take pleasure in wickedness* (2 Thessalonians 2:12). *And for this reason God will send upon them a deluding influence so that they might believe what is false* (2 Thessalonians 2:11). This is also revealed to us in Revelation 13:13 and 14: *And he performs great signs, so that he even makes fire come down out of heaven to the earth in the presence of men, and he deceives those who dwell on earth because of the signs which it was given him to perform in the presence of the beast...* Sin and deception are a package deal. (See also 2 Peter 2:1; Mark 13:22.)

No matter how hard he tries, I don't think Satan can deceive an obedient Christian. In Matthew 24:24 we read, *For false Christs and false prophets will arise and will show great signs and wonders, so as to mislead **if possible** even the elect*. This implies it is not possible if we are walking as one of His elect. However, if we are living and praying from a life of disobedience, we are a sure candidate for deception (see James 1:21-22). If the Holy Spirit is not in control of our lives, we will believe lies, one lie being that we don't have to get right with God to get our needs met.

Satan gets good mileage out of this lie because it is partially true. Jesus did not have to go to the cross for God to meet our temporal needs. God gives to all people *life and breath and all things,* according to Acts 17:25. Jesus and the disciples met many needs before He went to the cross, but He had to go to the cross in order that every aspect of our earthly needs would have an eternal purpose. God is sovereign. He creates or allows our temporal circumstances so that we are being conformed to the image of Christ, which is His ultimate, eternal goal.

The question that comes to mind is, "How would a being be like God if he were not associated with prayer in some way?" Most of us would not have a problem believing Satan can answer a prayer prayed to him. This is the basis of occult practice. The problem is in someone assuming an "answer to prayer" came from God when it may have been a deception from Satan.

In a recent Bible study I led, someone made the statement, "God has answered all my prayers from a very early age!" In sharing some of these supposed answers, it was obvious that the prayers were for temporal needs. This person was attempting to prove that if you get answers to your prayers, you must be a Christian. We know that God will bless whomever He pleases. *But our God is in the heavens; He does whatever He pleases,* according to Psalm 115:3. It's tempting to view any blessing of common grace as an answer to prayer because it feels good to think, "I am okay with God." When we do that, we are using prayer to prove who God is in our own minds. The deceiver loves such a train of thought because it gives him an opportunity to trick us into thinking we have had an answer to our prayer.

Prayer not based on Calvary, that is, on the righteousness of Christ available because of His work on the cross, is a major tool of Satan. A church member, who was living in immorality, shared with me that he was praying and fasting about his relationship with his wife. He said that God's answer to his prayer was to leave his wife. As hard as I tried, I could not convince him that his answer was not from God. How did I know that he had a counterfeit answer?

Here are some of the reasons:

☐ Righteousness had not preceded his prayer and fasting. (Matthew 6:33)

☐ His prayer was not based on the Word of God. God never violates His Word. (Isaiah 40:8)

☐ His goal in prayer was to satisfy the flesh, not to glorify the Father. (James 4:3)

☐ He was not abiding in Christ at the time. (Matthew 15:7)

☐ We can become vulnerable to temptation and deception during times of physical deprivation. (Matthew 4:3, 1 Corinthians 7:5)

☐ He did not seek a righteous man to pray with him in agreement. (James 5:16)

☐ He was not walking in obedience, and was open to deception. (James 1:22)

It should not surprise us that this man believed a lie. The deceiver had been successful in sealing his fate.

If someone calls to ask you to pray for him to get a job, and you do so without ministering to his spirit, and he gets a job, where do you think he will go the next time he has a need? He will go to you, the pray-er, right? Unknowingly perhaps, we have taught this person that going to Calvary is not necessary. We have allowed him to put his dependence on the pray-er, giving credit to the pray-er rather than giving glory to God. This attitude is often demonstrated by those who seek out a pray-er who has a reputation of having a "hot line" to God.

Not convinced? Where does it say in the Bible that Satan can counterfeit answers to prayer? As far as I know, it does not. For years I did not share any of my thoughts about this concern because the Bible does not use those words. I asked myself, "If my thoughts have any validity, why does the Bible not record that Satan falsifies and counterfeits answers to a believer's or an unbeliever's false or unbiblical prayers?"

I am currently convinced the Bible does not use these terms because prayer from a biblical perspective is "communion with God." Unbelievers and sinful believers have broken fellowship with God and have no communion with Him, according to I John 1:6-7. Their "prayers" are not prayer from God's perspective. The Bible does not address prayer to God that is false. So, that this concept is not spoken about in so many words, does not mean that the idea of Satan's deception in prayer is invalid or unbiblical.

Another term in relationship to prayer that is not used in the Bible is "prayer partners." However, the Bible teaches that we are to pray for one another (James 5:16), to bear one another's burdens (Galatians 6:2), and to confess faults to each other (James 5:16). Clearly the teaching is there to back up our modern phraseology, as we discussed earlier in the book.

I think it is dangerous for a Christian not to consider the possibility of the deceiver counterfeiting answers to prayers that God does not hear. Why is this teaching so important? By accepting a counterfeit answer, we undermine the very foundation of Calvary. Christ died on Calvary to free us from our sinful lifestyles, not just the eternal consequences of that lifestyle. His plan is not that we should remain in sin and justify it through pseudo-spiritual activities (Romans 6:1-2). Such a view cheapens the cross and discourages other Christians from praying.

God's will for us is holiness. Anything that keeps us from going to Calvary, including so-called "answers" to prayer, is not His will. *Just as He chose us in Him before the foundation of the world, that we should be holy and blameless before Him* (Ephesians 1:4). *But like the Holy One who called you, be holy yourselves also in all your behavior; because it is written, 'You shall be holy, for I am holy.'* (1 Peter 1:15,16). Your view of the holiness and importance of prayer determines your view of God.

A counterfeit answer to prayer has the potential to take the responsibility of man to be holy out of the equation. When that happens, a floodgate opens of misunderstandings about biblical prayer, because now your view of prayer is based on what you do or don't get from God in the temporal realm. It doesn't matter who prays, as long as someone prays. Prayer is just a way to get what I want or need. God is good because He answered my prayer, etc.

All these kinds of myths pave the way to negate the work of Christ on the cross and ease our pain for putting Him there. If I can get my needs met without confessing my sins, Jesus would not have had to die. Think what that means. It means that the deceiver has successfully robbed the Christian of the necessity and ability to live the Christian life. Who would want to be a Christian if there were no way to live it?

By God's grace, I am not sharing this to frighten or shock you, but to enlighten you to the possibility of deception in so-called prayer. I am not saying whether or not Satan has answered some of your prayers: I am just asking you to consider the possibility.

Chapter 12
Praying Scripturally for the Sick

My maternal grandmother died of cancer in the 1950's. My mother went to church and did good works, and I know my mother prayed for her mother. She was my grandmother's caregiver. In those days, dying of cancer was a very painful experience. I can't say my grandmother's death had a great impact on my life as a nominal Christian. However, I saw the devastating effect of her pain in my mother.

When my father died of cancer, I was just beginning to yield myself to the Lord. His doctor told us as a family that my father's cancer was terminal and left us alone for a time. My older unbelieving brother asked me to pray. I did, and asked the Lord for His grace and mercy. We all experienced the presence of the Lord.

There were seven kids in my family, five boys and two girls. One brother died in a plane crash. The oldest brother died of an aneurysm during cancer surgery. The oldest sister died a painful death of cancer. I was a dedicated Christian by that time and was just beginning to understand something about prayer.

My oldest sister, Betty, and her husband, Glen, were the first ones to take Shirley and me to church. They loved the Lord. After she got sick, she begged me to pray that the Lord would ease the pain or take her home. I prayed with all that was within me, and the pain just got worse. I had no answers.

However, years later when my youngest sister, Lois, died of cancer, it was different because we had learned to pray from the inside out, from the spirit to the soul (mind, will, and emotions), and out to the body. When the spirit is strong, the soul will have a positive effect on the body (Proverbs 18:14). It always produces peace when the soul and spirit are in harmony with God's plan and purpose. As the Bible says, God will never allow us in a circumstance He can't handle in our degree of maturity. He will, however, allow us in circumstances *we* can't handle on our own.

Lois and her husband Chuck had a son, Stanley, who took drugs and had a lot of problems. The courts told them they would need to take responsibility for him or he would go to prison. As a result, Lois and Chuck finished their basement and made an apartment for him. He liked it and seemed to be doing okay. Then in the midst of Lois' physical trauma, he committed suicide. His note said that he could no longer be a burden to his mom. It seemed to me that was more than anyone should be asked to endure. It was amazing to us how Lois was able to praise the Lord in the midst of it all. I witnessed her spirit getting stronger and stronger as we prayed for her spirit to be able to take every thought captive to the obedience of Christ (2 Corinthians 10:5).

I remember my oldest brother, Floyd (but called 'Gil'), would say, "Let's go see Sis." Gil knew Lois didn't have much time left on earth, but she was radiant with the love of Jesus. After being there just a few minutes, Gil would say, "Let's go. I have to go." So we would leave, and when we got home, he would want to go back. He could not stand to be with her and he couldn't stand not to be with her. I believe Gil is with the Lord today partly because of Lois' strong witness. Lois knew her Savior, knew she was forgiven, and she knew she was filled with the Holy Spirit and was on praying ground.

This was quite unlike when Betty was dying. Then Shirley and I didn't understand about being on praying ground. We didn't know how to pray according to the will of God. Betty had begun to feel God hadn't forgiven her of sins she had committed before she became born again. That guilt just added to her lack of faith because of unanswered prayer on her part and mine. The enemy loves to work on a weak body. Satan attempts to get our minds fixed on the body so that our thoughts of God are based on what

God does or does not do in the body. The Bible says in Proverbs 18:14, *The spirit of a man can endure his sickness, but a broken spirit who can bear?*

Our faith is ultimately weakened by praying ineffectively for illness. Why? Because men are so physically minded. I am presently persuaded that praying ineffectively for illnesses is more damaging to the cause of Christ than gross immorality. By way of Biblical example, one of the thieves crucified with Jesus challenged Jesus to get out of His suffering by getting down from the cross. In the thief's mind, the removal of suffering was the proof of Christ's Godhood. The removal of bodily suffering remains the ultimate test in many minds today. But I also come to that conclusion because of personal experience.

Many years ago Shirley and I were working hard and joyously with the high school group of our church. The church was growing and good things were happening. Then all of a sudden, the pastor was found guilty of having affairs with a number of women in the church. Needless to say, the church split several ways, but what was most difficult for us was the way different deacons were coming to see us, wanting to know which group we were siding with. I got so mad, not about what the pastor had or had not done, but about the way the leadership treated us, that we left. We thought, "If that's Christianity, we don't need it."

My point is this: After a week or so, my wife and I realized we had our eyes on man and not on the Lord. We began to pray and ask God where He would have us serve.

This alleged act of gross immorality caused us to stumble for a short time. But praying ineffectively for my sister Betty took a toll I could not get over. It is with me today. Every time I teach this material, I like to think in my mind's eye that Betty and Lois are in the presence of our heavenly Father praying for me to do the very best I can because it is so very important!

Would you agree with me that our praying for those who are sick is often ineffective? We pray and some die. We forget to pray and they get well. We really don't know how to pray for the sick; we have never been taught. You and I need to understand that our faith is ultimately weakened by praying ineffectively for those who are sick.

I believe in divine healing. This is not an attempt to deny or limit God's sovereignty in healing; God will heal whom He pleases. However, I think it will help us understand our role in prayer if we understand the problems associated with praying for the sick. We will not be motivated to learn how to pray for them effectively until we realize the grave spiritual ramifications of ineffective prayer.

Christians are often tempted to form doctrine from experiences in prayer. We all have a tendency to believe that God is the Great Physician only when we pray for someone's healing and they get well. But if we pray and they don't get well, then maybe God didn't hear or our faith was not strong enough. But God *is* the Great Physician whether He heals in a specific case or not, because the Bible says He is the Great Physician.

We must form our view of God from Scripture and NOT from our experience because our experiences change; **God does not.** We may have a good experience or we may have a bad experience: God is good all the time. There are ways we can pray, whatever our degree of Christian maturity, that will consistently glorify the Father rather than the pray-er, and which will testify to the goodness of God and the truthfulness and His word.

Scripture teaches us that God will never allow a sickness to touch one of His children that is not ultimately for the child's good. He cares that much. When a sickness is from God, it always has an eternal purpose— to glorify the Father.

A man in one of our seminars said, "Mr. Gillam, I think you are taking this thing of the Sovereignty of God too far. What about the common cold?" I answered, "Nothing touches us that hasn't been filtered through the love of God. If I have a cold, it may be because someone needs to see how a Christian handles a snotty nose!" It seems to be an adversity to me; sicknesses would all fall under the broader heading of "adversity."

Our first response to adversity should not be to remove it. This is especially so if one is walking with the Lord to the best of his or her ability. Our first response should be to allow it to draw us near to the Lord, to seek through the Word and prayer God's purpose for the adversity, that is, to determine what the Lord would like to do *in* me in any given trial.

Remember Paul's thorn in the flesh? We read about it in 2 Corinthians 12:7-10:

> *And because of the surpassing greatness of the revelations, for this reason, to keep me from exalting myself, there was given me a thorn in the flesh, a messenger of Satan to buffet me—to keep me from exalting my self! Concerning this I entreated the Lord three times that it might depart from me. And He has said to me, "My grace is sufficient for you, for power is perfected in weakness." Most gladly, therefore, I will rather boast about my weaknesses, that the power of Christ may dwell in me. Therefore I am well content with weaknesses, with insults, with distresses, with persecutions, with difficulties, for Christ's sake; for when I am weak, then I am strong.*

God allows or brings sickness that we may be made stronger or more pure for a broader service and a higher platform from which to minister.

Our second response should be to realize we are fighting unseen spiritual powers. When we focus on the spiritual issues and not on the outward physical situation, we will pray accordingly from and through the will of God. From Ephesians 6:12-20 we pray, understanding that:

> . . . *our struggle is not against flesh and blood, but against the rulers, against the powers, against the world-forces of this darkness, against the spiritual forces of wickedness in the heavenly places. Therefore take up the full armor of God, that you may be able to resist in the evil day, and having done everything, to stand firm. Stand firm therefore, having girded your loins with truth, and having put on the breastplate of righteousness, and having shod your feet with the preparation of the gospel of peace, in addition to all, taking up the shield of faith with which you will be able to extinguish all the flaming missiles of the evil one. And take the helmet of salvation, and the sword of the Spirit, which is the word of God. With all prayer and petition pray at all times in the Spirit, and with this in view, be on the alert with all perseverance and petition for all the saints, and **pray on my behalf**, that utterance may be given to me in the opening of my mouth, to make known with boldness the mystery of the gospel, for which I am an ambassador in chains; that in proclaiming it I may speak boldly, as I ought to speak.*

That's praying from the inside out!

Our third response should be to allow Christ to live within us through the power of the Holy Spirit, not through self-effort. Remember Galatians 2:20: *I have been crucified with Christ; and it is no longer I who live, but Christ lives in me; and the life which I now live in the flesh I live by faith in the Son of God, who loved me, and delivered Himself up for me.*

We must keep in mind that our response to a sickness or adversity is to glorify Christ, not only in the future or in the past, but right now, because He died to make that a result. When we look to the cross of Calvary, it will give us a proper perspective that allows us spiritual stability, like a pilot that picks a spot on the horizon to help him fly a straight course to his destination regardless of the wind. It may blow one way and then another, but when the pilot keeps his eye on the spot on the horizon, he is able to stay the course. That's what Christ does for us; He empowers us to stay the course when we keep our mind, will, and emotions on Calvary. His death and resurrection give everything in our lives an eternal purpose.

When praying for the sick we should keep in mind that the deceiver can and will falsify or counterfeit answers to "generic" prayers, that is, prayers that are not based on what Christ did on the cross. Satan does this in an attempt to convince us that righteousness is not a pre-requisite to God answering prayer. (For a fuller discussion, see the chapter "Prayer: Who Hears? Who Answers?")

The Apostle John says in 1 John 5:13-15,

> *These things I have written to you who believe in the name of the Son of God, in order that you may **know** (not guess or hope) that you have eternal life. And this is the **confidence** which we have before Him, that if we ask anything according to His will, He hears us. And if we*

know that He hears us in whatever we ask, we know we have the requests which we have asked from Him.

Our confidence in praying for the sick must come from our relationship with the Father. That relationship enables us to obey His commands in Romans 8:28, 1 Thessalonians 5:18, and Ephesians 5:20. Giving thanks in all things is the first step in effective praying. This will lead us to assurance of being on praying ground. Remember, "praying ground" is:

> Being sure that you are a child of God.
> Being sure that you have no unconfessed **revealed** sin.
> Being sure that you are filled with the Holy Spirit.

When these things are true of us, we are in a right relationship to pray effectively. You can tell you are praying effectively by the fruit of the Spirit revealed in you. If you become a little more loving, joyous, peaceful, patient, kind, and faithful, a little more Christ-like, that is proof that your prayers are effective. The proof is *not* in receiving what you prayed for in the temporal realm: it is what is happening in your spirit.

It is helpful to realize that there are three kinds of sicknesses for Christians:

1. A sickness unto death.

Near the end of life many people have the sense that death is near. Many experience a sickness that they know will lead to their departure from this life. Those who are born again can face this final sickness with assurance and joy that they will soon be done with the trials of life and experience eternal blessedness with God. For such people, their "sickness unto death" is also a final "sickness unto the glory of God."

But for unbelievers and for some disobedient believers, what is in view scripturally is a sickness unto *premature* death. This is God's judgment for one who is in direct disobedience to His will as revealed in Scripture. We read in 1 Corinthians 11:24–30

The night in which He was betrayed He took bread and when He had given thanks, He broke it, and said, "This is My body, which is for you; do this in remembrance of Me." In the same way the cup also, after supper, saying, "This cup is the new covenant in My blood; do this, as often as you drink it, in remembrance of Me." For as often as you eat this bread and drink the cup, you proclaim the Lord's death until He comes. Therefore whoever eats the bread and drinks the cup of the Lord in an unworthy manner, shall be guilty of the body and the blood of the Lord. But let a man examine himself, and so let him eat of the bread and drink of the cup. For he who eats and drinks, eats and drinks judgment to himself, if he does not judge the body rightly. For this reason many among you are weak and sick, and a number sleep.

Notice in verse 28 it says, *But let a man examine **himself**.* Do not say to anyone, "I know why you are sick; it's because of your sin." The one who is sick determines that for himself. We can only pray for God's grace and mercy for him. It seems to me that this is the one sickness we are least asked to pray about. God's decision is final and always right. Psalm 103:9: *He will not always strive with us; nor will He keep His anger forever.* When God has used every effort to bring a man to repentance and he refuses, we must not try to stand in the Lord's way.

The Apostle Paul gave us examples. 1 Corinthians 5:5 states, *I have decided to deliver such a one to Satan for the destruction of his flesh, that his spirit may be saved in the day of the Lord Jesus.*

And in 1 Timothy 1:20 he says, *Among these are Hymenaeus and Alexander, whom I have delivered to Satan, so that they may be taught not to blaspheme.*

These are heavy words and should never taken lightly. Remember with whom you are dealing.

2. Sickness unto chastisement.

Look at the following scriptures about this category of sickness. John 5:14 says, *Afterward Jesus found him in the temple, and said to him, "Behold, you have become well; do not sin any more, so that nothing worse may befall you."*

Luke 5:20 says, *And seeing their faith, He said, "Friend, your sins are forgiven you."* Verses 24-26: *But in order that you may know that the Son of Man has authority on earth to forgive sins"—He said to the paralytic, "I say to you, rise, and take up your stretcher and go home." And at once he rose up before them, and took up what he had been lying on, and went home, glorifying God. And they were all seized with astonishment and began glorifying God; and they were filled with fear, saying, "We have seen remarkable things today."*

Repentance is always healthy – never unhealthy.

Proverbs 3:1-8 says, *My son, do not forget my teaching, but let your heart keep my commandments; for length of days and years of life, and peace they will add to you. Do not let kindness and truth leave you; bind them around your neck, write them on the tablet of your heart, so you will find favor and good repute in the sight of God and man. Trust in the Lord with all your heart, and do not lean on your own understanding. In all your ways acknowledge Him, and He will make your paths straight. Do not be wise in your own eyes; fear the Lord and turn away from evil. It will be healing to your body and refreshment to your bones.*

Repentance and restoration, both spiritual and physical, always result in glorifying the Lord, not the pray-ers.

3. Sickness unto the glory of God.

John 11:1-4 tells us, *Now a certain man was sick, Lazarus of Bethany, of the village of Mary and her sister Martha. And it was the Mary who anointed the Lord with ointment, and wiped His feet with her hair, whose brother Lazarus was sick. The sisters therefore sent to Him, saying, "Lord, behold, he whom you love is sick." But when Jesus heard it, He said, "This sickness is not unto death, but for the glory of God, that the Son of God may be glorified by it."*

John 9:1-3 states, *And as He passed by, He saw a man blind from birth. And His disciples asked Him, saying, "Rabbi, who sinned, this man, or his parents, that he should be born blind?" Jesus answered, "It was neither that this man sinned, nor his parents; but it was in order that the works of God might be displayed in him."*

Let's review the three kinds of sicknesses: first, the sickness that leads to premature death. If there is no remorse or interest in repentance, a person's sickness could be unto death. Second, by repenting we can eliminate the sickness for chastisement with confidence. That leaves the sickness for the glory of God; only by His grace and mercy can we be a part of glorifying the Lord through the sickness. It is a high calling and a holy occupation.

Problems in Praying for the Sick

Let's look now at some of the problems encountered in praying for those who are sick.

1. Seeds of doubt

The counterfeiter, Satan, will use ineffective praying to plant seeds of doubt like:

Now, Christian, where is your God?
Do you really think it pays to be a Christian?
Why is your loving God punishing you?

2. False confidence based on a favorable change

Praying ineffectively gives the deceiver an opportunity to deceive us into thinking we've had an answer from God because of a favorable change in circumstances. Have you prayed for someone's healing and they seemed to get better for a time and then die? The deceiver will use a spiritual high, followed by a great fall, to his advantage to weaken our faith and create doubt. Can the falsifier make you feel better? Yes, think of Scientology, Jim Jones, the Toronto blessing, the Brownsville revival, etc. These movements made people feel better for a time, but they are right out of the pit.

3. Praying only FOR and not WITH.

If you pray FOR me effectively, I will be led to believe I can get my needs met through you, without getting right with God. I may develop more faith in you, the pray-er, than in God. I will lose the benefit of seeing and hearing the Lord through my prayer partner's view of Him as we pray together.

4. The possibility of miraculous divine healing

This has always been a problem for man because we all know and believe the Lord can heal; but will He, and when, and how? Jesus was not crucified because of His healing ministry, but because He forgave sin. Man has always been more interested in physical help than in spiritual help. God is more interested in the eternal. (2 Corinthians 4:18)

> Mark 2:5–11: *And Jesus seeing their faith said to the paralytic, "My son, your sins are forgiven." But there were some of the scribes sitting there and reasoning in their hearts, "Why does this man speak that way? He is blaspheming; who can forgive sins but God alone?" And immediately Jesus, perceiving in His spirit that they were reasoning that way within themselves, said to them, "Why are you reasoning about these things in your hearts? Which is easier, to say to the paralytic, 'Your sins are forgiven;' or to say, 'Arise, and take up your pallet and walk?' but in order that you may know that the Son of Man has authority on earth to forgive sins"—He said to the paralytic, 'I say to you, rise, take up your pallet and go home.'"*

5. Wrong motives

Sometimes we pray for healing seeking to create the impression that we are more spiritual than another person. God cannot honor spiritual arrogance in any way. He always *resists the proud, but gives grace to the humble.* (I Peter 5:5)

6. The power of positive thinking

The teaching of the "power of positive thinking," such as practiced by various cults—Mary Baker Eddy, Christian Science, "faith healers," etc., puts more faith in individuals than even in their own prayers to God. This erroneously teaches that the healing power resides in certain individuals, rather than God.

7. A wrong view of God

Our view of God must be based on Scripture, not on our circumstances or our ability to change them. When Jesus told Peter that he was going to the cross to suffer and die, Peter took

Him aside and rebuked Him for His statement. Jesus said to Peter, *"Get behind Me, Satan! You are a stumbling block to Me; for you are not setting your mind on God's interests, but man's"* (Matthew 16:23). Viewing physical illness and death with man's interest only in mind will hinder our understanding of God's purpose. It will eat away at our faith in prayer. When praying becomes void of faith, it is powerless. Satan loves powerless praying. Examples include couching everything in, "If it be Thy will," when God has made His will clear, or at the other extreme, commanding God to heal, violating Proverbs 3:5- 8:

> *Trust in the Lord with all your heart, and do not lean on your own understanding. In all your ways acknowledge Him, and He will make your paths straight. Do not be wise in your own eyes; fear the Lord and turn away from evil. It will be healing to your body and refreshment to your bones.*

E. M. Bounds, a great prayer warrior said, "Religion and God are dishonored, doubt and unbelief are strengthened by much asking and no getting."

8. An erroneous idea that it is not God's will for any to be sick. Job shows that the righteous suffer as much as the unrighteous. God's purpose for many sicknesses is to give us pause, and to make us consider our mortality.

There was a man several years ago who was told he had inoperable terminal cancer. He heard about the fact that laughing puts more oxygen in the blood and that empowers the blood to fight the cancer cells. He bought all the slapstick movies and material he could find that would cause him to laugh. He laughed 6 to 8 hours a day and he actually laughed himself well. As a result of his work and research, he was invited to be on the medical research team at Stanford. There is healing in a joyous spirit. Nehemiah 8:10b says, "... *Do not be grieved, for the joy of the Lord in your strength.*"

My point in sharing this story is that there are positive things man can do to strengthen his health, but he is still going to die! If we are cured seven times, it has no eternal value unless we turn to the Lord. We will never sustain a meaningful prayer life unless we by an act of our will develop an eternal mind-set.

9. The reality of God's sovereignty

As I said earlier, to pray effectively for the sick means we accept God's sovereignty. If we refuse to accept that a sickness is from God or that He has allowed a sickness, we will focus on the enemy; we will attempt to "bind the enemy" through prayer, which we cannot do. We will be content with some physical result that does not conform us to the image of Christ.

Ray Stedman, in *Spiritual Warfare,* wrote:

"I must say I feel there is altogether too much concern among Christians about this matter of demon possession. I know certain Christians who feel they must bind the enemy before they do anything. When they go into a room to have a meeting, they will pray to bind the powers of darkness. I know others who ascribe every common problem of human life to some manifestation of demon activity."

"The New Testament gives absolutely no warrant for this type of approach... the major attack of the Devil and his powers against human life is not by direct means, but indirect—by satanic suggestions through the natural and commonplace events of life."[17]

10. Not being on praying ground

"Praying ground" is a right relationship with the Lord. Confidence in prayer, prayer for any kind of need, not just in sickness, only comes through Calvary-based prayer. We can only be in a right relationship with God because of the finished work of Christ.

11. My humanity says heal the body.

But God says, *For momentary light affliction is producing for us an eternal weight of glory far beyond all comparison* (2 Corinthians 4:17). I would be inhuman if I didn't want a sick person to be healed, especially loved ones. The closer the relationship, the more difficult this problem is for us. I think this is one of the reasons that the Word says to call for the elders, the most spiritual leaders you know, to pray. There is wisdom in the counsel of many.

James 5:14-16 says, *Is anyone among you sick? Let him call for the elders of the church, and let them pray over him, anointing him with oil in the name of the Lord* (I view the oil as the fire of the Holy Spirit to cleanse. The Lord does the healing), *and the prayer offered in faith will restore the one who is sick, and the Lord will raise him up, and if he has committed sins, they will be forgiven him. Therefore, confess your sins to one another, and pray for one another, so that you may be healed. The effective, fervent prayer of a righteous man can accomplish much.*

The following is a testimony of how God used this teaching in my life.

Several years ago Shirley, and I taught a week long Prayer Enrichment Seminar in a large Baptist Church in Chula Vista, Mexico. When a church and its leadership cancel everything on the church's schedule for a week of meetings on prayer, you can expect God to work in an amazing way. Often revival of the saints breaks out.

When we begin, people come for various reasons, some out of curiosity, some out of duty. When we break up in small groups to put into practice what we have learned, we do lose a few. Then as we start teaching that biblical prayer will always reveal every secret sin, we lose a few more. After the discipline of silence and the cleansing takes place, the Holy Spirit takes over. We will generally have a revival. *Where the Spirit of the Lord is, there is liberty* (2 Corinthians 3:17), liberty to be transparent with the Lord and with each other. We sing, "Spirit of the Living God, fall afresh on me."

However, in this church there was no spirit of revival. There seemed to be a heavy black cloud over the church. I thought it probably was me. I thought, "Maybe I am not being clear. Maybe my translator isn't hearing me." I didn't know, so I asked to meet with the pastor and a couple of the elders. I shared how I felt about the heaviness I sensed. The pastor was quick to respond. He said, "There is a heaviness over this church. It's not you. It's because we are broken over a burden we are carrying about a family who was in this church."

He said that this family had been pillars in the church. They were real soul winners. A good number of the church's membership were Christians because of the love and faithfulness of this couple.

Then about a year earlier, they were looking forward to a cousin's *quinceanera*.(coming of age celebration). Their son was going on 14 and the father worked two and sometimes three jobs in order to buy his son a new suit and shoes for this upcoming 15th birthday. The pastor went on to explain that in their culture this is a very special time, especially for the young lady. In fact,

I learned that the gown for the young lady might very well be more beautiful and costly than her wedding gown.

On the night of the big celebration, the father didn't get home on time and his son got angry. When his father did get home, the son refused to go. However, the father was persistent and they went. Soon after they arrived, the son found his best friend and off they went to join all the festivities.

The boys were horsing around–in Nebraska we say "horse playing"–one picked up the knife that was on the table for the cutting of the cake and the boy's best friend fell on the knife. Evidently it hit his heart or something and he died instantly.

The son went into deep depression. He got very little sleep and when he did eat, he often vomited. The doctors said there was no physical problem. They took him for therapy, to a physiologist and a psychologist. They even took him back to the Catholic Church, in case the priest could help. No one could help.

The wife blamed the husband for not coming home on time. The husband blamed the wife for not understanding that he had done all he could. They were now discussing divorce. They no longer came to church. The congregation were so hurt by all of this. They were hoping that I could pray for the boy. The pastor said, "Will you pray for this boy?"

I said, "No, I can't do that. If I understand you right, these people are Christians?"

"Yes," he said, "they are."

"Then what I'd like very much to do is pray WITH them. Do you think they would be open to that?"

"Yes, Yes. They are open."

So the pastor, two elders, and I went to their home. It was about 8:30 p.m. I was concerned that it was too late, but the pastor assured me it would be okay. When we arrived, the husband was sitting on one side of the room and the wife on the other. It was obvious that they had a strained relationship.

I asked the husband if he still loved the Lord. He said yes. I asked the wife the same question and she said yes. I said, "Now, since you both say you love the Lord, and your pastor, two elders, and I also love the Lord, could we begin our time of prayer by focusing on Scriptures and praising Him for who He is?" We all were in agreement.

This is a very important principle of prayer: where two or more are gathered together and agree, the Lord is in their midst (Matthew 18:19-20). Coming to a unity of spirit in prayer is one of God's prerequisites of praying effectively.

Based on Psalm 100:4 I endeavor to help whatever group I am working with come into His presence with thanksgiving and praise. I will ask the group to take their Bibles and turn with me to Psalm 103. We form a small circle and begin to praise the Lord from His Word. I read the first verse and praise the Lord that He is holy. Then the person on my left reads verse two and praises Him for being love and we continue around the circle. After about twenty minutes we all agree God is good - always.

Then I asked the husband and wife, "If you were to die tonight, do you know for sure that you would go to heaven?"

The wife was confident that she would. The husband hesitated for some time and finally said, "I think so."

"You THINK so?"

"Well," he said, "I have done some good things and some that aren't so good." This was the couple who had led many to the Lord; now because of their circumstances he was not sure. God did not answer his prayers for his boy and did answer the prayers of all the other Christians who were praying. He really felt God had given up on him.

I very carefully went through the gospel with him. I told him a prayer to receive Christ and asked if it expressed the desire of his heart? "Yes, it does," he said.

We prayed and I asked him again, "Do you know where you are going to spend eternity?" He didn't know for sure!

The pastor couldn't believe what he was hearing. The pastor went through the gospel again. Still this man couldn't come to assurance of his salvation. I asked the husband, "Do you believe that God is sovereign? Do you believe that God is all powerful?" He said that he did. "Then you must understand," I said, "that if you had taken that knife and killed the boy yourself on purpose and you repented, that you would still spend eternity with the Father. Your salvation is not dependent on your performance but on Christ's shed blood on the cross."

I soon realized that no small miracle was taking place. The lights came on and he got a sparkle in his eyes, and we knew we were in the presence of the Lord. *Where two or more gather together and agree, the Lord is in their midst* (Matthew 18:19-20).

Next I asked the wife about her salvation. She knew for sure she was a Christian. She said," I have a bitterness in my heart. Will you pray for me?"

"No, we are here to pray WITH each other. Let me share with you the 'discipline of silence.'" I had several copies in Spanish. I said, "This outline is designed to spend a half or one hour alone with the Lord. Take a pencil and paper, your Bible and follow the outline. First pray from Psalm 111:1-6, praising Him for who He is just as we did earlier, then ask God to search your heart from Psalm 139:23-24. Write down any sin the Lord reveals and claim 1 John 1:9. Then leave His presence praising Him from Psalm 111:7-10."

Then I asked each one to find a place to meet alone with the Lord. After awhile we all came back together and thanked the Lord for filling us with His Holy Spirit.

The husband fell on his knees before his wife, asking her to please forgive him. With tears, she said she did, if he would do the same. As they shared and prayed together we were all greatly blessed.

Then the husband asked me if I would pray for their son. "No, let me explain, my brother," I said, "You are the high priest of this home." He almost could not take it in. In fact, I had to quit using "high" priest and talk about him being head of his home, as in 1 Peter 2:5, 9. He was the head, not because he earned it or because he was qualified, but because God ordained that he should be the head of his family.

After some time he got it and said, "Now I must pray for my son."

I said, "Yes, and we are going to pray for you." We prayed for him from Ephesians 1:15-19: "Father God, we know of Jose's renewed faith in You and his love for the saints, his wife especially. We thank You for him and for giving him a spirit of wisdom and enlightenment of his eyes for his calling of head priest of his family to pray for his son with joy, encouragement, and love working in the strength of the Lord's might. We come in Jesus' name. Amen"

By that late hour, 2 a.m., the mother was hesitant to awaken the son. The husband knew, however, that moment was the time to pray with his son. I smiled inside because now he was in charge.

We went to the boy's room and found him cuddled in the corner of his cot, in a fetal position and his pillow was stained with tears. His father got on his knees and asked his son to forgive him for not being the praying father he needed. "I am sorry, so sorry. Will you please forgive me? I know God has —will you?" His son rolled over and hugged his daddy and with many tears began praying for his dad. I can't tell you what that was like, what they prayed, but I knew that a father and son were doing business with their Heavenly Father.

I will never forget that moment in time. Whenever I become timid about attempting to minister to someone through prayer, this scene comes back to me and strengthens me. It has been and always will be a reminder not to do other people's praying for them. No two people on the earth could have prayed the prayers they prayed for each other that early morning. When we left, we knew we had been with Jesus.

The next Sunday, that whole family was in church testifying how **their** God had answered **their** prayers and they thanked the congregation for all the prayers they had prayed for them. There was no talk about the prayer teacher from North America. Had I done the praying for them, I could have robbed them of all the spiritual blessings derived from the husband functioning as the head priest of his home.

> "Whenever you find sickness in a house or death in a darkened chamber, seize the opportunity to speak for your Lord. Your voice for the truth will be likely to be heard, for God Himself is speaking and men must hear Him whether they will or no." —Charles H. Spurgeon

How to Begin Praying for the Sick
How and where do we begin to pray in adverse circumstances, including sickness?

1. Our first response to sickness should not be to remove it, but to focus on God.

> *Therefore we do not lose heart, but though our outer man is decaying, yet our inner man is being renewed day by day. For momentary, light affliction is producing for us an eternal weight of glory far beyond all comparison, while we look not at the things which are seen, but at the things which are not seen; for the things which are seen are temporal, but the things which are not seen are eternal* (2 Corinthians 4:16–18).

2. Our second response is to determine the spiritual issues.

> *For our struggle is not against flesh and blood, but against the rulers, against the powers, against the world-forces of this darkness, against the spiritual forces of wickedness in the heavenly places* (Ephesians 6:12).

3. Our third response is to realize who we are in Christ.

> *I have been crucified with Christ; and it is no longer I who live, but Christ lives in me; and the life which I now live in the flesh I live by faith in the Son of God, who loved me, and delivered Himself up for me* (Galatians 2:20).

Let's apply what we have learned about effective prayer specifically to praying for the sick.

We begin on the basis of Romans 8:28, 1 Thessalonians 5:18, and Ephesians 5:20. We are to give thanks in all things, for all things, and rejoice always. This is the will of God for us. We praise the Lord by faith for the great and mighty things He is going to bring out of this sickness, even if it is unto death. Praise will lay a foundation for the pray-er's confidence of being on praying ground. 1 Corinthians 4:4 says, *I am conscious of nothing against my self, yet I am not by this acquitted; but the one who examines me is the Lord.*

A Christian prays claiming Psalm 139:23-24: *Search me, O God, and know my heart; try me and know my anxious thoughts; and see if there be any hurtful way in me, and lead me in the everlasting way.* Does God hear and answer that prayer? Yes, 10,000 times out of 10,000. If the Holy Spirit reveals anything, we claim 1 John 1:9: *If we confess our sins, He is faithful and righteous to forgive us our sins and to cleanse us from all unrighteousness.* Then we praise Him for forgiving us and cleansing us. Next we pray for God to fill us with His Holy Spirit. Now we can be confident we are on praying ground. When a Spirit-filled Christian seeks the heart and mind of God, he, through the Word and prayer, will be able to discern the spiritual issues involved in the sickness.

What about the non-Christian? He cannot have a sickness that is to the glory of God (unless it causes him to repent). My concept of praying for the sick is based on a spiritual Christian's ability to determine the cause or purpose of the illness by a process of elimination. *But he who is spiritual appraises all things, yet he himself is appraised by no man. For WHO HAS KNOWN THE MIND OF THE LORD, THAT HE SHOULD INSTRUCT HIM? But we have the mind of Christ* (I Corinthians 2:15,16).

Discernment begins by determining whether or not the person making the request is a Christian. Unenlightened people cannot rightly identify a need because they are blinded to the things of God. We must not allow unregenerate people to tell us how to or what to pray about. *And even if our gospel is veiled, it is veiled to those who are perishing, in whose case the god of this world has blinded the minds of the unbelieving, that they might not see the light of the gospel of the glory of Christ, who is the image of God* (2 Corinthians 4:4).

If the person making the request is a Christian, we must minister to the spirit first, helping him determine if he is on praying ground —that is, cleansed, filled, and directed by the Holy Spirit. Once assured of that relationship, we may use our position in Christ to discern what we can about the sickness.

The sickness to death is the one we are least asked to pray about. When a disobedient or non-Christian has a sickness to death, he has rejected truth and has turned his back on God, who has utilized every effort to bring him to repentance. *He will not always strive with us,* according to Psalm 103:9. (Also see 2 Thessalonians 2:11-12 and Isaiah 1:15.) When spiritual Christians have a sickness to death, their only desire is to glorify God. We must join them in their praise.

The two types remaining are sickness to chastisement and to God's glory. Through prayer, Christians can know (not guess or hope) which they have because God has promised to give us wisdom when we seek it in faith. (James 1:5-6) The Christian must confess all known sin revealed by the Holy Spirit. (Psalm 139:23-24 and Psalm 51) God promises to always forgive if we ask in faith. (1 John 1:9) Sometimes it might be necessary to guide the sick person in making restitution for particular sins in order to clear his conscience. By this Biblical process, we can eliminate the spiritual causes of sickness to chastisement.

Then we ask God for healing (James 5:15). If He doesn't heal, the sickness is to the glory of God (2 Corinthians 4:15-18). At that point, we should stop asking for healing and start thanking Him and seeking His power to glorify Him in the illness, seeking His will and guidance to share with others what He is doing in our life. We need prayer not so much for the sickness but rather for giving God the glory! We know God has a purpose in everything, even suffering, that we might be able to minister to others who suffer. Sick ones need our prayers to show them how, in their sickness, they can win their loved ones to Christ!

> *Blessed be the God and Father of our Lord Jesus Christ, the Father of mercies and God of all comfort; who comforts us in all our affliction so that we may be able to comfort those who are in any affliction with the comfort with which we ourselves are comforted by God. For just as the sufferings of Christ are ours in abundance, so also our comfort is abundant through Christ. But if we are afflicted, it is for your comfort and salvation; or if we are comforted, it is for your comfort, which is effective in the patient enduring of the same sufferings which we also suffer; and our hope for you is firmly grounded, knowing that as you are sharers of our sufferings, so also you are sharers of our comfort. For we do not want you to be unaware, brethren, of our affliction which came to us in Asia, that we were burdened excessively, beyond our strength, so that we despaired even of life; indeed, we had the sentence of death within ourselves in order that we should not trust in ourselves, but in God who raises the dead; who delivered us from so great a peril of death, and will deliver us, He on whom we have set our hope. And He will yet deliver us, you also joining in helping us through your prayers, that thanks may be given by many persons on our behalf for the favor bestowed upon us through the prayers of many* (2 Corinthians 1:3-11).

Urge the sick person to pray on his own behalf. Praying **with** the sick one is often more effective than just praying **for** him. Praying for those who are sick should not be the responsibility of only the pastor or elders; it should be a normal part of prayer of every spirit-filled Christian (Isaiah 56:7). The prayer ministry of the church should be a ministry through which God's will is determined and the ultimate power source is utilized to see that God's kingdom purpose is carried out on earth as it is in heaven.

If a church prayer chain has sin in the camp, it will very quickly become the work of the deceiver to produce fruit of the flesh such as guilt, worry, jealousy, impure thoughts, critical spirit, discouragement, and legalistic attitude. Sin will cause prayer to become a vehicle through which a non-Christian or worldly Christian will be led to believe they can get their needs met without getting right with God. Praying with sin in the camp will effectively communicate that a needy person really doesn't need to be in a right relationship with the Father as long as he knows someone that is. A church prayer chain which is not based on righteousness will be used by the counterfeiter to falsify answers to prayers.

How then should we pray? **Unity in Christ is the first security against the devices of Satan.** When we pray in the will of God, for the will of God, the will of God cannot fail, nor can it be inconsistent! Our prayer will accomplish that which God intends, that is, to glorify the Great Physician, not those who are praying.

Praying from the inside out (from the spirit out to the body), is a concept that I have found very helpful. It is not the only way to pray, but it is a way that is supported by Scripture even though it is not directly taught. If you find yourself not agreeing with it, that's okay. I am sharing it as a useful tool, not as a clear command. The Word of God says in 2 Timothy 2:7, *Consider what I say, for the Lord will give you understanding in everything.* John 16:13 says, *When He, the Spirit of truth, comes, He will guide you into all the truth; for He will not speak on His own initiative, but whatever He hears, He will speak; and He will disclose to you what is to come.* This is my prayer for you as you read and study this concept; God, the Spirit of all truth, will bless you.

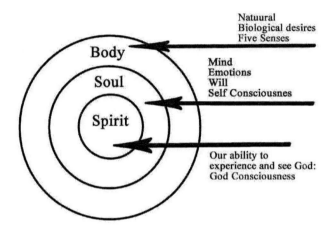

We do not study an enemy's strategies and attack him in his strength. We attack him in his weakness. Where is man weaker than in his body? The Word of God teaches that the flesh is weak.

The three concentric circles in the following diagram represent man's body, soul, and spirit. The body is the source of our natural biological desires; the five senses give us consciousness of the world around us. The soul is our mind, will, and emotions, the self-conscience. The spirit is our ability to see and experience God, our God-consciousness. Let's look at each of these.

The Body

Satan attacks the body in an attempt to get the mind to focus on the body. If you happen to think about God when your mind is focused on your body, your thoughts will be based on what God is or is not doing in or for the body. It's a trap! Satan knows that when the mind is set on the flesh it cannot please God. *Because the mind set on the flesh is hostile toward God; for it does not subject itself to the Law of God, for it is not even able to do so; and those who are in the flesh cannot please God.* (Romans 8:7-8)

☐ The body is decaying. *Therefore we do not lose heart, but though our outer man is decaying, yet our inner man is being renewed day by day.* (2 Corinthians 4:16)

☐ The body is temporal. *While we look not at the things which are seen, but at the things which are not seen; for the things which are seen are temporal, but the things which are not seen are eternal.* (2 Corinthians 4:18)

☐ The body is created and belongs to God. *For they* (the wicked) *exchanged the truth of God for a lie, and worshiped and served the creature rather than the Creator, who is blessed forever. Amen.* (Romans 1:25)

☐ The body is wasting away. *When I kept silent about my sin, my body wasted away through my groaning all day long. For day and night Thy hand was heavy upon me: my vitality was drained away as with the fever-heat of summer. Selah.* [Pause and think on these things.] *Therefore, let everyone who is godly pray to Thee in a time when Thou mayest be found; surely in a flood of great waters they shall not reach him.* (Psalm 32:3, 4, 6)

☐ The body is as durable as grass. *All flesh is grass, and all its loveliness is like the flower of the field.* It counts for nothing. (Isaiah 40:6b) *It is the Spirit who gives life; the flesh profits nothing.* (John 6:63a)

☐ Fleshly (bodily, material) weapons are useless. *For the weapons of our warfare are not of the flesh, divinely powerful for the destruction of fortresses.* (2 Corinthians 10:4)

☐ The flesh is weak. *Keep watching and praying, that you may not enter into temptation; the spirit is willing, but the flesh is weak.* (Matthew 26:41)

In contrast, God does not want us consumed with what is going on in our bodies. Our greatest battle is not a material battle against flesh and blood, not even our own flesh and blood. *For the weapons of our warfare are not of the flesh, but divinely powerful for the destruction of fortresses.* (2 Corinthians 10:4) *For our struggle is not against flesh and blood, but against the rulers, against the powers, against the world-forces of this darkness, against the spiritual forces of wickedness in the heavenly places.* (Ephesians 6:12)

The Soul

The soul consists of the mind, will, and emotions. The flesh wars against the soul ...*abstain from fleshly lusts, which war against the soul.* (1 Peter 2:11) *The mind set on the flesh is death, but the mind set on the Spirit is life and peace.* (Romans 8:6–11) In this battle with eternal ramifications, we are armed with the Word of God. *For the Word of God is living and active and sharper than any two-edged sword, and piercing as far as the division of soul and spirit, of both joints and marrow, and able to judge the thoughts and intentions of the heart.* (Hebrews 4:12)

The Spirit

The spirit is our God-consciousness, our ability to see and experience God. Satan is the destroyer, the accuser, the deceiver, the blasphemer, and author of wickedness. His ultimate goal in troubling our bodies is to eternally destroy our spirits. But God is willing to sacrifice the comfort and integrity of our bodies for the greater spiritual good. *I have decided to deliver such a one to Satan for the destruction of his flesh, that his spirit may be saved in the day of the Lord Jesus* (1 Corinthians 5:5).

☐ The spirit can endure sickness. *The Spirit of a man can endure his sickness, but a broken spirit who can bear?* (Proverbs 18:14)

☐ The spirit opposes the flesh. *But I say, walk by the spirit, and you will not carry out the desire of the flesh, for the flesh sets its desire against the Spirit, and the Spirit against the flesh; for these are in opposition to one another, so that you may not do the things that you please.* (Galatians 5:17-18)

☐ Persevere to stay in the Spirit. *Are you so foolish? Having begun by the Spirit, are you now being perfected by the flesh?* (Galatians 3:3)

Would you allow me to make an application with my paraphrase? "You foolish Christians, do you think just because you pray for this sick person and he gets well, that he will repent and become a Christian?" Don't be foolish. After all the miracles Jesus did, the people said, *show us a sign and we will believe.* (John 6:30)

God is working within you to perfect you: *For I am confident of this very thing, that He who began a good work in you will perfect it until the day of Christ Jesus.* (Philippians 1:6 and 2:13) God is infinitely more interested and committed to the completion of His work in our spirits than He is concerned with any level of discomfort to our bodies.

Pray for the spirit, the inner man, to be strong first and foremost. This is what I mean by praying from the inside out. Look at Paul's prayers. As an example, look at Ephesians 1:15-19. In this passage, he did not say the people in view were sick, but his words show his pattern of prayer for believers: *For this reason I too having heard of the faith in the Lord Jesus which exists among you, and your love for all the saints, do not cease giving thanks for you, while making mention of you in my prayers; that the God of our Lord Jesus Christ, the Father of glory, may give to you a spirit of wisdom and of revelation in the knowledge of Him. I pray that the eyes of your heart may be enlightened, so that you may know what is the hope of His calling, what are the riches of the glory of His inheritance in the saints, and what is the surpassing greatness of His power toward us who believe. These are in accordance with the working of the strength of His might.*

Ephesians 3:14-20 is similar. So is Colossians 1:9-12: *For this reason also, since the day we heard of it, we have not ceased to pray for you and to ask that you may be filled with the knowledge of His will in all spiritual wisdom and understanding, so that you may walk in a manner worthy of the Lord, to please Him in all respects, bearing fruit in every good work and increasing in the knowledge of God; strengthened with all power, according to his glorious might, for the attaining of all steadfastness and patience, joyously giving thanks to the Father, who has qualified us to share in the inheritance of the saints in light.*

We have seen how Satan likes to trouble the body in order to get at our soul and spirit. God, however, works from the spirit out to the body. When our spirit is in conformity to the Spirit of God, and our soul (mind, will, and emotions) is subject to the spirit, healing can come to our bodies when it is in God's plan. When it is not in His plan, the Spirit will always influence the mind to take every thought captive, and we will be able to find contentment and peace in our weakened physical condition.

For though we walk in the flesh, we do not war according to the flesh, for the weapons of our warfare are not of the flesh, but divinely powerful for the destruction of fortresses. We are destroying speculations and every lofty thing raised up against the knowledge of God, and we are taking every thought captive to the obedience of Christ. (2 Corinthians 10:3-5)

Therefore we do not lose heart, but though our outer man is decaying, yet our inner man is being renewed day by day. For momentary, light affliction is producing for us an eternal weight of glory far beyond all comparison, while we look not at the things which are seen, but at the things which are not seen; for the things which are seen are temporal, but the things which are not seen are eternal. (2 Corinthians 4:16-18)

*And do not fear those who kill the body, but are unable to kill the soul: but rather fear Him who is able to destroy both soul and body in hell. (*Matthew 10:28*)* Satan's ploy is always to get us to fear the weaknesses in our body.

But if the Spirit of Him who raised Jesus from the dead dwells in you, He who raised Christ Jesus from the dead will also give life to your mortal bodies through His Spirit who indwells you. (Romans 8:11)

Before I was afflicted I went astray, but now I keep Thy word. (Psalm 119:67)

Now may the God of peace Himself sanctify you entirely; and may your spirit and soul and body be preserved complete, without blame at the coming of our Lord Jesus Christ. (1 Thessalonians 5:23)

Let's review the "gaze and glance" principle in the context of the body, soul, and spirit.

When our focus or "gaze" is on our physical condition, the temporal body is more important than the eternal spirit, and our emotions take over. Our will is subject to our emotions and our mind is vulnerable to being tossed about by every wind of doctrine (Ephesians 4:14).

The following is an example of the "gaze and glance" principal in proper order. When our focus is on our spiritual condition, on things eternal, our mind is able to take every thought captive to the obedience of Christ. Truth known and obeyed can bring healing.

Angie's story illustrates this. It's about Jason, a ten year old. His father left the family. Angie led Jason and his mother to the Lord through neighborhood outreach. For a few weeks Jason had been staying with Angie after school until his mom came home. They became great friends as Angie discipled him.

One day Jason came to her door, wearing a serious look. He said, "Angie, Mom has a ringing in her ears and a big lump behind one of them. I've been praying for her, but I don't think God is hearing my prayer. Will you pray for her?"

"Of course, I will, " Angie said, "but you know, honey, sometimes when two or more pray together they have a greater effect. I would like for us both to pray together for your mother."

Jason loved that; so into the kitchen they went as Angie explained that in Psalm 100:4 God says we are to enter His gates with thanksgiving and His courts with praise. "Let's praise the Lord for who He is first of all and then thank Him for all He has done for us." They took time to consciously come into God's presence through praise.

Angie went on, "Now, Jason, God's word says in Psalm 66:18 and John 9:31 that if we have sin in our lives, the Lord will not hear us."

"What's sin?" Jason asked.

After thinking for a few minutes, because she had not defined sin to a ten year old before, she said, "Sin is anything in our lives that is displeasing to the Lord."

"Oh," Jason replied, "some friends of mine were mean to me today so I called them some bad names. Is that what you mean?"

"Yes, honey, that's what God would call sin," she said. He admitted having some of that. Angie instructed Jason to take paper and pencil and write down what he had just said. As they continued in their time of preparation for prayer, Angie explained rebellion.

"Oh, yeah, I have some of that too," Jason said. Angie told him to write it down. After more time of searching and writing, Jason said, "I think I'm ready to pray!"

"Great!" Angie replied. "Let's pray claiming 1 John 1:9 and ask God to cleanse us." They did, and Jason's long face was gone!

Then Angie said, "Now, let's pray for your mother. But before we do, let me ask you, if God doesn't answer our prayers just the way we think He should, are you going to be upset with Him?"

After a few minutes of serious thought, he said, "No, because I know God loves Mommy and He will do what's best."

"That's right, Jason. I'm sure the Lord is pleased with your willingness to trust Him in this area. Let's pray."

After an uplifting prayer time, Jason bounced out of the house with a twinkle in his eye and joy in his heart.

Angie shared how meaningful it had been for her to take the time to pray with Jason. It had been encouraging and she enjoyed it so much that she didn't realize how late it was. She went to the Lord again, asking Him to help her to be creative, maximize her time, so that she would be prepared to meet Cliff, her husband, coming home to dinner.

Just then the doorbell rang.

There was Jason with two friends. He said, "God isn't answering their prayers either!"

Angie was confronted with another interruption in her schedule. Was this really necessary? Could she take the time? One look into those questioning eyes and she knew she must. "Come in. Tell me what you would like to pray about."

Mary, eleven years old, said both her grandpas had cancer and she didn't know what she would do if she lost both of them. Sue didn't know much about prayer and had lots of questions. Angie took them into the kitchen and shared that when Christians unite their hearts in prayer, they have a powerful effect, but they must be sure they have no unconfessed sin in their lives. As Angie continued to explain about sin and interact with them, Sue got nervous, looking from one side to another, getting up and going to the next room. Angie called her back and asked, "Does this make sense to you?"

"No," Sue replied.

So Angie asked her when she had invited Christ into her life. Angie had assumed she was a Christian because she regularly attended the neighborhood Good News Club©. With a tear or two, Sue said she never had trusted Christ; she had just been pretending at those meetings.

"Would you like to invite Him in right now?"

"Oh, yes, I would," Sue proclaimed. They prayed and Sue trusted the Lord to do what He had promised. She asked Him to save her and believed that He did!

Angie went on to share the importance of asking God if there was any unconfessed sin in their lives and the need to take care of that before praying for others. Jason said, "Don't forget to tell them about rebellion!" They all prayed and made sure they were on praying ground.

Angie asked, "If God doesn't answer the way we think He should, are you going to be mad at Him?"

"No, we are trusting Jesus because He knows best," they said.

Their prayer was based on God's Word, in unity and commitment to God's will. What a dynamic prayer time that was! The kids left with the joy of the Lord and an experience in prayer they would never forget. Angie said that because of this time, intimate prayer was becoming more and more a part of their neighborhood Good News Club©.

Angie went on to say that before the training in one of our prayer workshops, she would have just taken their requests and prayed for them. She would not have even thought of ministering in this way.

This testimony illustrates the need of ministering to others in prayer. In accepting a request, first I must consider how God would have me pray. I am learning more and more how to effectively communicate with others through praying from God's Word. I've discovered that my ability to effectively communicate with man is incredibly dependent upon my desire and willingness to communicate with God.

In summation, I now realize that accepting prayer requests from others without ministering to them is really second best. When I take the time to learn about and minister to their spiritual condition, as well as to learn about their prayer burdens, their confidence in God and prayer will be strengthened. Remember, often people making requests of you have little or no confidence in their prayer effectiveness; they want someone else who they perceive as effective to do the praying. But their most pressing spiritual need is to have assurance of their own relationship with God.

Praying for the sick is a ministry to the soul of man –his mind, will, and emotions, so that God is glorified. Anything that touches a child of God has an eternal purpose. Prayer, biblical prayer, can transform any sickness into a sickness unto the glory of God.

> *I now rejoice, not that you were made sorrowful, but*
> *that you were made sorrowful to the point of repentance;*
> *for you were made sorrowful according to the will of God,*

in order that you might not suffer loss in anything through us. For the sorrow that is according to the will of God produces a repentance without regret, leading to salvation; but the sorrow of the world produces death (2 Corinthians 7:9–10).

The specific outcome for each sick person is in the Lord's hands. There can never be just one human formula for how to pray in every situation. And I realize, as my daughter, Bonnie, has said, "Not everything my dad says is scriptural." (Smile!) I feel I am on the fringe of the fringe of really learning how to pray for the sick, but I also know if I am willing for the Lord Jesus to teach me how to pray for the sick, He will, because that is part of who He is. And He will teach you too.

Chapter 13
The Word and Prayer for the Lost

After being merely a church-attending Christian for 24 years, the next four years I was heavily involved in Christian activity, including several nationwide evangelistic efforts. I was trained to share the gospel and how to lead a person to Christ, but after all that training, I had never been taught how to pray for the unbeliever. What do you do after you ask the Lord to save someone or after you have him or her on a prayer list for salvation? Most would agree that prayer has to be the foundation of evangelism, but few know or have experienced what praying for the lost will entail. I am afraid most of our praying for the lost is just vain repetition; at least, mine was.

We frequently have a human tendency to pray for the lost in the flesh, i.e. "change them, convict them," maybe even "make them sick." In most sparsely attended prayer meetings, after praying for the sick, if there is any time remaining, someone will know someone who is lost and needs salvation. Often a lengthy discussion follows about the person (sometimes bordering on gossip). Then there is a prayer or two asking God to convict that person of their sin. There may even be a bold one asking God to bankrupt his business or break his leg saying, "Lord, do whatever you have to do to bring him to Yourself." The pray-er's focus is on changing the sinner. I can't say this is wrong, but I believe with all my heart that there is a much better and more effective way to pray. Who wouldn't want to do that? Besides, if we pray for God to break their leg, it may come back to bite us! Be cautious about what you pray.

Natural man can see things that are wrong, but only a spiritual man will be able to view the man as God sees him. A spiritual man will know and understand the purpose for which God created the sinner and will see his good points and positive attributes. The Word is divinely powerful to destroy the fortresses of the enemy; the fortresses of unbelief, anger, hatred, a critical spirit, cruelty, an empty unfulfilled life, etc. When we experience change in our own attitude toward the sinner and gain a spirit of expectancy as we pray, we are taking spiritual ground, making our every thought in alignment with Christ. We begin to see the sinner in light of Calvary and why Christ died for him—because God has a wonderful plan for his life, which is to glorify God and enjoy Him forever!

As we contemplate praying for the lost, it is good to remind ourselves that we are declaring war, not on the sinner but on the power that holds the sinner. According to 2 Corinthians 10:5, we are destroying speculations and every lofty thing raised up against the knowledge of God, and we are taking every thought captive to the obedience of Christ. Praying effectively for the lost is a battle.

The major battle is walking in the Spirit. When we begin to pray earnestly for the lost, we may find ourselves being tempted in ways we couldn't imagine and proceeding on our own, telling God what to do according to what we see is wrong with the unbeliever. It's essential to understand God's will is to teach us how and what to pray for. Psalm 25 says, *Make me know Thy ways, O Lord; teach me Thy paths. Lead me in Thy truth and teach me, for Thou art the God of my salvation; for Thee I wait all the day.*

Also I've been reminded time and time again not to lean on my own understanding. *Trust in the Lord with all your heart and do not lean on your own understanding. In all your ways acknowledge Him, and He will make your paths straight.* (Proverbs 3:5-6) I might need to pray, "Father God, forgive me for trying to tell You what to do. Help me trust You as You teach me how to pray for the lost."

We must also count the cost of praying for a lost sinner. The enemy does not give up or back off without a fight. If we don't encounter resistance we are probably not praying in the Spirit.

Why is the enemy willing to fight so hard for this soul? Can you believe God for how He will use the sinner once he's saved? Can you envision God using him to bring 100,000 people to Himself? How about 100? Or maybe 10? Envision according to your faith. Start praising God now, by faith, for each one of those souls that will be in the kingdom when this one comes to Christ. Praising God, by faith and in advance, destroys Satan's hope.

The Sovereignty of God and the Responsibility of Man

Some who have a limited view of God's sovereignty sometimes say, "If God is sovereign and has elected those He will save, why should we pray?" We must pray because we don't know who He has chosen, and it is God's command for us to pray for the lost. The body of Christ needs to recognize and understand the responsibility of praying in unity —oneness with Christ for the lost. To effectively pray for the lost, we must come to grips with the sovereignty of God and the responsibility of man, which is an antinomy.

The Shorter Oxford English Dictionary defines *antinomy* as "a contradiction between conclusions which seem equally logical, reasonable, or necessary." This definition is not quite accurate. Biblically, there is no real contradiction, though it looks like one.

The antinomy we are concerned with is the appearance of contradiction between divine sovereignty and human responsibility. The Bible teaches that, as King, He orders and controls all things, including human actions, in accordance with His own eternal purpose. (Romans 9) But as Judge, He holds every man accountable for his own actions. (Romans 2:1-16) God's sovereignty and man's responsibility are presented to us as standing side by side, sometimes in the same passage.

It has helped me to picture the two concepts as a railroad track. The two rails of the track are the sovereignty of God and man's responsibility. They begin and end at the same place and run side by side. The thing that holds them together is the railroad tie, which symbolizes the Word of God and prayer, allowing the train to reach its destination by the power of the Holy Spirit.

Prayer is God's means of harmonizing His sovereignty with man's responsibility. They cannot be harmonized any other way. Our Heavenly Father has ordained for His will to be fulfilled through man.

Someone has said, "Not one soul will be found in heaven unless someone prays." Does this mean that God is impotent apart from man? Absolutely not! I believe that God has chosen, in His sovereign will, not to work apart from man. I believe the Lord could have led the Israelites out of Egypt some other way, but He chose to spend forty years training Moses to do the job. Truly, God has given man a will, but where (on earth!) did we get the idea that man's will is any match for the sovereignty (the supreme authority) of God? God desires that man choose the right way, but if he doesn't, God's mercy, love, patience, and longsuffering take over (see Psalm 145:8, 9, 18, 19).

Spurgeon writes in *Twelve Sermons on Prayer*:

> "But another objection has been raised which is very ancient indeed, and has a great appearance of force. It is raised not so much by skeptics, as by those who hold a part of the truth; it is this—that prayer can certainly produce no results, because the decrees of God have settled everything, and those decrees are immutable.

Now we have no desire to deny the assertion that the decrees of God have settled all events. It is our full belief that God has foreknown and predestinated everything that happeneth in heaven above or in the earth beneath, and that the foreknown station of a reed by the river is as fixed as the station of a king, and the chaff from the hand of the winnower is steered as the stars in their courses.

Predestination embraceth the great and the little, and reacheth unto all things; the question is wherefore pray? Might it not as logically be asked wherefore breathe, eat, move, or do anything? We have an answer which satisfies us, namely, that our prayers are in the predestination, and that God has as much ordained His people's prayers as anything else, and when we pray we are producing links in the chain of ordained facts. Destiny decrees that I should pray—I pray; destiny decrees that I shall be answered, and the answer comes to me." [18]

In my first forty years as a Christian I struggled with praying for the lost, partly because I appeared to be asking God to violate men's will. You can't make a man do something he doesn't want to do.

When I was a child, my dad told me to do specific things. Sometimes I responded by saying, "You can't make me do that!"

He would reply, "You're probably right, but I can make sure you wish you had." The old adage, "You can lead a horse to water, but you can't make him drink," may be true; but if you feed him salt, he will drink like crazy! I know that's true. As a young boy in Scottsbluff, Nebraska, I worked at the cattle auctions on Mondays. Cattle are sold by the pound. It didn't take me long to learn that some men had a way to get their cattle to drink a lot of water just before they were sold. The crafty ones were able to increase their cattle's weight by five to ten percent simply by feeding them salt. Scripture tells us to be the salt of the earth. I believe that's what we become as we manifest attributes of God in our life that dispel the unsaved's wrong view of God so that they will thirst for Him.

Prior to understanding this, my praying for the lost was a duty. Thus, to stay "spiritual" and ease my conscience, I would make sure that my lost family members and friends were on several "needs salvation" prayer lists, oblivious of my obligation to do more. At times I fell into the trap of assuming that I had done my spiritual duty by just "feeling bad" about my loved ones being unsaved. God help me!

I know now that God has chosen to bring others to Himself through the prayers of His obedient children. The highest purpose of prayer is not just to get an answer, it is communion: communication with our Heavenly Father. God's purpose for prayer is that we get to know Him. The Lord is more concerned about our relationship with Him than He is with the unbeliever's circumstances. Therefore, our role is first to know God through His attributes, then to make those attributes visible to the unbeliever as we pray for his salvation. Dr. Lloyd Ogilvie said, "Successful prayer is not measured by how much we get from God, but how much of Him gets into us."

We cannot sustain a vibrant walk with God or a movement of prayer without praying fervently and effectively for the lost, because *He is patient with us, not wanting anyone to perish, but everyone to come to repentance* (2 Peter 3:9b, *NIV)*. When we pray effectively for the lost, we will be in harmony with God's will.

When we are in a right relationship with the Lord, He will burden our heart for the lost. In fact, if a Christian does not have a burden for the lost, we might question his relationship with the Lord. It is evident in Scripture that the mark of a true Christian is a sincere concern for others. As we take that concern to the Lord, He will bring us into new light, both about ourselves and about others. The depth of our concern for the unbeliever will reveal our true weaknesses. For example, when we pray for the unregenerate, we may sometimes find ourselves asking how much we really care—i.e., do we care enough to share our car, our home, our fishing gear or whatever else the Lord requires of us? Do we even find the time to spend an evening with the person we are praying for? Praying for the lost will require us to make changes in our lifestyles that we may not be ready to make. That brings us to repentance and a clear view of our need to be filled with the Holy Spirit. Only a Spirit-filled Christian can continually pray for the lost and be at peace with his own walk.

Beware of getting caught in the devil's trap of measuring the effectiveness of your prayers only by the changes you observe in those who are the object of those prayers. The changes in the unbeliever's life are important and can be wonderful; however, if we measure the effectiveness of our prayers only by what we see in them, we will have an up-and-down emotional ride. Such experiences can give us a distorted view of God. We will find ourselves asking questions such as, "What kind of God would save the most undeserving sinner with very little prayer, but would not save a most deserving person, from man's perspective, with much prayer?"

For example, I might begin praying for a boy deep in sin and drugs, and, after only six weeks, God saves him. Had I also been praying earnestly for six years for the salvation of my son, who is really a "good kid," I might begin asking myself, "What kind of God works like that?" Our view of God is often determined by perceived answers or non-answers to our prayers. When we pray and God answers, we think one way about Him. When we pray and God doesn't answer, then we think another way about Him. When the thoughts we get of God are at odds with objective truth about Him as revealed in the Bible, we have a problem, because God is the same yesterday, today, and forever (Hebrews 13:8). He never changes; He is immutable, consistent, and faithful.

Then how do we measure the effectiveness of our praying for the lost? As I have said before, we do that by measuring what God is doing in us, the pray-er, not by what God may or my not be doing in the life of the unbeliever. If the fruit of the Spirit—love, joy, peace, patience, kindness, goodness, faithfulness (Galatians 5:22-23)—is being made visible in me, the pray-er, then I have confidence that I am praying effectively. When I become a little more loving toward the unsaved, toward everyone, a little more patient, a little more caring, etc., my prayers are being answered. But if, after praying for some time for the unbeliever, I become less loving, less caring, less patient, etc., or if any one of the fruit of the flesh (Galatians 5:19-21) becomes visible, it's a sure sign that my eyes are on what God is doing *for* me rather than on what God is doing in me. It is *natural* for us to be motivated by what God is doing *for* us; it is *supernatural* to be motivated by what God is doing *in* us.

Shirley and I have four children, three girls and one boy. The boy is the youngest, and he was spoiled the most! When Shirley and I applied this principle of prayer, we finally stopped asking God to change our son and started asking Him to change us. We praised Him with the Bible as our prayer book. Increasing our time of praise caused us to place more trust in the Lord. Eventually, we saw and experienced in each other the fruit of the Spirit rather than the fruit of the flesh. The old cliché, "Prayer changes things," has an element of truth; but more often than not, prayer changes us, and then God gives us solutions to change things.

Perhaps you have had an experience similar to ours. It seemed the more determined my wife and I were in our prayers for our son, the worse he became. Either he was getting worse or we were being enlightened as to how far he was from the Lord all along. One thing was certain, the more we prayed, the more difficult it was for us to be patient and caring. This was a sign to us to be diligent to focus on praising God for our son's positive traits. We asked the Lord to help us see the good in our son. We asked ourselves, "What's the most positive thing we know about him?" Then we asked the Holy Spirit to enlighten and empower us to convey our insights to our son. As it says in *Proverbs 25:11, Like apples of gold in settings of silver is a word spoken in right circumstances.* Our prayers in part were to help our son comprehend his worth in Jesus Christ.

Praying for the lost isn't always so revealing or uncomfortable, but quite often it is. There is usually a price to be paid, sometimes a sacrifice needs to be made. It is scriptural that prayer enlightens the soul to show us the action we need to take. True prayer enlightens the soul to the works of God as well as the works of the Devil. War brings out both the good and bad in man. The more adverse the circumstances are, the more visible are the attributes of God and the Devil.

When our relationship to the Lord is number one, and nothing is more important to us than getting to know Him, then our obedience, both to the Father and to man, becomes an enriching experience. In fact, our obedience leads us out of the "have-to-seek-God" camp into the "want-to-seek-God" camp.

We pray for the lost because:

> ☐ God has ordained for us to pray for the lost. It is His will. The strength of our faith will not grow if we are unwilling to allow God to teach us to pray for the lost.
>
> ☐ We need to be obedient to the Great Commission (Matthew 28:19-20). How can we be obedient if we are not learning how to pray scripturally for the lost?*".... beseech the Lord of the harvest to send out laborers into His harvest."* (Luke 10:2)
>
> ☐ Praying for the lost is a vital part of laboring in the harvest field.
>
> ☐ Our view of God's plan for our life will be blurred if we have no heart to pray for the lost.

Let's look at each of these factors more fully:

1. Praying for the lost is a holy occupation and is God-ordained. The Lord is the Prayer Teacher. He will teach us if we seek Him to do so. Prayer is and always will be a mystery, because if we knew all there is to know about prayer, we would know all there is to know about God. That is not possible in this life. But one thing I've learned is that there is a right way and a wrong way to pray. An example of the wrong way is praying for a sinner that I do not really love. *But I say to you who hear, love your enemies, do good to those who hate you, bless those who curse you, pray for those who mistreat you.* (Luke 6:27-28) Someone has said, "One who is well loved is well prayed for." I believe this to be true. Praying for a lost person must flow from a heart of compassion. Christ's love led him to die for us "while we were yet sinners." Our love should compel us to pray for even the most unlovely of sinners.

2. The strength of our faith is proportional to praying as God has taught us to pray in any given situation. If God has shown us how to pray for a certain need or a certain person, our faith is

strengthened and we pray confidently. If we pray thoughtlessly, carelessly, or according to our fleshly desires, we cannot be sure God will hear or answer, and our faith is weakened. The thoughts I am sharing will be of little value apart from your prayer asking God to teach you to pray (Luke 11:1), and from your obedience to His leading. Faith without works is dead (James 2:20). Biblical prayer almost always leads to an action. As Oswald Chambers said, "Understanding spiritually does not come from knowledge but rather from obedience."

3. Christ himself gave us the Great Commission in Matthew 28:19-20. He also gave us the command to pray for laborers in his harvest (Luke 10:2). He is also our example in his work as an intercessor. Isaiah 53:12 tells us that Jesus ...*bore the sin of many, and interceded for the transgressors.* Also the Apostle Paul says, *I urge ... that intercession ... be made for everyone ... This is good, and pleases God our Savior, who wants all men to be saved and to come to the knowledge of the truth* (1 Timothy 2:1-4 NIV). John MacArthur elucidates the role of intercessor in his Bible study on 1 Timothy 2:1-8, entitled *Evangelistic Praying.* He states:

> "To intercede for others is not to coldly request the salvation of those we care about. It is to sympathetically enter into the depth of their anxiety and pain and to cry out to God on their behalf. We need to be compassionately involved in the problems of the lost. I am convinced that our praying tends to be shallow and impotent because we don't live with a sobering awareness of man's need and the desperate state of the lost. Neither do we live with an all-consuming desire to see God glorified in the salvation of souls. We tend to be so self-centered that we avoid getting involved in the lives of those who need our prayers."[19]

By Christ's example and by direct command, we understand that we must be about praying and laboring for the lost in order to be in God's will.

4. We will have a distorted view of God's plan for our life if we have no desire to pray for the lost. What is God's purpose for us in praying for the lost? The first and foremost reason is to glorify Him by:
- A. Conforming us to His image by making His attributes visible to others in our sphere of influence.
- B. Bringing us to a greater dependence on Him as we learn not to lean on our own understanding.
- C. Strengthening the cause of Christ by increasing the Spirit-filled fighting force.

God is ready to perform a new and deeper work in us, which is the fulfillment of His plan for our life. He works in our soul before He works through us. You see, praying for the lost almost always requires dying to self. In John 12:24, Jesus says, *Truly, truly, I say to you, unless a grain of wheat falls into the earth and dies, it remains by itself alone; but if it dies, it bears much fruit.*

John 15:13 sounds this theme again: *Greater love has no one than this, that one lay down his life for his friends.* Then in 1 John 3:16 we read that Jesus is the example: *We know love by this, that He laid down His life for us; and we ought to lay down our lives for the brethren.*

I believe that God uses prayer for the lost to conform the pray-ers to the image of Christ, so that He Himself may be made visible—and desirable—to the unbeliever. God works in our inner being before He works through our body. Praying for the lost, without a commitment or availability to be used in answer to your prayer, leads to a distorted view of prayer and of God, because prayer is not an end in itself. True prayer will lead to an action. (James 2:20)

Are you willing to be changed by God in order to be used of God? Derek Prince, in his book *Everything by Prayer*, says prayer is both a science that has to be studied and an art that needs to be cultivated. In my opinion, his statement is especially true in praying for the lost. The science is an understanding of God and how He works; the art is learning to apply what you've learned (sanctification). Some may say, "God's elect will be saved." True! But, God in His sovereign will has chosen not to work apart from the prayers of Spirit-filled believers.[20]

The road map to victory in praying for the lost
Prepare for war. Spiritually, how do you prepare for war?

1. Be sure you are on praying ground (in a right relationship with the Lord). *The prayers of a righteous man availeth much...* (James 5:16b)

2. Pray Scripture. *The Word of God is powerful.* (Hebrews 1:3)

3. Pray according to or in harmony with the sovereignty of God and the responsibility of man.

☐ Is the person elect? Who gave you the burden?

☐ Is it God's will? It is not God's will for any to perish. (2 Peter 3:9b)

☐ Will God answer? *No good thing will He withhold from those who walk uprightly.* (Psalm 84:11b)

☐ Will you praise Him, no matter what? *Oh, give thanks to the Lord.* (Psalms. 105:1-9)

4. Identify and praise the Lord for positive traits in the unbeliever.

5. Identify the wrong view of God he has.

6. Internalize an attribute of God that dispels the wrong view.

7. Avoid vain repetition; be creative and persistent. How do I know when my persistence becomes vain repetition? One sign could be when I lose my spirit of expectancy.

8. By faith, rejoice and thank God now as though they are already saved. (Thessalonians. 5:16, 18)

While this is not the only way to pray, it is very effective. It may seem a bit awkward at first, but as you persist, it will help you transition your prayers from focusing on temporal needs to eternal issues, from negative circumstances to positive facts!

Some people have said, "You're making prayer too hard, too complicated." Their view of prayer often is "just talking to a friend" or "talking to the man upstairs." "After all," they argue, "Jesus said, *You are my friends if you do what I command.*" (John 15:14, *NIV*) Certainly this is true; He is our friend. But prayer is much more than talking to a friend, especially when we are praying for the lost. Some have said, "It seems, Mr. Gillam, you're saying that we need our Ph.D's in prayer before we can pray effectively for the lost." I don't intend to communicate that. I know, for example, that the simplicity of a child's prayer for Grandpa can be very effective, but we must not build our total philosophy of prayer on that kind of experience.

God does not send children to war. There are times when we need more than childish prayer. We need to be growing up in our prayer lives (2 Timothy 2:15). We don't have to have a Ph.D. in prayer before we can pray effectively for others, but I do believe with all my heart that we had better be working toward our Ph.D.'s in prayer. A soul winner must be a master pray-er. The body of Christ desperately needs committed, trained, skilled, biblically-based intercessors who can teach others (2 Timothy 2:2).

If you find yourself resisting this teaching, that's understandable. I resisted more than you can imagine and had a lifetime of self-sufficiency to overcome, and I still have a long way to go. But God will always meet us where we are spiritually, and then move us to where we need to be. He is the Prayer Teacher.

Internalizing God's Attributes as Witnesses to God

Would you agree that every non-Christian and every backslidden (carnal, worldly) Christian has a distorted view of God? You must agree because if the unbeliever had a right view of God, he would come running to the Lord. Rightly identifying that misconception or distorted view is a work of God's grace in answer to a believer's prayers. Someone has said that a problem well defined is 90% solved! When the wrong view is identified, we may claim an attribute of God that dispels it and pray that attribute into the life of the Christian who is closest to the unbeliever, so that the unbeliever can see it modeled before him. This is the heart of what it means to pray effectively for the lost.

People have many wrong ideas of God and what it means to be a Christian. Some of the distorted views could include:

☐ God is more a harsh judge than a loving father.
☐ My sins are too big to be forgiven.
☐ I have problems bigger than God can handle.
☐ God helps those who help themselves.
☐ I hope to be saved by works.
☐ Only "good" things happen to "good" people.
☐ I have to clean up my act before I can become a Christian.
☐ The Christian life is just a crutch to help us through life.
☐ I will have to give up so much, i.e., wealth, friends, habits, fun, and "the good life", if I accept Christ.
☐ My earthly father didn't love me, so how can I trust a Heavenly Father?

In addition to such misconceptions, other stumbling blocks that the lost have to overcome are within themselves: hypocrisy, low self-acceptance, self-sufficiency, pride. If we sincerely desire to pray for an unbeliever, we need to ask God to make known to us the unbeliever's misconception of God. Then we can focus on internalizing an attribute that corrects and dispels our unbelieving friend's wrong view. The intercession of the Son of God found in John 17, the "high-priestly prayer," that the Lord prays for us is our mandate.

When we pray an attribute of God into our life or into the life of other Christians who are in the unbeliever's sphere of influence, we bring light into the unbeliever's darkness. In answer to a believer's prayer, God prepares a sinner. He also burdens an obedient Christian who is in the sinner's sphere of influence to pray for him and He brings them together. He said to His disciples in Matthew 9:37-38, *The harvest is plentiful, but the workers are few. Therefore beseech the Lord of the harvest to send out workers into His harvest.* The work in God's harvest is making His attributes visible in life's situations. Being in the world but not of it and allowing God's attributes to work through us are not only blessings in our own lives, but also destroy the work of the Devil!

Workers prepare the ground for the seed to be planted —different seeds require different soil preparation. The seed is planted, it is watered and nurtured, and the Lord causes the growth. Then comes the harvest! What's the point? Praying for the lost is a process. Helping the unbeliever to see and understand or comprehend his worth in Christ is a vital part of learning to pray for the lost. When the irresistible blessings of the Lord are clear to the non-Christian, he will surrender his heart to Christ. That's what happened as God taught me to pray for my mother.

I prayed for my mother for years without much affect. When I started asking the Lord to teach me to pray, my burden for my mother increased. As I prayed, the thought came to ask God to show me what were her misconceptions of God. Through my prayers and praying with my wife, I began to see that one of my mom's misconceptions of God concerned His love.

Mom was a very loving person from the world's perspective. People would tell me how loving my mother was and what she had done for them. That was the key; her view of love was based on what she could do for others. If she could do more for you than you could do for her, she loved you more. This was always a problem for me as I was growing up. I couldn't understand how my parents could love the down-and-outers more than they seemed to love their own kids. That was not always true, of course, because she did great things for me, like making a cover for my boat and an awning for my motor home to name a few. When I was in high school she made me and my friends Levi-type pants out of awning material, stripes and all. They were outlandish. We were the talk of the town. We wore them with white shirts and broad, gaudy suspenders. I think those pants would be a status symbol even today!

Anyway, I started asking the Lord to empower me to love my mom with His kind of love—unconditional love, not an "if" or "because" kind of love, but the same love with which He loves me. God answered that prayer! I thanked God for the caring person my mother was and how her modeling had helped me so much through the years.

I told her that I loved her, but she didn't really receive it. So, always checking to be certain I was on praying ground, I began asking the Lord to show me how I could communicate my love to my mother in a way she could understand. I would always get the impression to tell her how much I loved her. Often, I found myself kind of arguing with the Lord: "Lord, I do tell her I love her."

The thought came, "Yes, but you told her you loved her when you were not a Christian, and although you didn't mean it like you do now, she doesn't see the difference. The enemy has blinded her eyes."

"Well, Lord, how can I tell her that I love her from her perspective?"

At once the thought came to send her cut flowers. Oops, short circuit there! Not cut flowers for my mother! Maybe potted plants would do, but not cut flowers. My mother had loads of potted plants. For weddings, funerals and hospital visits, she always gave potted plants, not cut flowers. After a wedding or funeral they could always be planted and enjoyed. Cut flowers just don't last! Maybe the plastic ones would do. They are the same today, yesterday, and forever!

As I persisted praying about how to communicate my love, I always got the same answer, send her a bouquet of flowers! I finally gave up and said, "Okay, Lord, I'm sending her a bouquet of cut flowers. She isn't going to like it, and it'll all be Your fault!"

When I sent that first bouquet of fresh flowers, she was 71 years old and no one had ever sent her flowers before. I thought cut flowers were an extravagance that she would not appreciate. Just the opposite was true! She loved them! She took them all around her neighborhood and said, "Look what my Christian son sent me!" She took them to church. All the walls between us came tumbling down! I will always be grateful to the Lord for the prayer times we had together before the Lord took her home.

My two unsaved brothers gave me permission to share the "Four Spiritual Laws" at her funeral. I believe one of them is now with the Lord, for he has passed on. I am trusting the Lord for my other brother, who has since passed on.

My ability to help others pray for their unsaved loved ones is a credit to my mother and father. They are both with the Lord today, and I believe they have left a heritage of prayers for me. As I continue to honor my father and mother, I am blessed as my kids honor their father and mother, and my grandkids are learning to honor their parents! That is a vital part of what it is all about to be a praying Christian family.

Why do many Christians avoid getting involved in the lives of the lost? There are probably more reasons than letters in the alphabet, but a major one is that involvement tends to reveal our spiritual weaknesses. That may be why God urges us to pray for the lost. Often, as we pray for the lost, an attitude or weakness is revealed in us that we had previously ignored. Prayer should bring us to the end of ourselves. If it doesn't, we ought to examine the way we are praying.

Perhaps another reason is the lack of being disciplined in prayer. Getting involved with unbelievers without being taught how to pray would be like enlisting in the army and going to war without weapons, or with weapons but no training in their use. If a Christian does not know how to internalize an attribute of God he is in a losing battle. The first step in internalizing an attribute of God is to choose, through prayer, to allow God to work His will and way in our life before we seek to remove some problem. God always has a purpose for our shortcomings and failures. He told Peter in Luke 22:31-32: *Simon, Simon, behold, Satan has demanded permission to sift you like wheat; but I have prayed for you, that your faith may not fail; and you, when once you have turned again, strengthen your brothers.*

To summarize, when we want to pray effectively for the lost, we should seek to:

1. Be in a right relationship with the Lord. If you have any doubt, take a day alone with the Lord and pray through the C.P.M.I. booklet, *Prayer Without Purity is Function Without Effect.* Known sin must be removed from our lives first and foremost. *If I regard wickedness in my heart, the Lord will not hear.* (Psalm 66:18) *The effective prayer of a righteous man can accomplish much.* (James 5:16b)

2. Become a prayer partner with an available Christian in your family or a friend who is right with the Lord, who, whenever possible, is also close to the unbeliever. Ask him to pray with you for your walk with the Lord (Ephesians 1:15-10; 3:14-19; Colossians 1:9-12, etc.), as you pray the same for your prayer partner. In Ecclesiastes 4:9-12, we read *"two are better than one."*

3. Identify the unbeliever's wrong idea of God. (Note that all backslidden carnal Christians also have distorted views of God.)

4. Put your faith in a promise of God that guarantees that attribute or assures victory. This will keep you from putting your faith in your works or performance.

5. Look for an action to take, for almost all prayer leads to action. ... *faith, without works, is dead...* (James 2:17, 20 and 26). One of the actions that will confirm that you're on track is recognizing a positive trait in the unbeliever. Then ask the Lord for the right words at the right time to share with him that you praise the Lord for him and these positive traits (Proverbs 25:11). Remember, your praying will likely lead you to do something you do not really want to do or that you feel totally incapable of doing. That's okay! You're on the right track. As long as you're willing, God will meet you at your point of need. *No good thing does He withhold from those who walk uprightly* (Psalm 84:11b). Be obedient! Spiritual understanding does not come from intellect but from obedience.

6. Monitor the results. Pray that the Lord will open your eyes to show you His work. I find it helpful to divide the results into two categories: desired results and actual results. My desire, of course, is to see someone come to the Lord, but I may discover that he is "turned off" temporarily! If I am praying in the Spirit, the "turn off" may be useful from God's perspective, because now I am more knowledgeable about his erroneous view of God.

We can be sure that God always desires to build more of Him in us, even before the unbeliever is open to Christ. As I monitor the difference between the desired results and the actual results, I will come to know better how God works. I can know and believe Him by His works (John 10:38). Armin Geswine, the Founder and President of Pastors Prayer Fellowship in southern California, has said that if we are no longer surprised by the way God answers prayer, we are maturing in prayer. I am still quite surprised by the way He answers at times, but not as much as I used to be, and I fully expect to be less surprised next week or next year. I can say that because I'm getting to know Him.

7. Pray more for the walk of a believer who is close to the unbeliever's life.

Praying for the lost will often require praying twice as much for our fellow believer's walk as we do for the unbelievers salvation. For example, let's assume that my mother knows the Lord and my father does not. Whose life is most exposed to my unbelieving father? My mother's life is constantly seen by my dad. So where is the enemy likely going to attack? He will attack the believer—my mother. Thus, the believer needs a lot of prayer to manifest the fruit of the Spirit–love, joy, peace, understanding, patience, etc., so that the unbeliever can see what it means to be Christ-like.

This principle of praying twice as much for the believer's walk as for the unbeliever's salvation was really brought home to me through praying intently for a person who was deep in sin, with almost cultish circumstances, drugs, etc. The Lord enlightened me to recognize a dedicated and gifted lady who had been saved out of an occult background. I introduced her to my unsaved friend and began to focus my primary prayers for her walk and her witness to my friend. I was quite surprised that, while she said and did a lot of the same things I did, she was much more effective. She also was able to say and do things my friend would have never accepted from me. This loving Christian lady had earned a right to be heard in this particular area by her life message. God used the combination of our prayers to help bring my friend to Him. It is seldom the prayer of only one person God will use to bring victory.

Praying twice as much for the believer's walk can be so encouraging because we are not just focusing on the unbeliever's disobedience, but on God, His Word, and what He desires to do in us and through us and other believers.

8. Praise God, by faith, no matter what the visible results. A praising Christian cannot pray ineffectively. Even a sinner's prayer of praise gets through to the Father and is pleasing to Him when it comes from a sincere heart. In praying for the lost, it has helped me to remember that I did not choose the Lord; He chose me. I did not love Him first; He first loved me. I cannot save anyone. I must be totally dependent on the Lord.

By faith in God's unchanging Word, we realize that we have the following things going for us:

We have the resources to **know** God.

We have the resources to **know** ourselves.

We have the resources to **know** our Christian friends in the body of Christ who are willing to share their various gifts to help us.

We have the resources to **know** our enemy.

We have the resources to **know** and reach our goal.

We have the **Holy Spirit,** who encourages us, empowers us to overthrow the enemy, enables us to rejoice in the midst of battle, and enlightens us to give credit to God, where it is due (see Psalm 25).

Will you pray with me, claiming Luke 11:1, "Lord, teach us to pray for the lost?"

Chapter 14
The First Command with a Promise

Honor (esteem and value as precious) your father and your mother; this is the first commandment with a promise: [Exodus 20:12] that all may be well with you and that you may live long on the earth. (Ephesians 6:23)

We have discussed in all of the previous chapters how having an effective prayer life is essential to our spiritual well-being. This verse in Ephesians, quoting from the Ten Commandments, gives us another essential of well-being: we must honor our parents. It is not a stretch to say that our ability to honor our parents and our ability to have an effective prayer life are linked.

When a Christian is living in disobedience to any of God's commands, his ability to pray effectively is reduced to nothing because God is not obligated to answer our prayers when we are in known sin. But this is especially true when praying for parents and/or children. Honoring our father and mother is more than just a good suggestion; it is a command, and our obedience will affect our ability to pray effectively. I am persuaded that much of our praying lacks creativity and power because we have been passive and uneducated in regard to the command of Exodus 20:12 (Old Testament) as reiterated in Ephesians 6:2-3 (New Testament).

When we give only lip service to honoring our father and mother, we forfeit the light needed to pray intelligently for our children and our grandchildren as well as others the Lord has laid on our heart. Because we are not utilizing the resources God has ordained for us, i.e. our parents, we are not bringing them into the power of our prayer life. Often the very attribute God would like to build in our life to enable us to honor our parents is the very attribute needed to pray effectively for our parents and our children and those in our sphere of influence.

When we are living in obedience to God's command to honor our father and mother, the Holy Spirit teaches us how to pray in harmony with God's will. He enlightens and empowers us to see life through an attribute of His. We then have insight to pray for others.

Let's look at a specific example of how this can work. Perhaps we seek the Lord's power to honor our father, who is an alcoholic, and when God hears and answers that prayer, we are then strengthened to pray specifically for him. The insights the Holy Spirit gives us in regard to our father then become the discernment we use to pray for other sinners with similar needs. A word of caution, however: we are given the spirit of knowledge to intercede and not to criticize!

How do children of God honor their fathers and mothers in ways that will ensure them long life and a life full of true joy? Most of what I have read and heard about honoring your parents involves remembering their birthdays, anniversaries, etc. by sending flowers or gifts. I believe God's Word requires much more than this. These actions are nice and we should do them, but even people who are not believers give nice gifts. What is God requiring of us, His children? I think the Lord is instructing us to do something that unbelievers and disobedient children of God cannot do, something which requires total trust and obedience to God and His Word for the resources to obey this command.

Children of God honor their parents by attributing eternal worth to them. When we attribute eternal worth we are glorifying the Lord who is worthy. Ephesians 6:2-3 does not say to honor them because they are Christians and that they are nice to us. Unbelievers can be grateful for loving parents. When we as Christians are obedient to the first commandment with a promise, and we love our parents just as if they were the most faithful Christians we know, God says we will be blessed with power to love them and show it. We will be blessed with insights to understanding, peace, joy, etc. One of the richest blessings in life is to be able to pray consistently and effectively for others, especially for our own families. It's not available if we aren't obeying this command.

Ephesians 6:2 is directed to children of God only, because only God's children have the resources to be obedient to that command. A non-Christian is more likely to get into heaven through his good works than he is to fully honor his father and mother from an eternal perspective. Of course, a non-Christian can succeed at neither.

What does it mean to attribute eternal worth to our parents? When a football player is honored for his passing ability, his number of completions in a game, he often says, "I learned that from my coach." That's good, but it's only temporal. When we bring attention to the mind, will, and emotions, which is our soul, and engage our spirit with positive attributes of God, which are eternal, we have the capacity to give honor from an eternal perspective.

If you realize, for example, that your mother is a very caring person, and that you have that quality too, ask the Lord to help you give credit to your mother the next time someone recognizes that characteristic in you. Let's assume that you have a non-Christian neighbor who needs to go to the doctor for a checkup. You offer to keep the baby for her while she is gone. She responds positively and is appreciative. When she comes back she says, "Thank you. You surely are a caring person." God has now given you an opportunity to tell her that is something you've gained from your mother.

Now you begin praying Proverbs 25:11: *Like apples of gold in settings of silver is a word spoken in right circumstances.* You may pray something like this: "Lord, thank You for helping me to share with my mother the right words at the right time about how her caring for others has enabled me to be caring too." You honored your mother when you spoke to your neighbor, but you can honor her again by sharing the incident with your mother. The communication with your mother might be something like this: "Mom, the other day my neighbor had a need for a baby sitter and I was able to help her. She was grateful and said that I am a caring person. I told her that this is something I inherited from you. I want you to know how God has used you in my life. Thanks, Mom." This is truly honoring your mother by attributing eternal worth to her. You have brought to light a quality of God in her life that has blessed you. When an attribute of God is made visible, God is honored. When God is honored, He is lifted up, as in John 12:32.

What does God mean when He says *"that all may be well with you and that you may live long on the earth?"* It means that our life may be blessed by drawing attention to an attribute of God. We are lifting Him up as He was lifted up on the cross. *And I, if I be lifted up from the earth, will draw all men to myself,* John 12:32. This is Calvary-based prayer, as we discussed earlier. Matthew Henry's commentary on this verse states,

> "(2) That by the death of Christ souls should be converted, and this would be the driving out of Satan (v.32) *But I, when I am lifted up from the earth, will draw all men to myself.* Here observe two things: –
> The great purpose of our Lord Jesus, which was to *draw all men to himself,* not the Jews only, but the Gentiles also. Observe here how Christ himself is all in all in the

conversion of a soul. It is Christ who draws. He does not drive by force, but draws as the loadstone [magnetic iron ore]; the soul is *made willing*. It is Christ to whom we are drawn. He who was shy and distrustful of him is brought to love him and trust in him—drawn up to his terms, into his arms.

The strange method he took to accomplish his purpose by being *lifted up from the earth. He said this to show the kind of death he was going to die,* the death of the cross. He who was crucified was first nailed to the cross, and then lifted upon it. The word here used signifies a honourable advancement; *If I am exalted;* he reckoned his sufferings his honour. Now Christ's drawing all men to himself followed after it in time.

The great increase of the church was after the death of Christ. It followed after it as a blessed consequence of it. The cross of Christ, though to some a *stumbling-stone,* is to others a *loadstone.* Some make it an allusion to the lifting up of the bronze snake in the desert, which drew all those to it who were bitten by venomous snakes. O what flocking was there to it! So there was to Christ, when salvation through him was preached to all nations; see ch. 3, 14, 15. Perhaps it has some reference to the posture in which Christ was crucified, with his arms stretched out, to invite all who come..."[21]

We must be totally dependent on Christ and His resurrected power to draw all men unto Him. Seeking the wisdom and discernment we need to honor our parents from His perspective requires diligence. God is the rewarder of those who diligently seek Him. Hebrews 11:6: *And without faith it is impossible to please Him, for he who comes to God must believe that He is, and that He is a rewarder of those who seek Him.* This is a part of what Paul is telling us in Ephesians 6:2-3, *That all may be well with you.* As we obey God, He blesses us, He rewards us. The Lord will empower us to follow through; He will renew our strength, restore our joy and confidence in our praying.

If your father is abusive, you will need a lot of God's power to love him. You cannot honor him if you don't really love him. You can't pray effectively for the salvation of someone you do not love. God enables you to love your father by praying His love for your father into your life. As a result you become a more loving person. You will become more effective in your praying. You'll be more sensitive, understanding and loving toward your kids, your spouse, and all those around you.

When you know how to do something right, you often notice when others do it wrong. It is easy then to express a critical attitude. Wisdom is required to use any of our God-given gifts for His glory, even the gift of love. *Love bears all things, believes all things, hopes all things, endures all things,* 1 Corinthians 13:7. As we are enlightened as to how to love in God's way, we will begin to develop an ability to look at people and circumstances from God's perspective. This guarantees a fulfilled life; that's a life that experiences the purpose for which God created us. Read on to see how God used Ephesians 6:2-3, the first command with a promise, in my life.

My Dad was not much of a conversationalist. Instead of telling me to be quiet at mealtime, he would just thump me on the head. He could thump hard. Thumping is using the middle finger to snap off the tip of the thumb with all your might! It would make me so mad.

Before I learned how to love my Dad in the power of the Holy Spirit, I, too, was a thumper. I think it should be written in the Bible, "No thumping allowed." When I was able to communicate

God's love for me with my Dad, I was able to communicate better with my kids and I stopped thumping them.

My father and I had a very strained relationship when I was growing up. We were a family of seven children. I was the middle one and the most rebellious. I left home the first time when I was 14 and permanently when I was 16. After I married in 1950 I worked for my Dad for a time and our relationship was somewhat better; however, it was not until after I began to surrender to the Lord that I really developed a burden for my Dad's salvation. I tried every way I knew to share about the Lord with him, but it only made things worse.

When I became a staff member of Campus Crusade for Christ, I began learning a lot. One was how to pray effectively for my Dad. I heard Josh McDowell share how God had convinced him that he could not really pray effectively for his Dad unless he loved him, which he didn't. His dad was a town drunk. How can you love someone that you can't respect? He began to ask God for His love for his dad. Josh prayed that the Lord would help him see his dad from His perspective. The first thing God began to reveal was that his dad was easy going and laid back.

Josh began to thank the Lord for this truth about his dad, even though it was hard to accept. Josh was the opposite, high-strung and on the go. But Josh prayed Proverbs 25:11, that God would give him the right words at the right time to tell his dad about this new revelation. He told him he was being used in his life by God to show him he needed to be more relaxed and slow down a bit.

I began to relate this testimony to my dad and me. My dad was a diesel truck mechanic, a very good one. But growing up I felt being a diesel truck mechanic was one step below a garbage collector, who could at least take a bath and smell better. Not so with a diesel mechanic; that diesel smell stayed on your body and in your clothes even though they were laundered. (But even my view of garbage collectors was based on my natural ignorance and non-Christian view. Early in their marriages, my granddaughters' husbands had that job. They were good men, hard working and trying to get ahead, which they did.)

Dad's shop in the 1940's was usually in a dark alley. I just didn't respect him, but I did learn a lot about being a mechanic and how to keep my cars running. To say that Dad was a great mechanic would be an understatement. Years later it was cool if you could work on your car or build a hotrod. As a committed Christian I began to realize that I had inherited, as well as learned, some of Dad's ability when I worked in his shop.

So that you get the full picture, I need to back up a bit. I graduated from high school, the first graduate in our family, at 154th out of 156. There were only two kids in my class dumber than me and they were my friends. We "studied" together. I was told I had an inferiority complex. An employer told me that was partly right, but I don't have a complex! I am just inferior! Apart from Jesus Christ, he was absolutely right. That is true of all of us, isn't it?

When I committed my life to Christian service, I was 40 years old and had never read a book cover to cover. In English class I had always read the first and last chapters, turned in a book report, got a D minus; I made it! When my wife and I joined the staff of Campus Crusade for Christ, we were required to take Institute of Biblical Studies. As you can imagine I was behind the eight ball. I knew I would never make it. We prayed asking God for help.

Most of the staff were college graduates who drove older clunker cars without knowing how to keep them running. It didn't take long to find out I could be of help to other staffers, and the word got around. One young man came to me and explained how his car would some times quit and other times it ran fine. He told me how it had caused him to miss meetings, classes, and speaking opportunities. He was a Christian brother God was really using. As he explained how his car was acting, I remembered a similar case my Dad had with a customer while I was working for him. Dad discovered that the customer's car had a crystallized distributor shaft and it broke very sharply. When the points fell together his car would run, but a bump or too much power would cause the shaft to rotate and slip out of place and the car would not run. So I checked the shaft in this student's car, and sure enough, that's exactly what had happened. We bought a new distributor shaft and had him going in no time. He thought I "walked on water." I shared with him that I was able to help him because of what I had inherited from my father and because of what he taught me. I asked him if he could help me with my books and he was more than glad to do that. Such a deal!

I had opportunity to honor my father by attributing worth to him. I prayed from Proverbs 25:11 before calling Dad that my words would be like "apples of gold in settings of silver", the right words of how God was using what I inherited from him and my gratefulness for his training and teaching me. This was the first time I shared this kind of news with Dad, and he didn't say much. However, I continued to tell him how I praised the Lord for his positive traits. His negative ones I saw fall by the wayside. Eventually Dad began to comprehend or see his worth in Christ, to see himself from God's perspective as I continued to praise and thank him. When I shared with Dad about the crystallized distributor shaft and how I was able to help a young man God was using mightily on the campus of Colorado University, I told him he was used of God through me. At that point I began to understand experientially what it meant to "honor your father and your mother."

Just as this command helped lay the foundation for Josh McDowell to lead his father to Christ the day before he died, my mother's pastor led my father to the Lord the day before he died. Even though my parents have passed on, we still endeavor to honor them whenever God uses what we've inherited from them. This perspective has helped us to pray more effectively in other cases because we are obeying the first command with a very precious promise.

Our pattern of thought might go something like this:

☐ What is a positive thing I know about my parents?

☐ Am I praising the Lord for them?

☐ What attributes or characteristics have I inherited from my parents?

☐ When has God used one of them in my life or ministry or work?

☐ How and when can I apply my faith to the command to honor my parents?

☐ With whom can I share what I have learned and thus give glory to the Lord? (Psalm 105:1)

If you don't know who your parents are, adopt some! And get to praying!

Appendix A

The following prayer resources are available from Church Prayer Ministry International or from Chambers College Press.

Lord, Teach Me To Pray, The DVD Series
    The goal of this Prayer Enrichment Seminar on DVD is to help Christians pray biblical prayer. Six discs contain 24 lessons. Each lesson requires 30 minutes viewing time and ten to fifteen minutes in small group prayer with Scripture plus discussion. The leader needs no experience. All the instructions are on the disc.

Suggested donation - $60.00

The Restoration of Biblical Prayer is the Gillams' written form of their Prayer Enrichment Seminar plus their life's experiences while teaching the material beginning in 1976.

Suggested donation - $20.00

The 2959 Prayer Notebook by Peter Lord is designed to apply the teachings on Biblical prayer; it is not a syllabus of the PES. Paul Billhimer said,"Any church without a systematic prayer program is simply operating a religious treadmill." Those who use the notebook will find it a great help in getting off of that treadmill.

Suggested donation - $30.00

Prayer Without Purity Is Function Without Effect. One of the biblical truths the PES focuses on is Psalm 66:18, God does not hear the prayers of a sinner, apart from a prayer of repentance. This booklet contains the biblical outline used of God in the Korean revival in the early 1940s. It's a step-by-step scriptural guideline for personal revival.

Suggested donation - $5.00

The Word and Prayer for the Lost is an abbreviated view of praying biblically for the lost and is contained in the book, *The Restoration of Biblical Prayer*.

Suggested donation - $10.00

Prayer Chains is a booklet addressing the good and the bad about prayer chains. "Man looks on prayer as a means of getting his needs met, the Bible idea of prayer is that we may get to know God Himself," said Oswald Chambers. This booklet offers Biblical solutions through the practice of scriptural praying.

Suggested donation - $5.00

The Ulti-Mate Adventure workbooks, based on 1 Peter 3:7, are guidelines for a private retreat with your mate.

Almost every married couple would agree that marriage takes work to make it fulfilling. Much listening and interaction help bring harmony to a marriage, and vision and planning give it direction and purpose.

It is necessary to take time out periodically to be alone with your partner to reflect, evaluate and plan for further growth and fulfillment in your relationship. *The Ulti-Mate Adventure* is designed to help you communicate clearly with your spouse, as well as give you a chance to get away together for a weekend to relax and be refreshed by each other's company.

Suggested donation - $20.00

Joint Heirs, a scriptural guideline for a couple's prayer time, was written to help couples learn to pray together, not for removing problems, but for each other's walk with the Lord.

Suggested donation - $3.00

The Gaze and Glance Song Book, by Jean Reiswig and Teresa Ong. As Jean taught the children's sessions at our seminars, they had a hard time relating to the GAZE and GLANCE, so she thought of the phrase"peek a little and look a lot", which stuck! Then Teresa wrote the music. This is a great tool.

Suggested donation - $5.00

Pastors Prayer Support Team Strategy booklet is a well-tested plan of action to disciple a core group of men in biblical prayer. This plan can also be adapted to build a prayer support team for the pastor's wife, Sunday school teachers, missionaries, etc. It is not designed to pray for the building program or the Easter Cantata or the lost. The prayers for these things will come as a by-product. The primary focus of the PPSTS is for the pastor's walk with the Lord.

Oswald Chambers has said,"There are a number of men who teach about prayer, but where is the man who sets men to praying?" This plan will do just that!

Suggested donation - $5.00

Spiritual Workouts for the Moral Athlete, by Stephen Ong. A rich daily devotional. Suggested donation - $12.00

40 Days of Solemn Prayer is a collection of relevant scriptures to guide individuals or small groups in praying for the needs of our nation. The readings were compiled during several times of national crisis and continue to be pertinent.

Suggested donation - $10.00

Prayer Therapy, by Teresa Ong. A helpful guide in handling problems by utilizing prayer to gain wisdom, comfort, and solutions to life's problems. 312 pages. Suggested donation $12.00

Endnotes

1. Reuel Howe, *Miracle of Dialogue*, (San Francisco: Harper, 1984) pp 3- 4.

2. Oswald Chambers, "August 6: The Cross in Prayer,"(ProverbsProverbs) *My Utmost for His Highest, (United Kingdom: Marshall Morgan & Scott, c1927).*

3. Oswald Chambers, *If Ye Shall Ask, (United Kingdom: Marshall Morgan & Scott, c1937).*

4. Paul Lee Tan, *Encyclopedia of 7700 illustrations* (Rockville, MD: Assurance Publishers, 1979), page 483.

5. For more detailed introspection and cleansing, see *Prayer Without Purity Is Function Without Effect* (published by Church Prayer Ministry International). This exercise is very beneficial before making any major decision or when dealing with a deep problem.

6. Oswald Chambers, "June 26:Always Now ", *My Utmost for His Highest, (United Kingdom: Marshall Morgan & Scott, c1927).*

7. Paul Billheimer, *Destined for the Throne* (Minneapolis: Bethany House, 1996).

8. Francis Roberts, *High Road to Surrender* (Uhrichsville, OH: Barbour Publishing , 1985).

9. Paul Billheimer, *Destined for the Throne* (Minneapolis: Bethany House, 1996).

10. Oswald Chambers, "July 27: The Way to Know ", *My Utmost for His Highest, (United Kingdom: Marshall Morgan & Scott, c1927).*

11. The Lord's personal name was Jesus, which signifies Savior. It is carefully accented by repetitions in the record as being highly important. (1) He was so called

prospectively by Gabriel to Mary: "And behold, you will conceive in your womb, and bear a son, and you shall name Him Jesus" (Luke 1:31, italics added). (2) He was so named by the angel to Joseph in his supernatural dream respecting Mary and the child: "And she will bear a Son; and you shall call His name Jesus, for it is He who will save His people from their sins " (Matt 1:21). (3) He was so called on the day of His birth: "She gave birth to a son; and he called His name Jesus " (Matt 1:25). (4) He was so called when His name was officially bestowed at circumcision: "His name was then called Jesus, the name given by the angel before he was conceived in the womb " (Luke 2:21).(The New Unger's Bible Dictionary, 1988.)

12. Oswald Chambers, *If You Will Ask, Reflections on the Power of Prayer*. Grand Rapids: Discovery House Publishing, p. 55.

13. Ibid. p. 28

14. A.T. Pierson, *George Mueller of Bristol*, Fleming H. Revell Co., no date, p 186.

15. Oswald Chambers, *The Servant as His Lord, United Kingdom: Marshall Morgan & Scott c1959.*

16. *Wycliffe Bible Commentary*, Chicago: Moody Press, 1975 p. 1364.

17. Ray Stedman, *Spiritual Warfare*, Discovery House Pub. 1999, p. 46.

18. Charles Haddon Spurgeon, *Twelve Sermons on Prayer*, (Michigan: Baker Book House, 1970.) p. 72.

19. John MacArthur, *Evangelistic Praying*, Chicago: Moody Press, 1988.

20. Derek Prince, *Everything by Prayer*

21. Matthew Henry Commentary, http://www.ccel.org/ccel/henry/mhc5.John.xiii.html.

Index

access to God. 130-133
adoration.. .... 52, 73, 88
alcoholic. 43, 262
all your heart. 208, 212, 238
answer. 20, 28, 35, 36, 42, 46, 50, 57, 58, 69, 76, 96, 106, 116, 119, 136, 138, 144, 150, 153, 155, 156, 159, 160, 187-190, 192, 194-197, 210, 217, 222, 233, 234, 241, 242, 244, 247-249, 251, 252, 254, 261
approaching. 19
asking.. 34, 42, 49, 52, 78, 90, 97, 100, 111, 114, 125, 136-140, 152, 153, 157, 184, 197, 212, 219, 223, 233, 234, 237, 241, 243, 244, 247, 253, 268
attack. 121-123, 169, 213, 226, 257
attributes of God... 13, 38, 55, 59, 81, 84, 93, 94, 99, 102, 130, 190, 242, 245, 263
battle.... 118, 119, 122, 123, 165, 166, 168, 171-173, 178, 228, 238, 255, 259
being denied. 137, 140
Bible... xii, 2-4, 14, 17, 19, 26, 29, 31, 37-39, 61, 66, 68, 69, 71, 73, 74, 76, 77, 79, 83, 89, 93, 94, 97, 99, 100, 103, 106, 107, 113, 114, 116, 122, 123, 126, 137, 156, 159, 165-168, 171, 175, 180, 182, 185, 189, 192, 194-196, 199, 201, 202, 218, 239, 244, 247, 266, 272
Calvary.... 26, 29, 33, 34, 36, 37, 49, 129, 130, 134, 135, 137, 141, 142, 188, 190, 194-196, 205, 214, 238, 264
change.. 13, 21, 34, 48, 54, 60, 66, 67, 69, 103, 114, 152, 157, 164, 175, 202, 210, 211, 238, 244, 245
chastisement. 127, 208, 209, 223
circumstances... 1, 13, 31, 34, 43, 44, 50, 82, 97, 99, 104, 107, 146, 157, 160, 184, 194, 200, 210, 211, 217, 220, 242, 245, 250, 258, 264, 266
claiming the promises of God.. 91
closet. 61, 160
comfort. 140, 224, 229
command... 38, 69, 73, 96, 109, 118, 135, 149, 150, 175, 178, 180, 185, 225, 239, 247, 248, 250, 261-263, 266, 270
compound words for God.. 87
confession.. .... 52, 73, 76, 88, 177, 181
conforming. 29, 94, 99, 159, 173, 248
co-workers. 135
defeat. 20, 101, 116, 166
deliverance. 119
difficulty. 10, 116, 131, 134, 141, 151276

direction. 82, 148, 167, 170, 178, 181, 272
divine healing. 202, 210
dying.. . . . . 20, 37, 130, 162, 169, 173, 199, 200, 248
faith. . . 1, 14, 39, 53, 60, 66, 78, 79, 95, 96, 100, 103, 105, 107-109,
    112, 114-116, 119, 122, 130, 132, 136, 143-153, 164, 200-
    202, 204, 205, 208, 210-212, 214, 219, 221, 223, 230, 239,
       246, 247, 250, 255, 256, 258, 265, 270
father. 5, 10, 20-22, 35, 36, 43, 53, 55, 59, 63, 64, 66, 67, 78, 80, 93,
    94, 102, 104-106, 109, 113, 122, 124, 129, 130, 133-136,
    138, 139, 147, 148, 162, 165, 174, 185, 188-192, 195, 199,
    202, 203, 206, 215, 216, 218-220, 224, 225, 230, 232, 240,
    242, 245, 251, 255, 257, 258, 261-263, 266, 267, 269, 270
finances. 52, 66, 160
focus. 13, 39, 40, 43, 47, 48, 51, 63, 95, 96, 103, 104, 120, 129, 176,
    204, 213, 220, 227, 231, 232, 237, 245, 252, 258, 273
forgiving. 4, 59, 94, 222
friends.. . . . 23, 32, 46, 113, 133, 135, 136, 144, 183, 188, 232, 233,
       242, 248, 250, 251, 253, 258, 268
fruit.. 15, 50, 59, 63, 68, 70, 71, 75, 79, 96, 102, 105, 107, 139, 164,
      173, 178, 206, 225, 230, 244, 248, 257
frustration. 68, 75, 116
fulfilled.. 12, 47, 55, 60, 180, 181, 240, 266
gaze and glance. 31, 39-41, 44, 49, 55, 58, 60, 68, 70, 273
glorify. . . . 17, 59, 67, 80, 93, 94, 128, 130, 134, 179, 195, 202, 203,
       205, 223, 225, 238, 248
gossip. 156, 237
grace.. 35, 36, 58, 71, 96, 97, 99, 102, 106, 109, 111, 123, 128, 130,
    138, 143, 149, 150, 174, 185, 188, 189, 194, 197, 199, 203,
       207, 209, 211, 251
great commission. 246, 247
growing in faith. 164
hear. . . x, 5, 6, 10, 12, 14, 19, 20, 35-37, 42, 43, 65, 78, 88, 127, 152,
    160, 170, 187, 189-192, 196, 202, 220, 222, 232, 246, 247,
       256, 271
holy.. 3, 7, 9, 12-15, 27, 32, 33, 35-37, 40, 52, 59, 63-66, 73, 76, 83,
    84, 92, 104, 109, 112, 119, 123, 124, 131, 133, 141, 142,
    151, 155, 159, 177, 179, 181, 183, 190, 193, 196, 197, 200,
    205, 206, 209, 214, 215, 217, 219, 222, 223, 240, 243, 245,
       246, 259, 262, 266
Holy Spirit. . . . 7, 12, 13, 15, 32, 33, 40, 52, 63-66, 73, 76, 123, 141,
    159, 177, 179, 181, 183, 190, 193, 200, 205, 206, 214, 215,
      219, 222, 223, 240, 243, 245, 259, 262, 266
husband. . 10, 60, 113, 124, 126, 156, 174-180, 184, 199, 200, 216-
       220, 233
immorality. 68, 158, 179, 194, 201

leukemia.. 173
life. ... 5, 9, 12-17, 19-21, 23-25, 29, 31-37, 40-46, 58-60, 63-71, 73,
79, 83, 85, 89, 93-96, 98-103, 105, 107, 113, 115, 119-124,
129, 141, 145, 148, 151, 160-163, 166, 169-174, 177, 178,
180-182, 185, 188-190, 192, 193, 197, 199, 205, 206, 208,
213, 214, 221, 223, 224, 227, 228, 231, 234, 238, 242-244,
246, 248, 251, 252, 255, 257, 258, 261-264, 266-268, 270
lost. ... 20, 28, 91, 102, 117, 152, 162, 169, 234, 237-239, 241-252,
255, 257-259, 272, 273
love.. xii, 2, 4-7, 11, 15, 21, 40, 41, 49, 50, 59, 63, 66-69, 71, 73, 77,
79, 80, 84, 85, 91, 93, 94, 96, 98, 99, 101, 102, 104, 107,
113, 114, 116, 121, 124, 126, 130, 146, 150, 152, 164, 168,
181, 184, 188, 192, 200, 203, 209, 215, 217, 219, 230, 240,
246, 248, 251, 253, 254, 258, 263, 265-267
manifesting..................................... 71, 97, 173
marriage....................... 10, 17, 32, 175, 177-183, 272
mind... ix, 1, 4, 23, 31, 32, 34, 36, 38, 39, 44-46, 48, 49, 51, 57, 63,
64, 68-70, 74, 79, 81, 88, 89, 91, 92, 99, 107, 108, 111, 120,
124, 127, 152, 167, 170, 194, 199, 201, 205, 212, 213, 222,
226-228, 230-232, 235, 263
mother. ... 20, 37, 65, 125, 127, 140, 174, 185, 199, 219, 232, 233,
252-255, 257, 261-264, 269
myths.. 27, 197
names of God.. 86
obedience. 48, 49, 112, 121, 122, 135, 152, 153, 195, 200, 231, 232,
238, 245, 247, 256, 261, 262
overcome............................... 116, 178, 251, 252
persistence................................... 78, 79, 250
power.. 9, 12, 19, 24, 31, 37, 40, 42, 46, 65, 66, 71, 85, 89, 93, 103,
104, 106, 108, 112, 115, 117, 120, 124, 125, 138, 141, 145,
146, 148, 153, 155, 176, 179, 188, 191-193, 203, 205, 211,
223, 225, 230, 238, 240, 261-263, 265, 266, 269
praise. ... xii, 3, 4, 15, 40, 47, 48, 57, 59, 67, 73, 76, 88, 89, 95, 102-
109, 111-117, 119-121, 124-127, 150, 152, 176, 177, 184,
187, 200, 217, 221-223, 232, 244, 249, 256, 258, 269
prayer.. 6, ix, x, xii, 1-4, 6, 7, 9, 10, 13-17, 19-21, 24-29, 31-38, 40-
45, 47-50, 52, 58-60, 63-71, 73-80, 88, 93-105, 107, 110-
112, 114-118, 121, 122, 126-130, 133, 136, 140-143, 149-
153, 155-178, 180, 182-197, 199, 200, 202-205, 210, 212-
215, 217, 218, 220-226, 230, 232-235, 237, 240-258, 261,
262, 264, 271-273
prayer partners.......... 155, 156, 159, 162-166, 172-174, 183-185
praying for. 1, 25, 27, 28, 70, 75, 110, 153, 156, 158, 168, 173, 188,
202, 205, 206, 209, 220-222, 224, 232, 234, 235, 237-239,
241-246, 248-250, 252, 257, 258, 261, 273

praying ground..... 13, 190, 200, 206, 214, 222, 223, 234, 249, 253
praying with.. 1, 19, 77, 155, 157, 165, 173-175, 180, 224, 225, 253
promises.... 20, 29, 71, 84, 91, 96, 99-103, 143, 147, 151, 153, 223
purity......................... 48, 88, 99, 180, 187, 256, 271
purpose. 9, 13, 28, 31, 49, 50, 55, 59, 63, 66, 71, 77, 93, 94, 98, 104,
    108, 121, 123, 125, 127, 128, 134, 135, 145, 152, 156, 159,
    181, 194, 199, 203, 205, 212, 218, 222, 223, 225, 235, 237,
    239, 242, 248, 255, 264-266, 272
reflecting...................................... 124, 125
refuge............................... 55, 99, 126, 139, 147
relationship... 1, 11-13, 31, 35, 36, 42, 43, 49, 50, 53, 58, 63, 64, 66,
    68, 70, 131-135, 137, 157, 158, 165, 181, 188, 194, 196, 206,
    214, 217, 223, 225, 235, 242, 243, 245, 249, 256, 267, 272
requests..... x, 1, 25, 34, 47, 48, 59, 74, 77, 80, 88, 95, 98, 107, 127,
    136, 139, 140, 157-159, 185, 206, 235
responsibility of man........................... 197, 239, 249
righteous. 37, 42, 47, 87, 94, 101, 104, 130, 172, 187, 189, 195, 212,
    214, 222, 249, 256
Satan. 36, 42, 107, 115, 120, 121, 123, 124, 132, 165, 168, 169, 175,
    178, 180, 190-197, 200, 203, 205, 207-209, 212, 225, 227-
    230, 255, 264
Satan's ploys.. 163
scripture.. vii, 12, 17, 29, 40, 53, 73, 74, 77, 79, 86, 87, 94, 98, 103,
    104, 113, 114, 117, 121, 156, 157, 159, 164, 168, 176, 178-
    180, 182, 184, 185, 192, 193, 202, 207, 211, 225, 242, 243,
    249, 271
service............ 24, 52, 110, 117, 132, 158, 172, 204, 261, 268
sick.. 25-27, 37, 50, 126, 199, 202, 205-207, 209, 212-214, 220-224,
    229, 235-237
sinful lifestyles....................................... 196
sovereignty of God..................... 95, 203, 239, 240, 249
strength. 34, 37, 55, 99, 105, 106, 109, 126, 149, 155, 161, 167, 213,
    219, 224, 226, 230, 246, 266
stumble............................... 158, 159, 184, 201
supplication..................... 47, 48, 52, 59, 73, 88, 90, 95
surrender............................... 105, 106, 252, 267
temporal... 1, 13, 33, 36, 38, 39, 44-48, 68, 69, 73, 75, 95, 120, 127,
    190, 193, 194, 197, 206, 221, 227, 231, 250, 263
thanksgiving.. 47, 48, 52, 59, 73, 76, 88, 89, 95, 104, 112, 161, 217,
    232
transform............................... 77, 104, 105, 235
trust. 9, 53, 58, 65, 67-69, 85, 95, 99, 119, 120, 127, 147, 149, 151-
    153, 182, 183, 208, 212, 224, 233, 238, 244, 251, 262, 265
truth... 12, 29, 31, 34, 35, 37, 38, 41, 42, 46, 64, 84, 109, 110, 118,
    147, 150, 160, 170, 185, 187, 192, 204, 208, 220, 223, 225-

                         227, 232, 238, 240, 244, 247, 267
unbelievers........................ 26, 196, 207, 255, 257, 262
understanding... 9, 20, 29, 31, 34, 35, 49, 53, 55, 58, 66, 83, 93, 96,
        121, 131, 137, 141, 153, 174, 175, 185, 204, 208, 212, 216,
                225, 230, 238, 242, 248, 249, 256, 257, 263, 266
unity in Christ....................................... 225
vain repetition............................ 78, 79, 237, 250
victory. 31, 36, 120, 122, 124, 145, 172, 249, 256, 258
warfare.......................... 11, 120, 178, 213, 228, 230
wife.. 10, 17, 20, 22, 23, 32, 51, 56, 60, 113, 114, 116-119, 125, 157,
        169, 170, 174-180, 184, 194, 201, 216-219, 245, 253, 268,
                                                    273
wisdom.. 83, 91, 92, 96, 136, 146, 161, 214, 219, 223, 230, 265, 266
Word.. 3, 5, 7, 9-11, 14, 24, 28, 31, 32, 37, 41, 63, 64, 66, 74, 75, 77,
        79, 80, 84, 85, 88, 92-99, 101-104, 108, 114, 116, 121, 123,
        127, 129, 143-148, 150, 151, 153, 155, 157, 165, 168, 174,
        176, 185, 195, 202-204, 214, 217, 222, 225, 226, 228, 231,
        232, 234, 235, 237, 238, 240, 245, 249, 258, 262, 264, 265,
                                                    268, 272